to margaret

HOW GREEN IS YOUR GARDEN?

editors	cj lim + ed liu
design + production	studio 8 95 greencroft gardens, london nw6 3pg mail@cjlim-studio8.com www.cjlim-studio8.com
publishing editor	maggie toy/wiley-academy
first published	*2003* by **WILEY-ACADEMY** great britain a division of JOHN WILEY + SONS atrium, southern gate, chichester west sussex po19 8sq www.wileyeurope.com
isbn	0-470-84539-2

printed + bound	peterhurst ltd, great britain

how green is your garden?

contents

THE FIRST GARDEN
a cj lim @ bartlett architectural lab production. design team: cj lim. jm kong. ed liu.

(LOOKING) GLASS HOUSE
a cj lim @ bartlett architectural lab production. design team: cj lim. rw cannon.

HANGING GARDENS of WANTON HARMONY
a studio 8 production. design team: cj lim. ed liu. jm kong.

GREEN PALACE
a christine hawley + cj lim @ bartlett architectural lab production.
design team: c hawley. cj lim. jm kong. ed liu. a abdulezer. b addy. w wong. m wells.

GREEN CROFT in NW6
a studio 8 production. design team: cj lim. j lam.

PARK of SAND
a cj lim @ bartlett architectural lab production. design team: cj lim. jm kong. m wells.

GALLERY of FOUR SEASONS
a cj lim @ bartlett architectural lab production. design team: cj lim. l findlay. ed liu. jm kong.

OASIS in the ATTIC
a cj lim @ bartlett architectural lab production. design team: cj lim. rw cannon.

GRASSHOPPER INN
a studio 8 production. design team: cj lim. jm kong.

ICEBERGS + FLOWER MAPS
a christine hawley + cj lim @ bartlett architectural lab production.
design team: c hawley. cj lim. p lam. t murray. ben addy. jm kong.
environmental engineer: k bode / bdsp. structural engineer: m wells / techniker

seasonal change	courtyard	human bodies	grasshopper	rotate + slide
butterflies	light	deck chairs	community	fork
microclimate	reconfiguration	planting	allotment	VDU
recycling	mechanical flowers	smell	sound	signage
water	green	fields	sofa	recording

lawn mower

FLOWERS of (LOOKING)GLASS HOUSE

Rose .... a rose
Hyacinth .... a hyacinth
Violet .... a violet
Jasmine .... a jasmine
Lily .... a lily

GARDENS (in order of appearance)

The First Garden .... a library, museum + community building in Sittingbourne, Kent
(Looking)GlassHouse .... a glazed garden in a suburban locale
Hanging Gardens of Wanton Harmony .... a modified HGV carrying a wall of plants
Green Palace .... an arts centre in Palos Verdes, California
Park of Sand .... a memorial garden on Lake Michigan (Dusable Park)
Gallery of Four Seasons .... a museum celebrating the work of Tomihiro Hoshino
Oasis in the Attic .... a housing complex in Bow, London (Circle 33)
Grasshopper Inn .... a country restaurant in Hokkaido, Japan
Icebergs + Flower Maps .... an aquacentre and landscape in Aalborg, northern Denmark

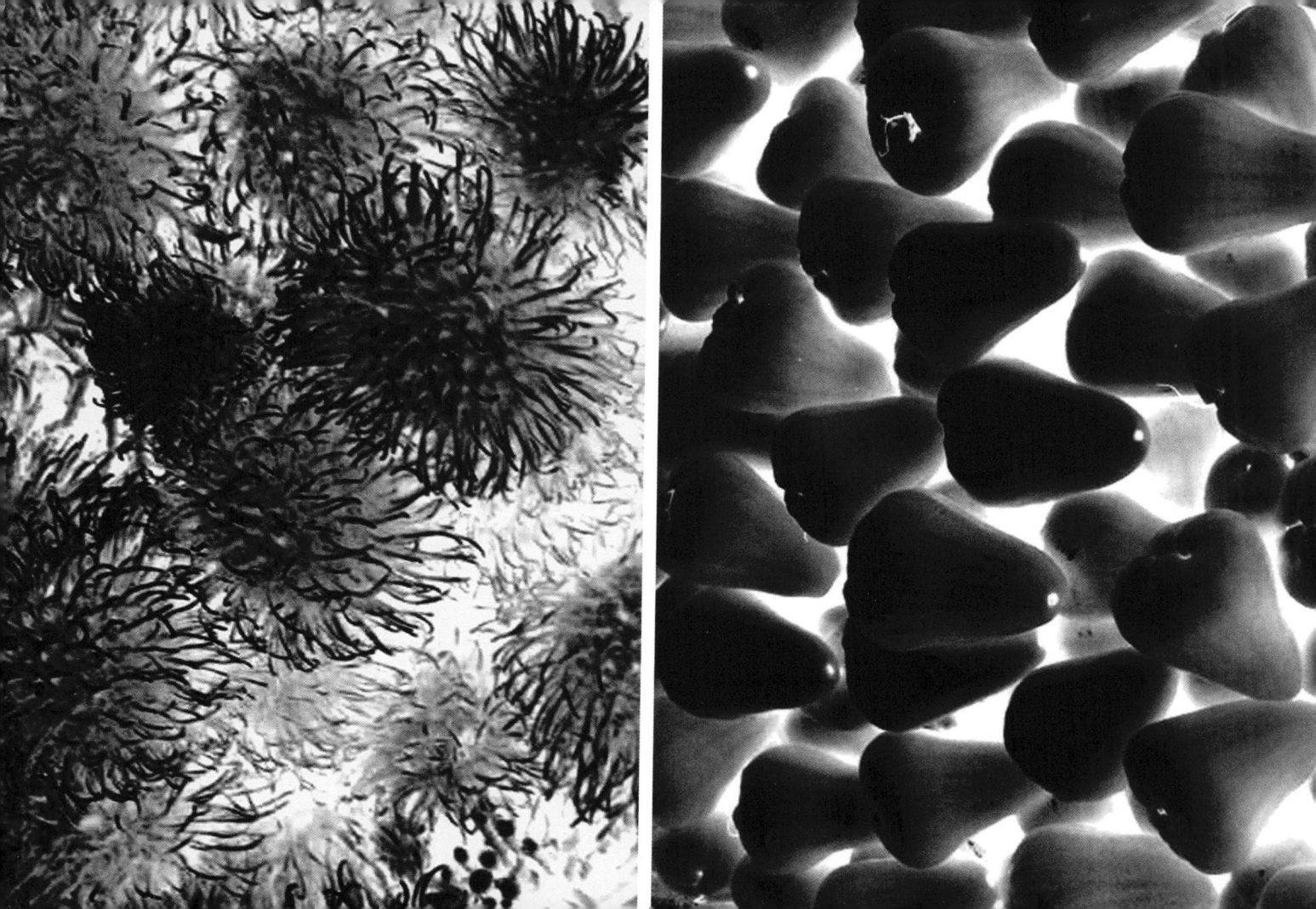

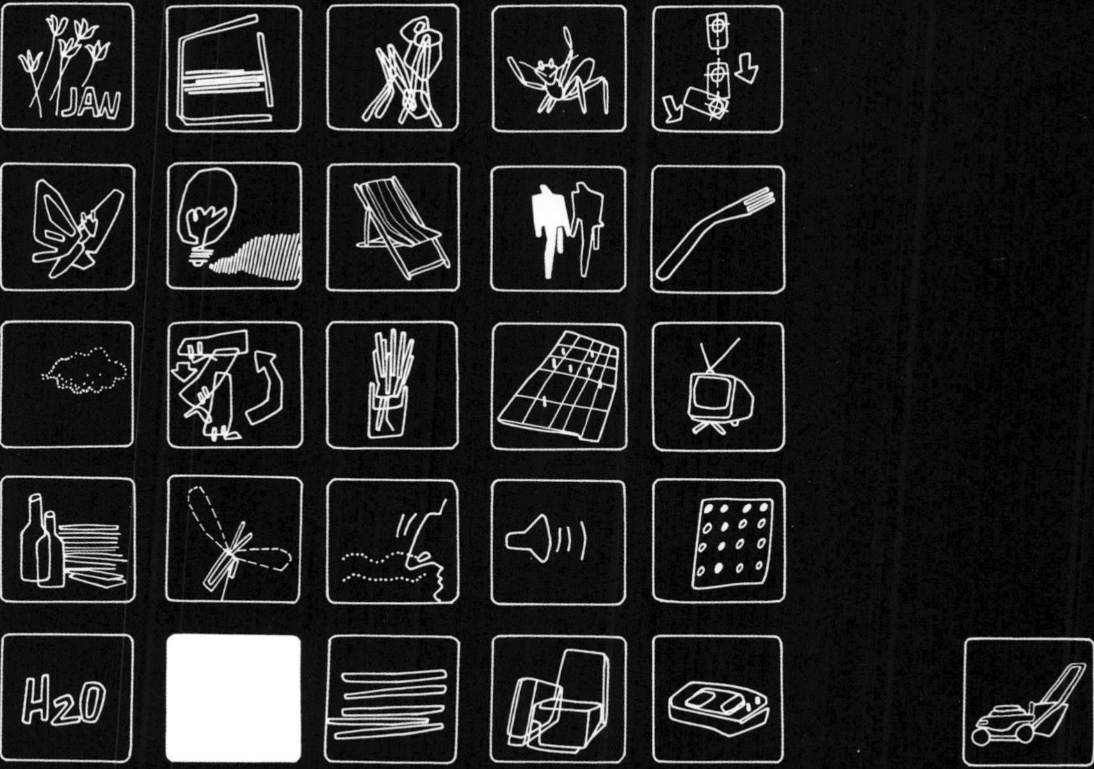

.... our heroine

CHARACTERS (in order of appearance)

.... elder sister of Alicia Liddell
.... father of Alicia + Edith Liddell
.... family friend of the Liddells'
.... an inhabitant of Sittingbourne library
.... two seasoned pugilist brothers

Carter .... an inventor

.... denizen of the Hanging Gardens of Wanton Harmony
.... mother of Alicia + Edith Liddell

.... an accident-prone handyman

.... a visitor at Dusable Park
oat .... an expert in edible flowers

ing girl .... tea attendant at the Tomihiro Museum of Shi-ga
r .... Japanese doppelgänger of Theosophilus Carter

.... a bird that flies and speaks backward

.... a grasshopper

erva .... two famous mice

+ the carpenter .... a salesman + a carpenter

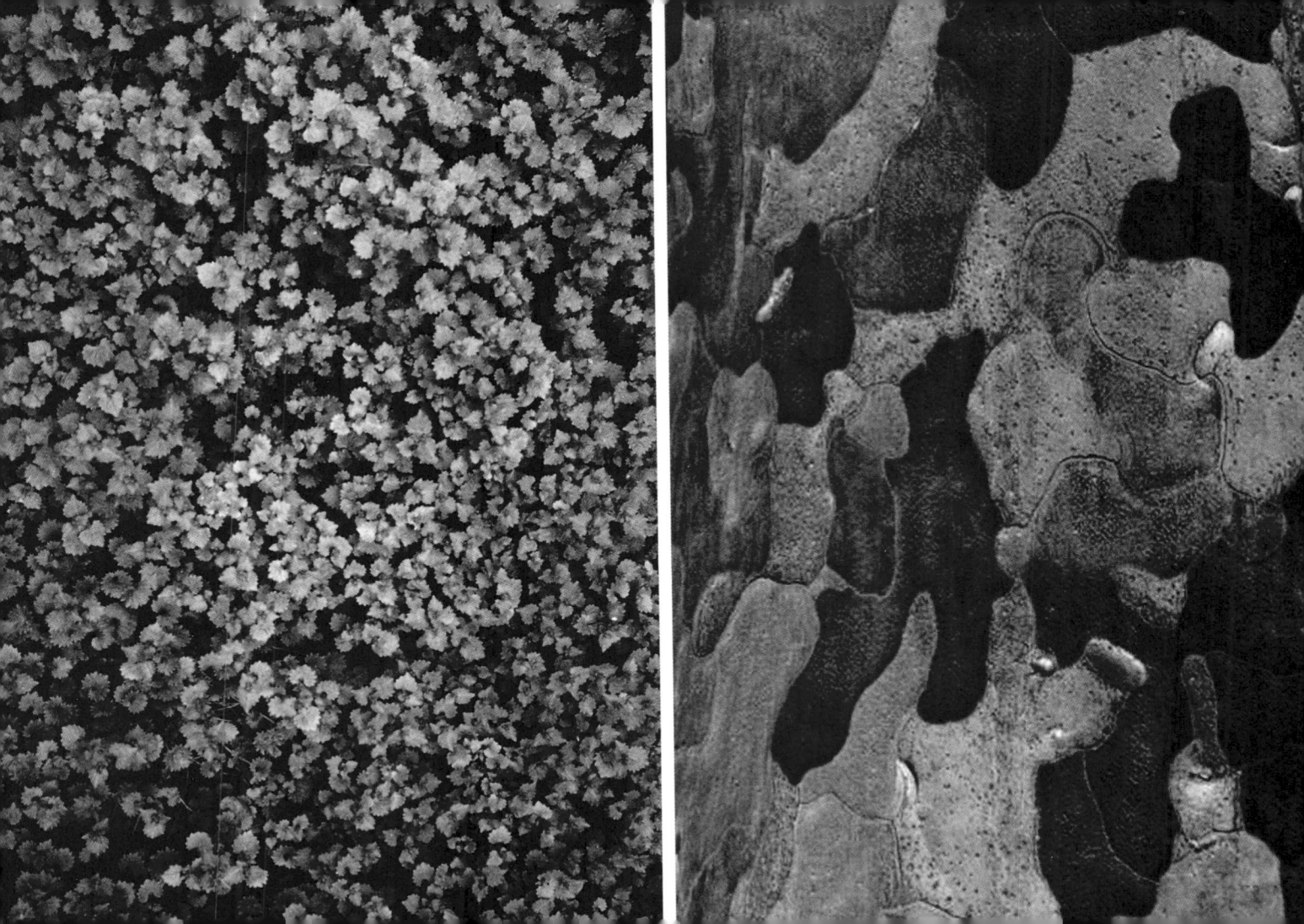

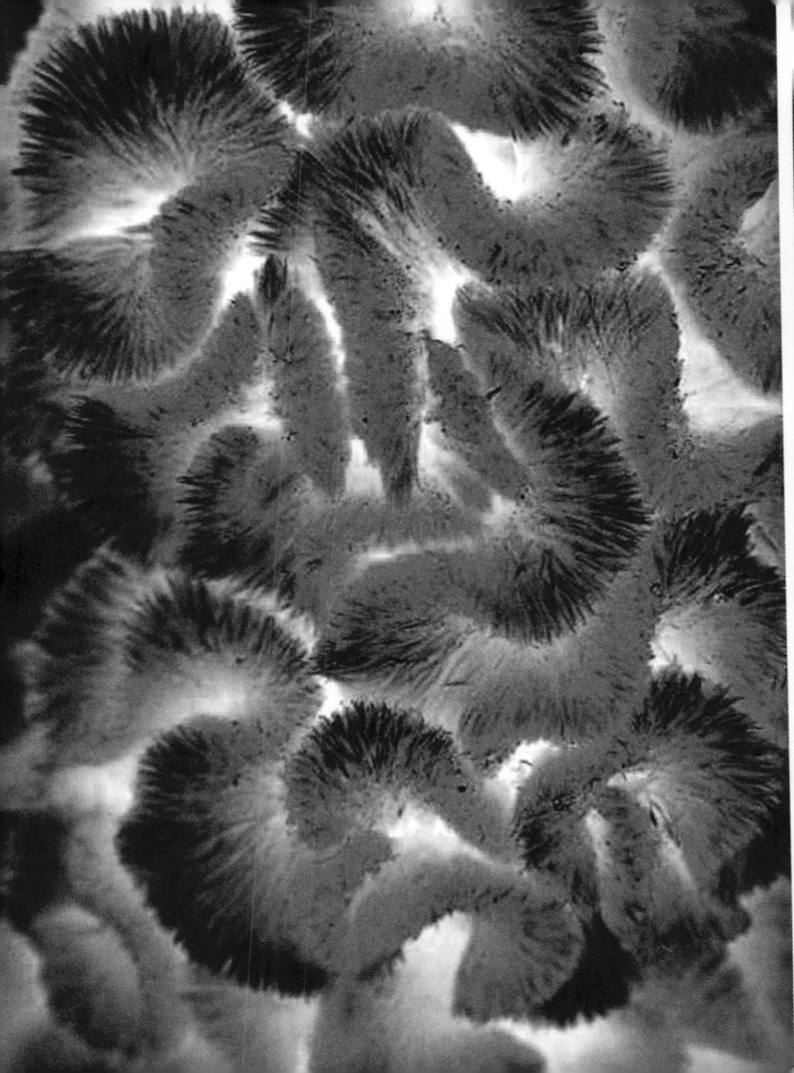
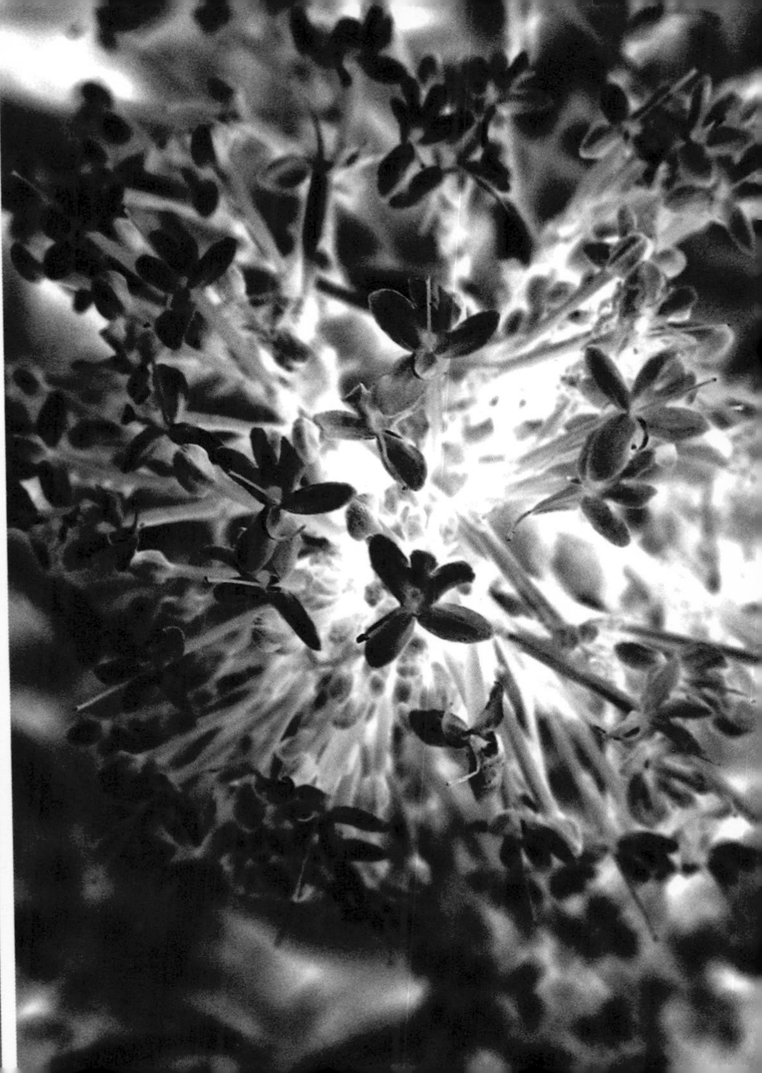

Alicia was feeling bored. It was raining cats and dogs outside, and her elder sister Edith was impersonating Adult Edith, her nose deep in some ever-so-dry treatise on architectural history from father's library of ever-so-dry first editions. Alicia made the silent wish that her over-serious sibling's enunciation of the words 'entablature', 'neo-classical' and 'pilaster' would dry out the horrid wet weather so that she could search for disorientated felines and canines in the community garden downstairs. When it soon became clear that the wish would remain ungranted, she sighed and turned her attention to her decrepit toy rabbit...

Degree and Diploma Show 2004

19. June - 9. July

Opening event: 5.30pm Friday 18. June

School of Architecture
University of Sheffield
Floor 15, The Arts Tower
Western Bank
Sheffield

0114 2220399

Photo: Detroit House, Live Project, 2003

The University of Sheffield

School of Architectural Studies
The Arts Tower
Sheffield S10 2TN

1
03
50
11
20
85

SHEFFIELD
11.06.04

GREAT BRITAIN

POSTAGE PAID

021

PB701761

KT

Kim Trogal
Fluid
100 De Beauvoir Road
London N1 4EN
United Kingdom

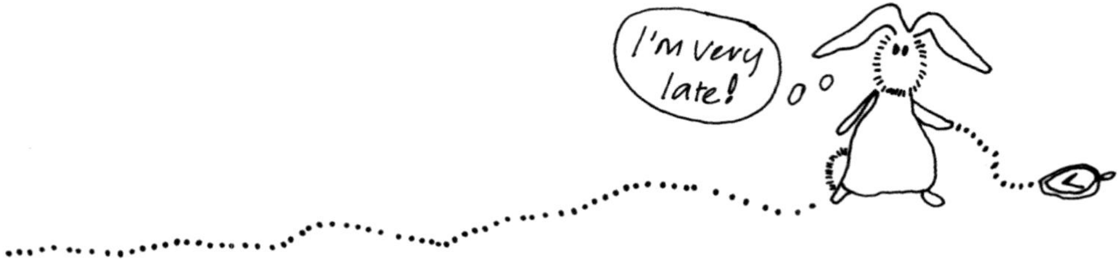
I'm very late!

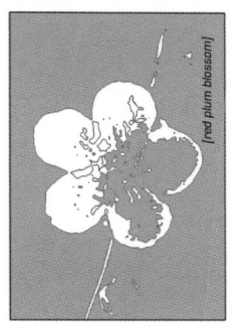

[red plum blossom]

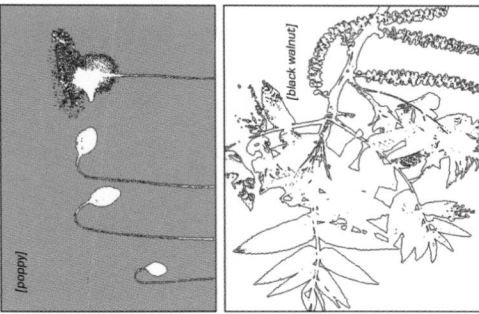

[poppy]

[black walnut]

spring

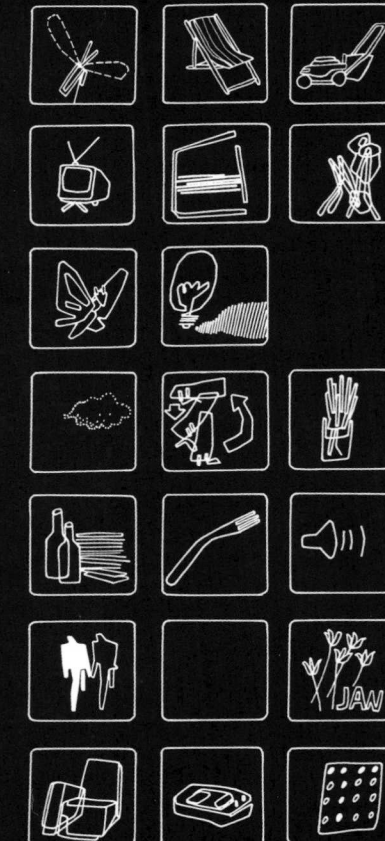

CHAPTER 1:
IN WHICH WE MEET ALICIA LIDDELL AS SHE STUMBLES ACROSS A GUIDEBOOK TO NINE MYSTERIOUS GARDENS

Alicia looked up at her father who was happily ensconced in his favourite sofa and staring at the television set. She was quite transfixed by the effect this queer device had on the other members of her family — it was capable of projecting them into wholly imaginary worlds innumerable and fantastic. Seated all the while in his red leather armchair, Father would oscillate from the thick of a cattle stampede to a spacecraft on final frontiers of space. Today, rather prosaically, he was in a common, surrounded by clusters of stripy deckchairs.

'Father? I'm bored,' announced Alicia.

'Hmm? Why don't you find yourself a nice book to read?' suggested her father. His eyes did not shift from the flickering screen. It began to dawn on her that Father would not be much fun that afternoon, so she took his advice and went for a wander in the library.

THE LIBRARY

A short stroll away from the common, Alicia lost herself in a never-ending corridor of books. As was her custom whenever she was in a bookshop or library, she went to see if they had any books by her Uncle Charles. Uncle Charles wasn't her real uncle, but an old friend of her parents who had written Alicia's two favourite books of all time. It did not take her long to find them, but it was another slim volume nearby that caught her eye. It had an appealingly ambiguous picture on its green cover (she always judged a book by its cover, at least until she had read it) and was marked on its

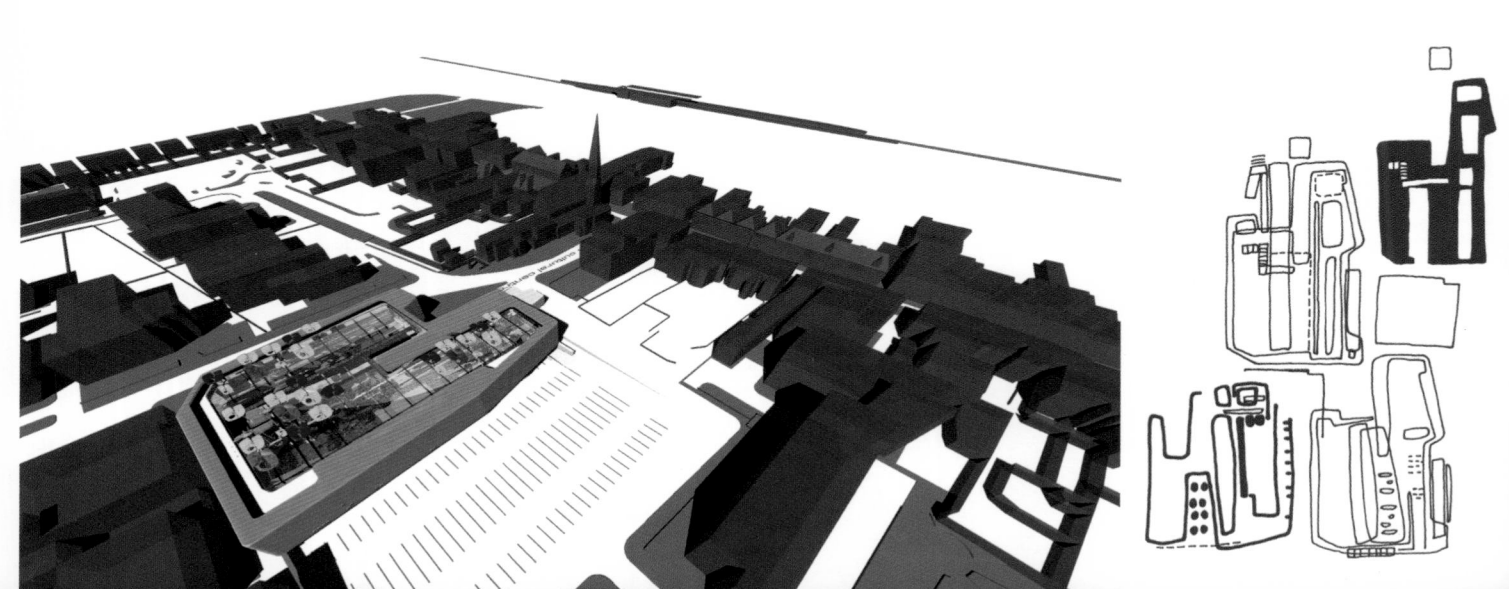

The First Garden

spine with a white tab bearing the letters:

ARC8
LI

Alicia nodded approvingly, noticing a pleasing number of illustrations and inverted commas as she leafed between the covers. As she never tired of saying: 'What is the use of a book without pictures or conversation?'

Just as she was turning to the first page, something white with extremely long ears appeared from the corridor, snatched the book out of her hands and scampered down the corridor.

'Excuse me!' said Alicia, her cry swooping to a sotto voce as she recalled that she was in a library. The woman at the issues desk looked at her sternly over her reading spectacles. Alicia looked down at her feet, forlorn and on the verge of bursting into tears at the unfairness of it all. Her self-pity quickly changed to self-righteous anger as she saw the creature with the long white ears coming towards her again. What was truly puzzling was that rather than returning from whence it had departed, it approached from the direction in which it had first arrived. At first she thought it was a case of mistaken identity, but there was no mistaking the fur and whiskers, let alone those ears and the fluffy stub of a tail behind them. Besides, how many rabbits do you see in public libraries, even ones with gardens in?

'I believe that belongs to me,' said Alicia

[The cultural complex takes the form of an inverted landscape, its physical boundary extending up to the site perimeter. The conventional urban strategy of a building surrounded by a forecourt is subverted; the public forum appears as a semi-enclosed and raised interior courtyard redolent of a secret garden out of children's literature.]

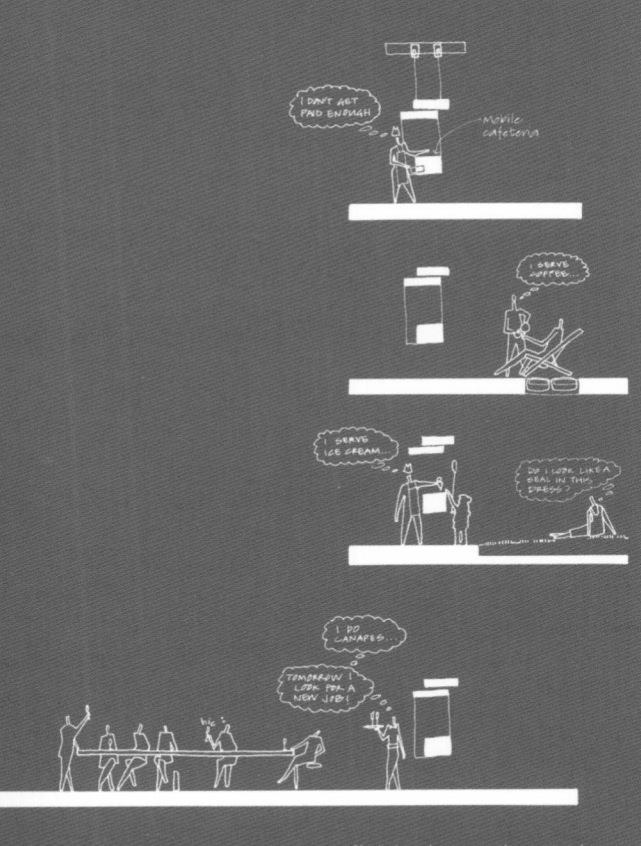

[A picnic pod traverses the courtyard on an overhead track; function is dependent on position in the courtyard. This mobile café/bar caters for formal gatherings as well as serving as a café, ice cream parlour, picnic supplier and wastebin.]

PLAN @ + 1.0m

NOTES: line drawn in green denotes optional elements and can be implemented in phases

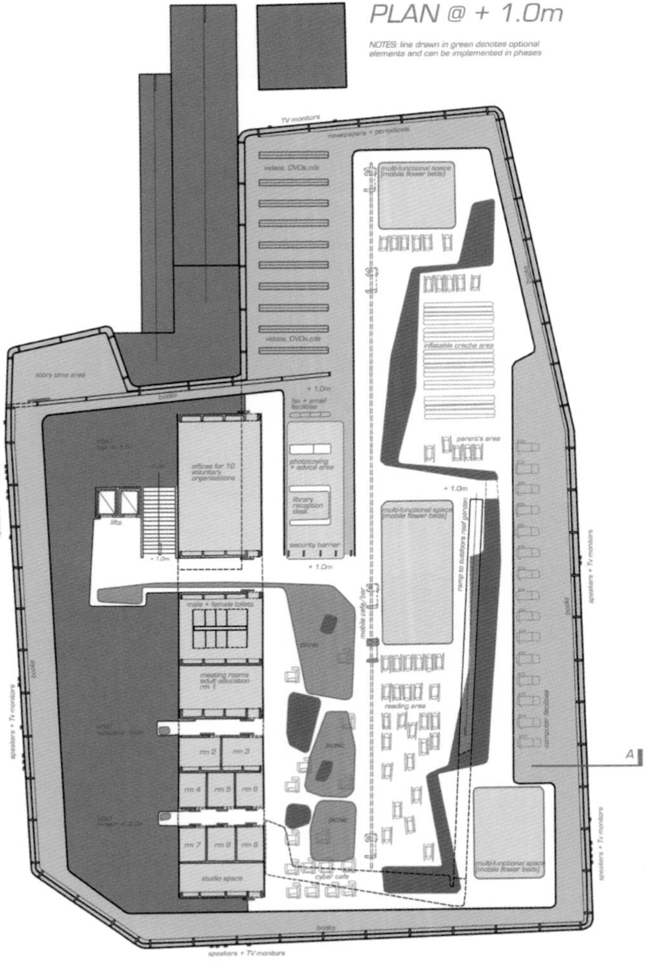

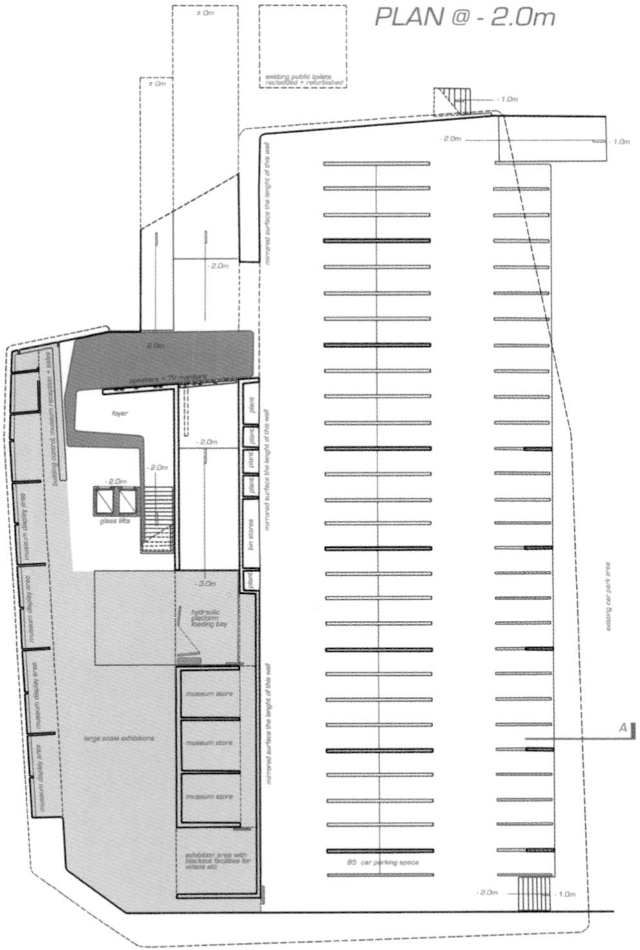

PLAN @ - 2.0m

The First Garden

haughtily, pointing to the green book that was still clasped in the rabbit's paws.

'Are you sure?' asked the rabbit, peering inside the book. 'What's your name?'

'My name is Alicia Liddell, not that it's any business of yours. Now give me my book back this instant!' Her hushed voice rose a discreet octave, ever wary of the librarian's hypersensitive ears.

'Hmmm,' considered the rabbit. 'There is a name here, but I'm afraid it bears no resemblance to yours...what kind of a name is this anyway? It only has two letters in and its dashedly difficult to pronounce to boot!'

'That, you silly creature...' said Alicia stiffly, '...is the name of the author,' and fully knowing that it was unladylike behaviour in the extreme, seized the book from the rabbit's clutches and strode off to the picnic area.

[grassy hillocks in courtyard]

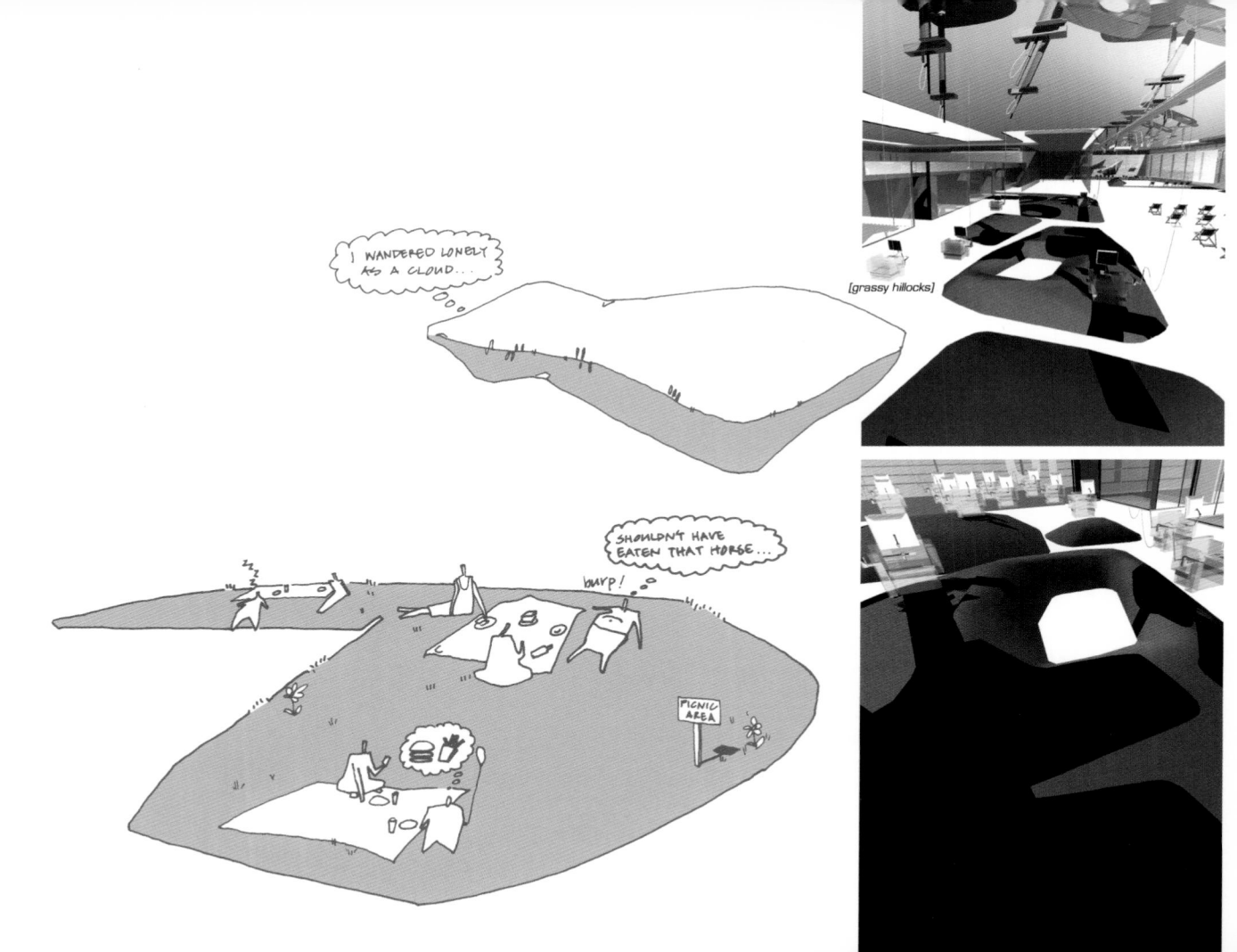

[grassy hillocks]

[internet sofas]

[Enclosed by the perimeter library, the
principal elements within the courtyard are
zoned in long parallel strips, mimicking
Sittingbourne's linear centre. Floor surfaces,
ranging from stone paving to grass to gravel
reflect this organisation, providing auditory
and tactile, as well as visual, indications of
boundary]

THE PICNIC AREA

Alicia found herself a nice spot on a grassy
knoll where she could read her book in peace. The
background chatter of picnickers clinking their
glasses and the call of an ice cream vendor barely
registered as Alicia perused the opening chapter:

The Sound of little children
laughing, bold letters unfurling
from the paving entice the public
towards a surreal edifice
consisting of processed paper.

The wall of literature extends
around the perimeter of the complex,
forming a continuous inner wall of
knowledge. This is mirrored by the
outer wall, a concentric ring of old
periodicals and newspapers - stacked,
layered and sealed into an external
envelope capable of withstanding the
elements. Inside, a glazed well encloses
the library, soundproofing the space
from the museum and courtyard. At
specific points, the library ring
widens to form a children's
storytelling area (with floor-
retractable headphones) and a bank of
after-school study terminals.

Alicia was suddenly overcome by a wave of
déjà do (a more intense version of déjà vu that
embraces smells, touch, taste, sounds, and a sixth

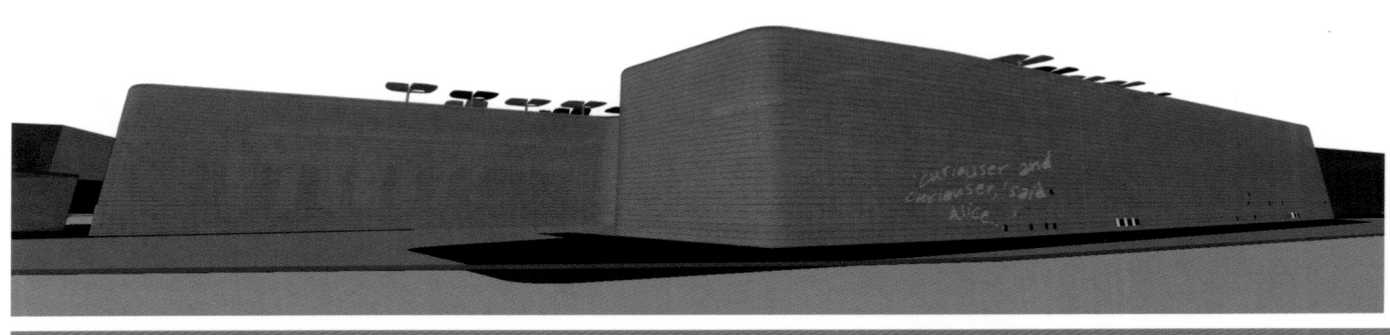

indefinable impression, as well as vision). This book appeared to be telling her about the very building she was in! How remarkable! (In time, Alicia would find the book to be indispensable, as it would guide her unerringly through nine otherwise impenetrable gardens - a trinity of botanical trinities.) As she read the first sentence again, the letters jumbled off the page and reassembled to form the name of the first garden:

Sittingbourne Cultural Centre

The entrance to the new cultural centre at Sittingbourne slopes gently into the structure's undercroft, the route peppered with whispered confidences, screened images and oblique glimpses into the garden's inverted underbelly. Subverting the conventional civic building with forecourt, the complex appears as a semi-enclosed and raised interior courtyard, redolent of a secret garden out of children's literature.

The monolithic 'garden wall' is a breathing entity, effecting an ethereal threshold between the municipal and the domestic, exterior and interior, urban and pastoral. Embedded with miniature speakers, video screens and colour, the edifice is a barrier that paradoxically welcomes the passer-by with a flurry of speech and imagery.

[The exterior recycled paper cladding is punctuated with miniature speakers and video screens, projecting the happenings within the garden out into the surrounding space. Congregating around the garden wall, then, will be crowds of passers-by, ears pressed to the speakers or eyes trained to the monitors forming a human landscape. At any one time, one may hear the sound of children giggling from the crèche area, a story being read from an audiotape.]

'did you say pig, or fig?' said the cat
'I said pig,' replied Alice

[*The informal and convivial nature of the den or secret garden extends into the interior; deckchairs, sofas and soft floors replace the staid uninviting furniture endemic of old municipal institutions. Fun replaces formality; oddity and delight are the order of the day.*]

'I've heard of wailing walls and whispering galleries,' mused Alicia, 'but never a building so outspoken as to announce itself to the entire world!' Alicia marked her page, closed the book and walked towards the voluminous courtyard.

THE COURTYARD

The floor of the cavernous courtyard shimmered with translucent shades of emerald and jade. Dotted sporadically amongst the shifting green bed lay ellipses of neutral white floor, as if the sun had missed a few spots with its sweeping brush.

'Why, if I didn't know better,' said Alicia, 'I would think that I were walking on the bed of an enormous pond.' The ceiling of oversize lily pads did little to disillusion her of this flight of fancy. She noticed that each leaf had a perfectly circular hole around two feet in diameter booleaned out of its top right corner.

'I certainly wouldn't like to meet the caterpillar that nibbled on those! And imagine what sharp incisors it must have to have cut such a clean round hole.' Her head engrossed in thoughts of monstrous Lepidoptera, she barely noticed the gargantuan butterfly wafting down from the ceiling to sit down beside her. Alicia gave a shriek and fled into the museum.

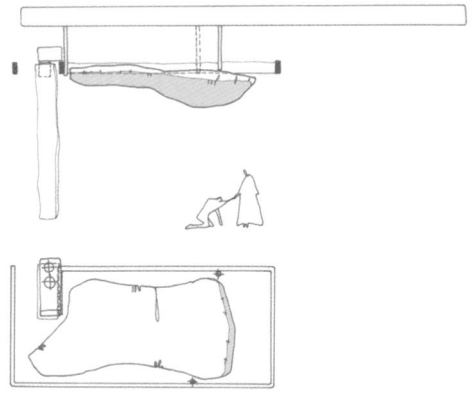

[paper pod-structure]

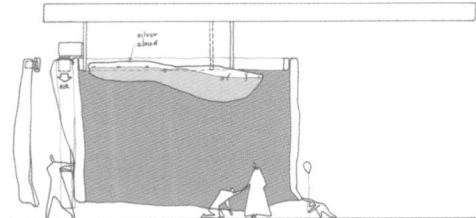

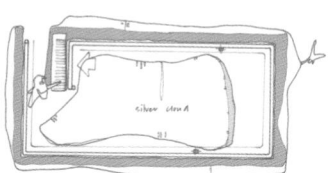

[The courtyard comprises a series of dedicated and flexible spaces that offer varying degrees of habitation, tranquillity and landscaping. These include a picnic/café area with gently contoured grassy hillocks with sofas and internet facilities, a deckchair reading area, a crèche with inflatable flooring strips, and three multi-function spaces that can be used for temporary exhibitions, formal gatherings or meetings. When privacy is required, a paper pod-structure unfolds and inflates into a flower-like structure. A ramp leading up to the terrace provides views over the town's roofscape, and a mobile catering unit provides refreshment to each area.]

drama

garden

cooking

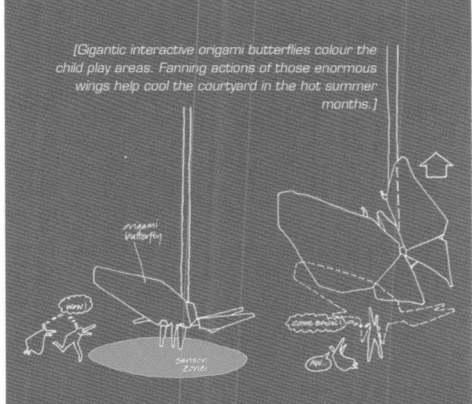

[Gigantic interactive origami butterflies colour the child play areas. Fanning actions of those enormous wings help cool the courtyard in the hot summer months.]

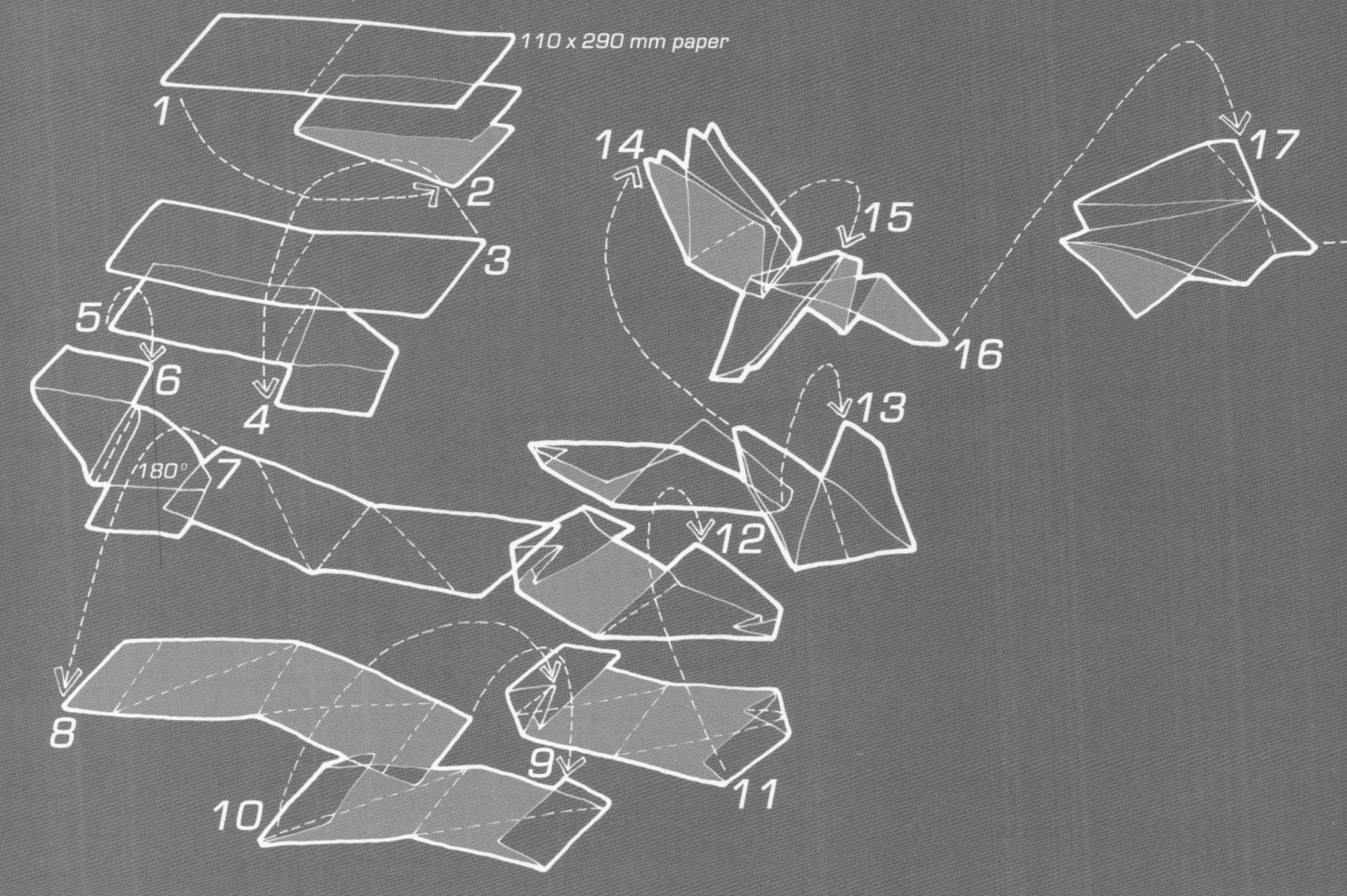

110 x 290 mm paper

1

2

3

5

6

4

180° 7

8

10

9

11

12

13

14

15

16

17

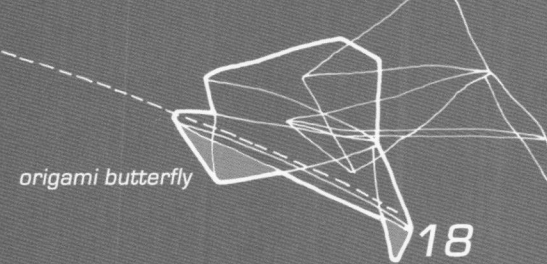

origami butterfly

18

biography   history

politics

art film

[assembly hall]

[A sea of miniature barges float overhead in the double-volume museum space, playfully questioning scale and natural order.]

THE MUSEUM

Hanging from the roof of the museum's great hall was a fleet of minute ships, floating on an imaginary ocean. They were not so tiny that they could fit in Alicia's hand, but they were certainly not large enough to sail on the open sea. Who could possibly use a boat this small? She consulted the little green book:

The historic heritage of Sittingbourne forms an integral part of the architecture. In lieu of a building where cultural objects are framed or placed on pedestals, brick, barges and paper from the long-established local industries constitute the very fabric of the complex.

The town's brickyard provides the building blocks for the surfaces of the museum. Brick walls, floors and ceilings flow into each other, dissolving the visitor's sense of orientation. An array of miniature replica barges representing the shipping industry further distorts one's sense of scale. Elsewhere, the paper-works provides the material for the textured and variegated external facade as well as giant origami butterflies and flowers that colour the child play areas, withdrawing above head-height when the space becomes over-peopled.

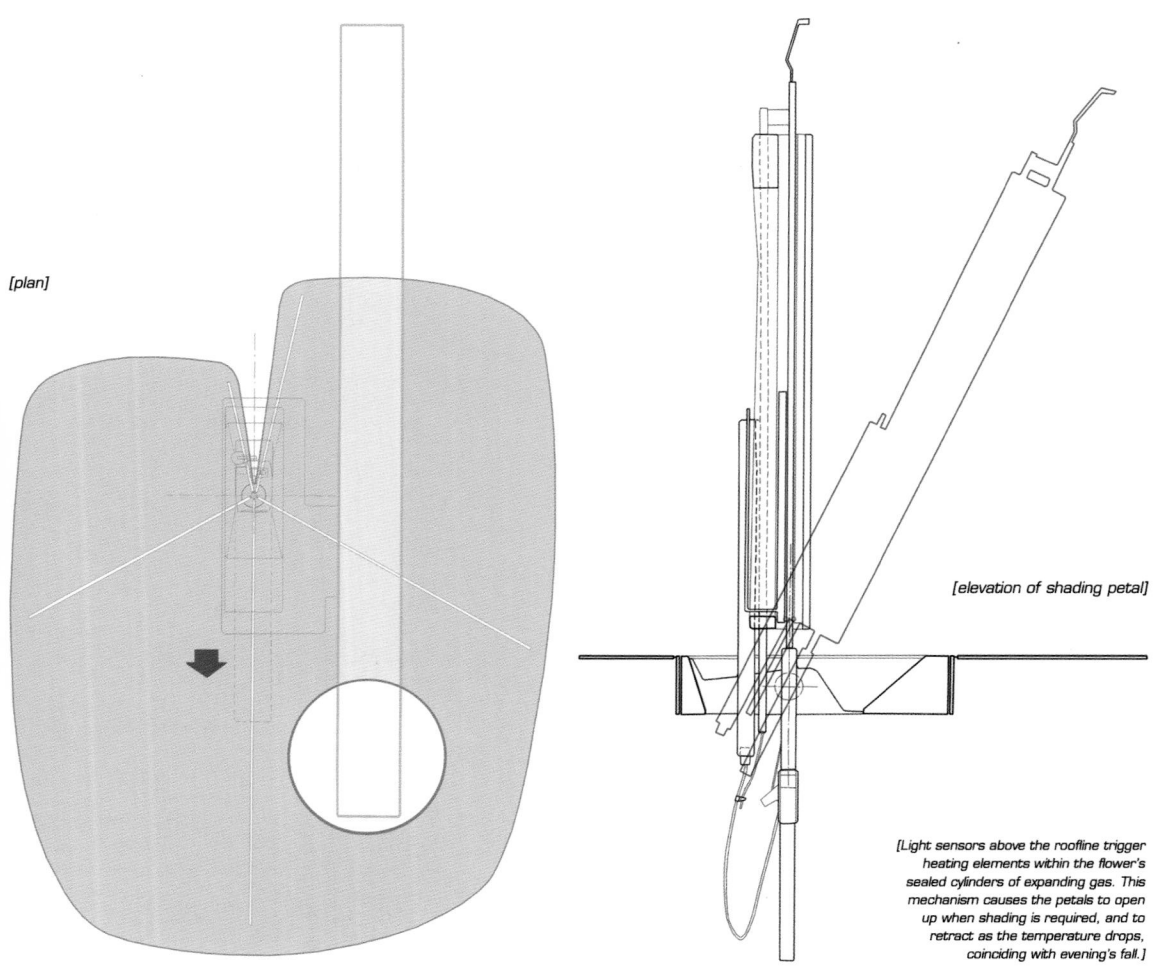

[plan]

[elevation of shading petal]

[Light sensors above the roofline trigger
heating elements within the flower's
sealed cylinders of expanding gas. This
mechanism causes the petals to open
up when shading is required, and to
retract as the temperature drops,
coinciding with evening's fall.]

Alicia came to the grave conclusion that she had fled from a folded piece of paper. On the other hand, she tried to persuade herself, nothing could be worse than horrid insects getting tangled up in her hair, particularly giant ones. On the verge of hanging her head in shame, she was interrupted by some very loud shouting. Alicia's irrepressible inquisitiveness quickly overcame any lingering pangs of embarrassment. Checking the map in the book, she worked out that the hubbub was coming from the direction of the forum.

THE FORUM

Displayed outside the assembly room was an events board made of dark green felt. White plastic letters had been inserted into the grooves spelling out a notice:

TODAY AT 10:30 TH TW DL BROTH RS
WILL D BAT TH FUTUR OF G N TIC NGIN RING

Somebody, it appeared, had stolen the e's.

To Alicia's left, standing aloft a crow's nest from a restored ship, was a small fat man in a jaunty multi-coloured cap. He was half-addressing and half-shouting at Alicia and the assembled crowd in the forum below. Alicia's eyes wandered over the gallery, and then did a double take, for on a second identical platform to her right was the spitting image of the first fat man.

'Twins are not like two peas in a pod,' said the fat man on the right, solemnly.

'No! No! You great nincompoop!' shouted the fat man on the left (evidently the first man's twin), his face turning a deep beetroot. How can you say we're like two peas in a pod? We're like chalk and cheese!'

Alicia was very confused, as they seemed to be disagreeing to agree rather than agreeing to disagree (which is generally more normal).

'Shut it, you 'orrible little man!' bawled the first twin, which Alicia thought was a somewhat backhanded insult coming from one twin to another.

The second twin took off one of his boots and hurled it at his brother.

It missed.

'Fancy throwing a tantrum just because you're on the losing end of an argument,' said Twin Number One insultingly.

'That's a shoe I threw you numskull! Fancy not knowing the difference between a shoe and a tantrum!' said Twin Number Two contemptuously.

'This isn't a debate at all!' observed Alicia. 'It's more like a slanging match!' Nevertheless, their infantile squabbling managed to incite the crowd around her. Before she knew what was happening, a furious brawl broke out and in the ensuing mêlée, Alicia was swept out of the building onto a path leading her to the second of the nine gardens.

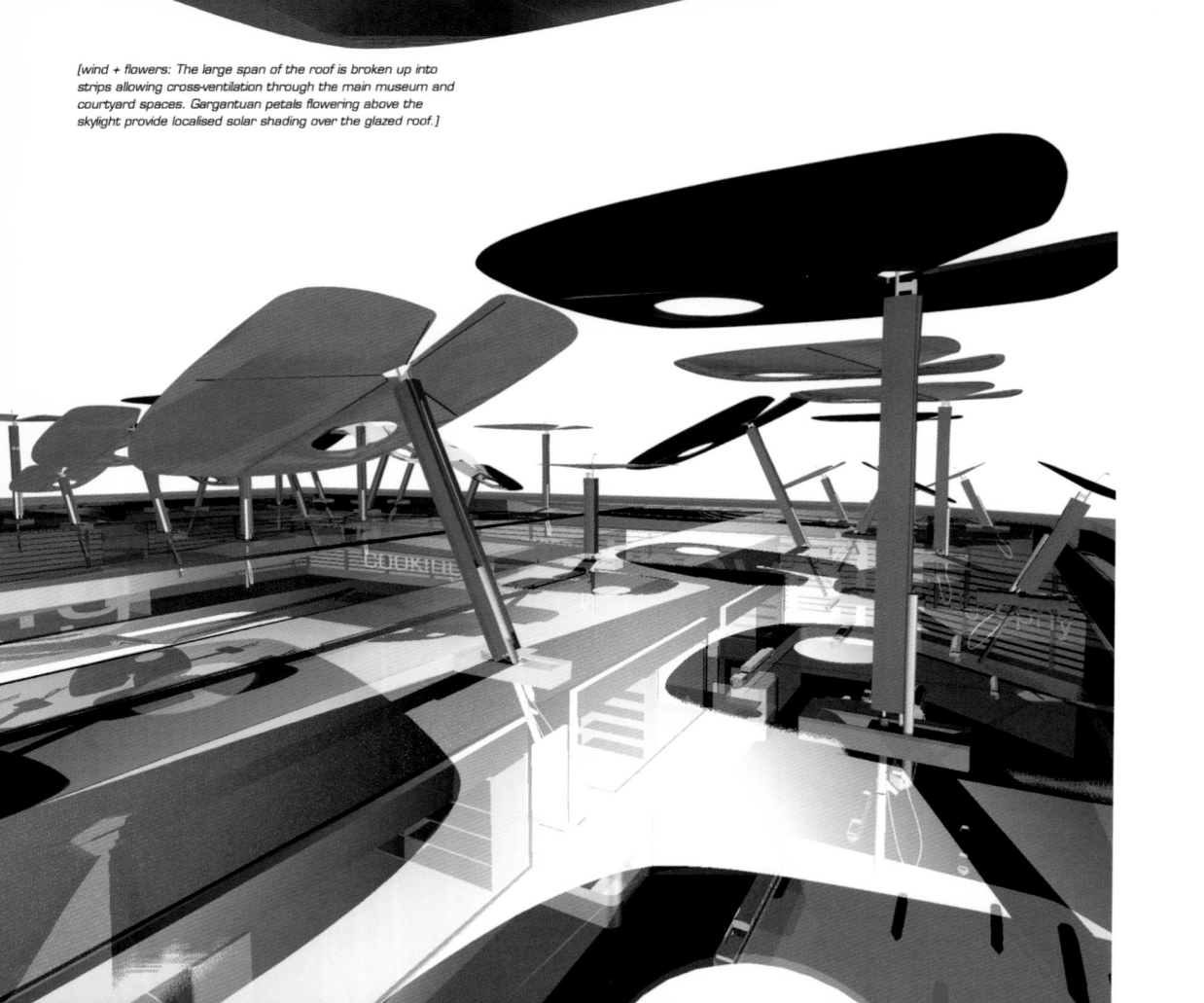

[wind + flowers: The large span of the roof is broken up into strips allowing cross-ventilation through the main museum and courtyard spaces. Gargantuan petals flowering above the skylight provide localised solar shading over the glazed roof.]

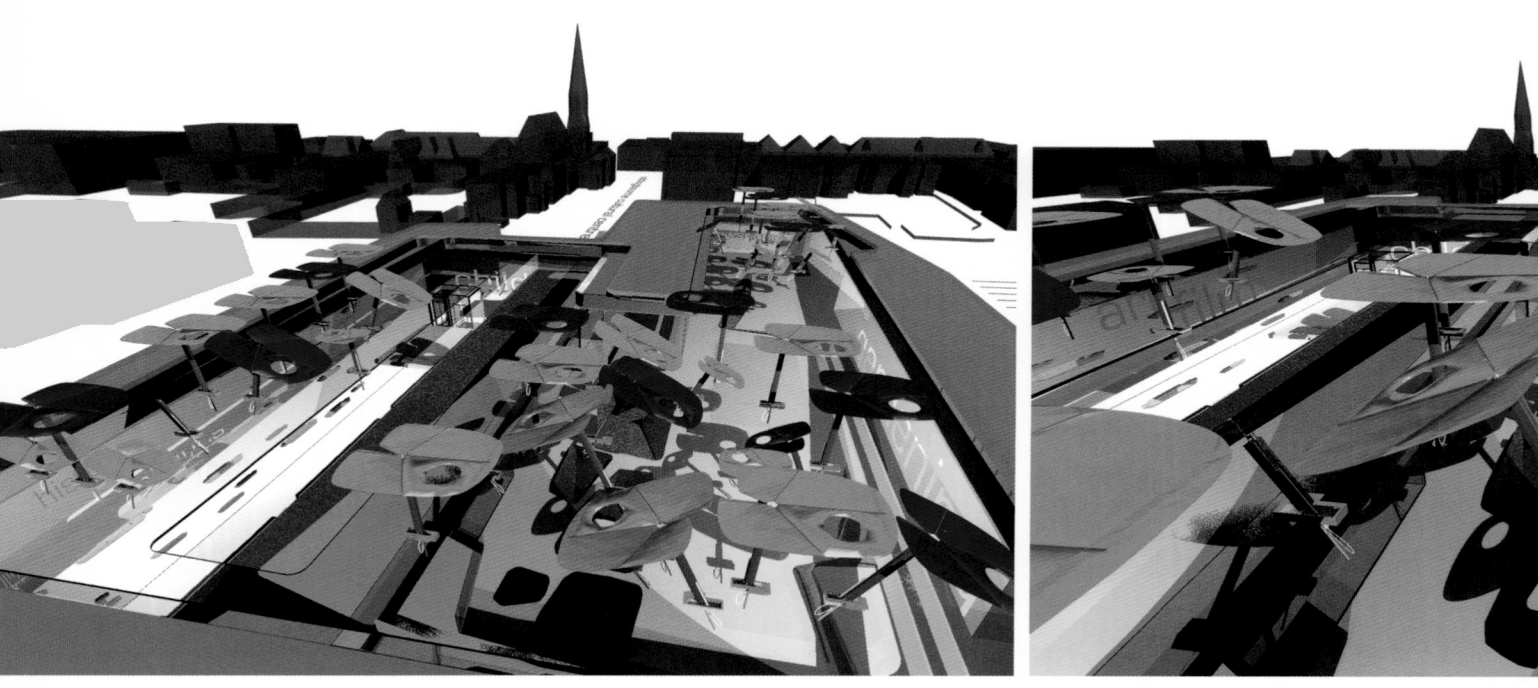

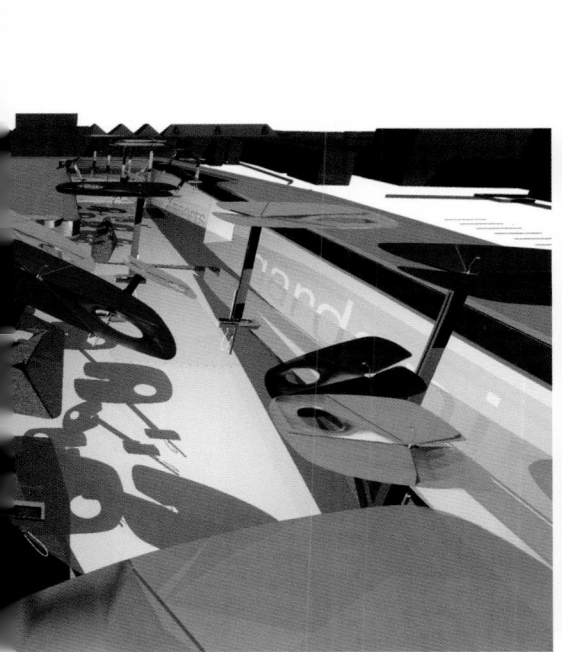

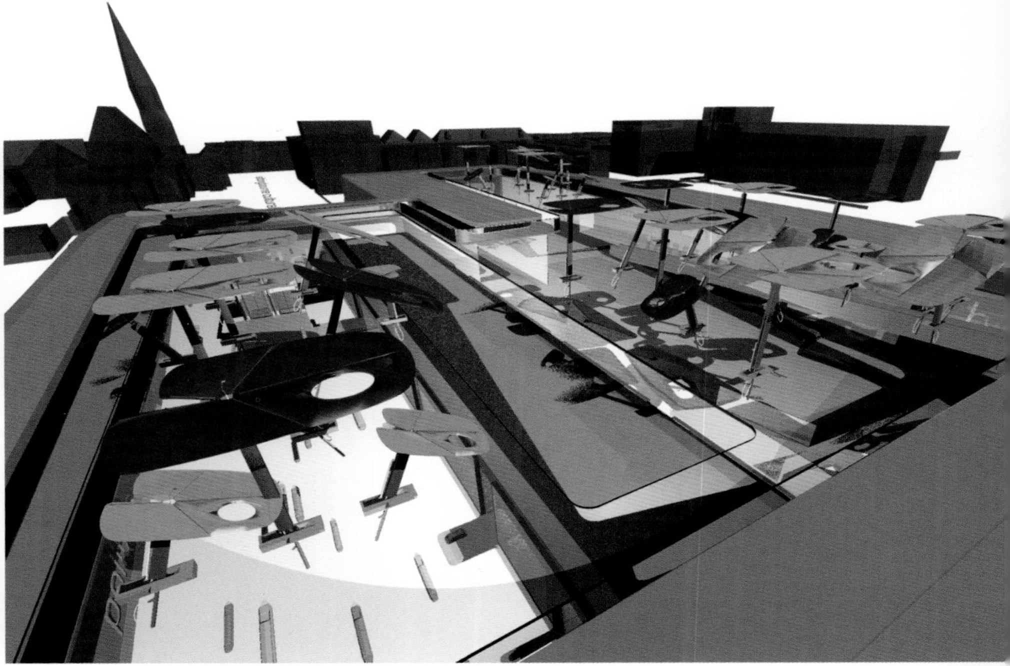

T he trail led through a thick bank of fog into another extraordinary green setting. Still entwined with misty tendrils, Alicia stared down at her rabbit-slippered toes with a mixture of comfortable recognition and embarrassment, opining that she should perhaps own something more sophisticated — glass slippers, for example, like her best friend Cindy's. The only glass in the garden, however, was on the floor, below which lay flowers of every description.

'Why, this is like a carpet of live flowers!' exclaimed Alicia with a delight that rapidly deflated as she forlornly recalled the dull floral affair that mother had picked out for the new flat.

'Wouldn't it be marvellous to have real flowers instead of pictures of them on the floor?' sighed Alicia. 'And wouldn't it be even more wonderful if I could smell them?'

As if in response to her wish, her nose entered what can only be described as a natural perfumery, assailed as it was by a myriad scents and fragrances a thousand times more ephemeral and tantalising than their synthesized facsimiles. Before her very eyes, the botanical carpet began to open up like petals, releasing the flowers within from their vitreous captivity. Swaying in the wind, they swished and sashayed in conversation with one another.

'What is that intoxicating odour?' asked Alicia.

'You are too kind,' said Rose. 'It is but I.'

CHAPTER 2:
IN WHICH ALICIA CONVERSES WITH A CARPET OF FLOWERS AND ALMOST LOSES HER REFLECTION

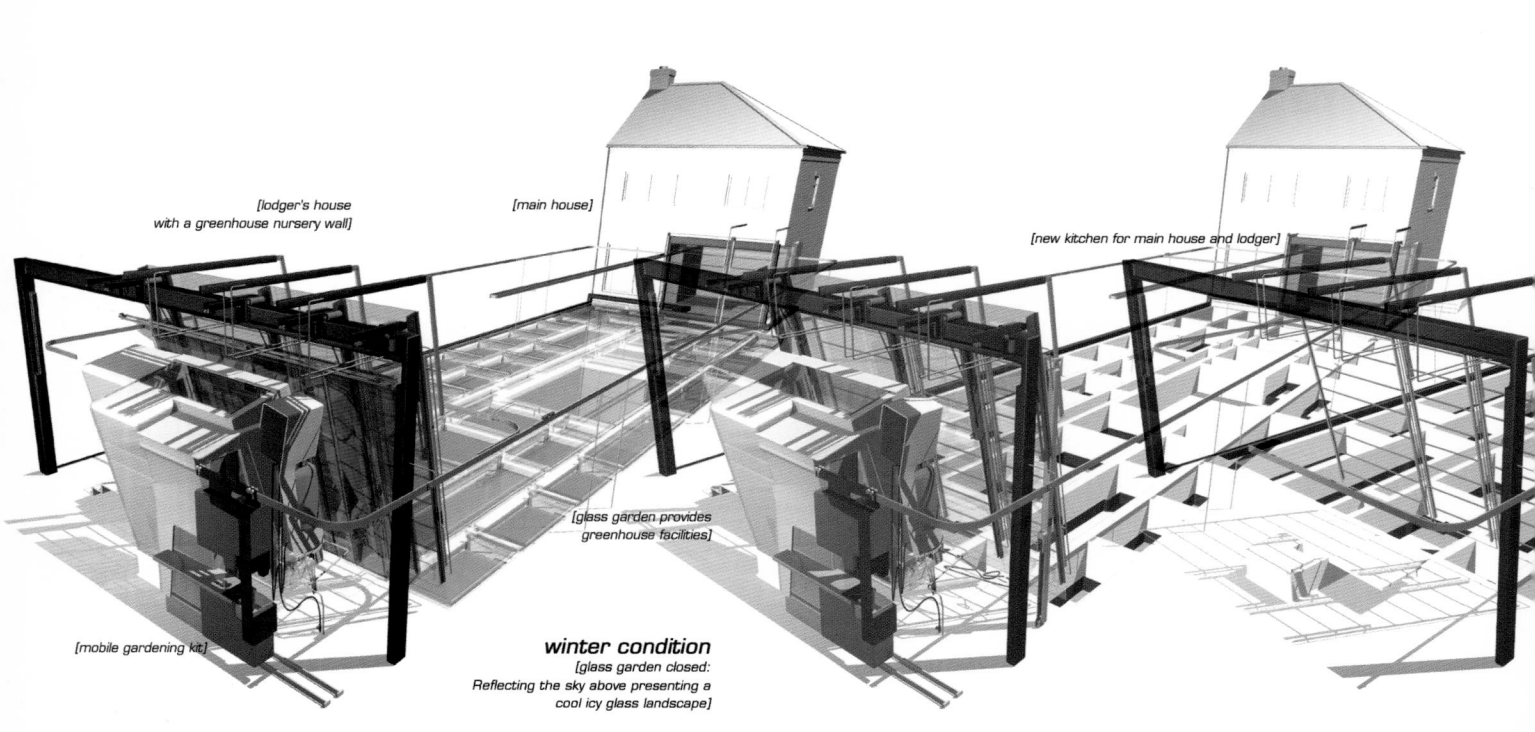

[lodger's house
with a greenhouse nursery wall]

[main house]

[new kitchen for main house and lodger]

[glass garden provides
greenhouse facilities]

[mobile gardening kit]

winter condition
[glass garden closed:
Reflecting the sky above presenting a
cool icy glass landscape]

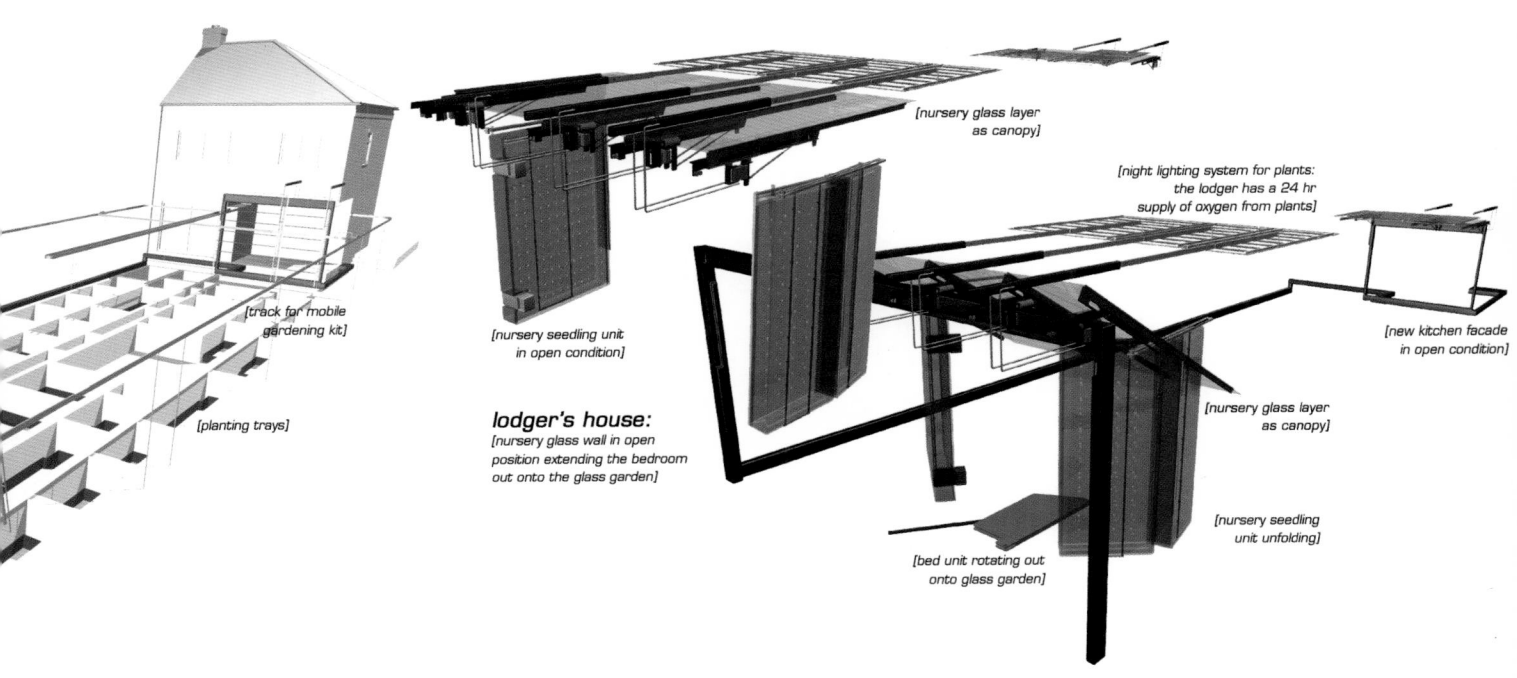

[nursery glass layer
as canopy]

[night lighting system for plants:
the lodger has a 24 hr
supply of oxygen from plants]

[track for mobile
gardening kit]

[nursery seedling unit
in open condition]

[new kitchen facade
in open condition]

[planting trays]

[nursery glass layer
as canopy]

lodger's house:
[nursery glass wall in open
position extending the bedroom
out onto the glass garden]

[nursery seedling
unit unfolding]

[bed unit rotating out
onto glass garden]

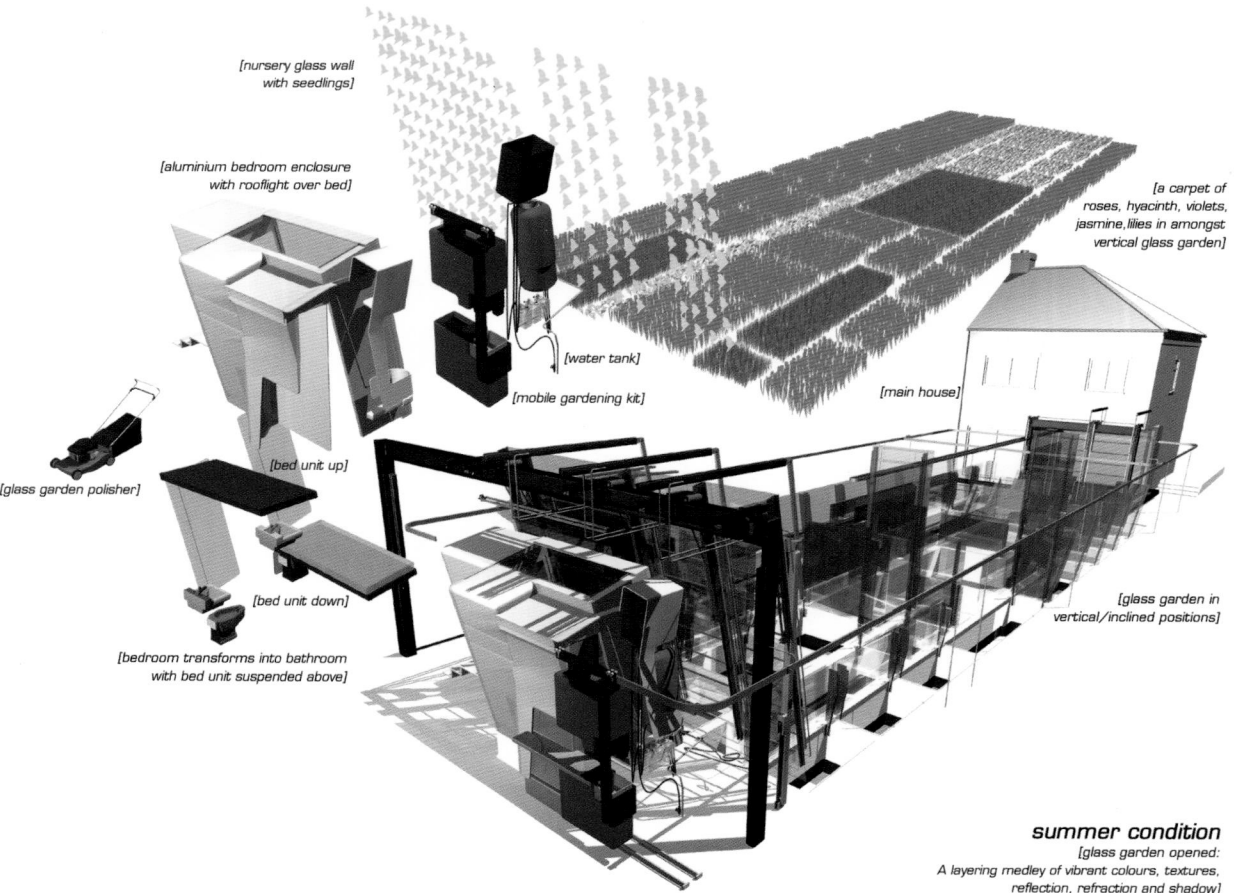

[nursery glass wall with seedlings]

[aluminium bedroom enclosure with rooflight over bed]

[a carpet of roses, hyacinth, violets, jasmine, lilies in amongst vertical glass garden]

[water tank]

[mobile gardening kit]

[main house]

[glass garden polisher]

[bed unit up]

[bed unit down]

[glass garden in vertical/inclined positions]

[bedroom transforms into bathroom with bed unit suspended above]

summer condition
[glass garden opened:
A layering medley of vibrant colours, textures, reflection, refraction and shadow]

'I believe she was referring to me,' huffed Hyacinth.

'She said intoxicating, dear, not toxic,' sniped Rose.

'Ladies, ladies! Let's not argue,' broke in a third voice that belonged to Violet. 'I'm sure she means all of us — Hyacinth, Jasmine and Lily included. Anyway, isn't it just marvellous to be out in the open once more, and feel the wind run through one's petals?'

'I suppose I was being a little snippy,' conceded Rose. 'I'm always a little piqued when waking from a nice dream. I dreamt I was a Queen, with thousands of suitors, all vying for my favour.'

'And I dreamt I was a princess!' added a higher pitched voice, which belonged to Jasmine.

Alicia stood stock-still, her mouth wide-open in astonishment, at the scene and scenery unfolding in front of her. She ventured closer to the squabbling flowers but as she approached, they became more subdued and indistinct until they could neither be seen nor heard at all.

'Where have you gone?' cried Alicia. 'I won't hurt you!'

'We are reflection flowers made of light,' said Rose from behind her. 'If you approach too close, your shadow makes us disappear.' Sure enough, as Alicia took a few paces back, the flowers re-emerged in their diaphanous glory. Much to her consternation, however, she could see her own reflection trapped in the folded carpet. Not only her reflection, but a reflection of her reflection, and a reflection of her reflection of her reflection.

'Where does it all end?' wailed Alicia. 'And how do I get out of this mess? If I'm not careful, I shall end up reflecting forever and ever!'

'I'm afraid you will have to wait till autumn when the carpet closes again,' said Violet.

'But it's only spring now!' wailed Alicia. 'And I'm expected home for elevenses!'

'Excuse me, Miss,' said a deep quavering voice behind her that made Alicia jump with a start before landing with a soft thud on her cushioned pink slippers. 'But who are you talking to?'

'The flowers, Sir. They were talking to me.'

'I have heard stories, although I have grave doubts apropos their scientific credibility, of plants flourishing when spoken to,' said a little man in a top hat and a grave voice (which might possibly be described as deep and quavering too). 'What I have not heard, even in the most esoteric circles, is a single instance of a flower talking to a human or indeed having an iota of influence on human behaviour.'

'Please, sir? How do I get out of this place?' asked Alicia.

'I really shouldn't do this. It's terribly

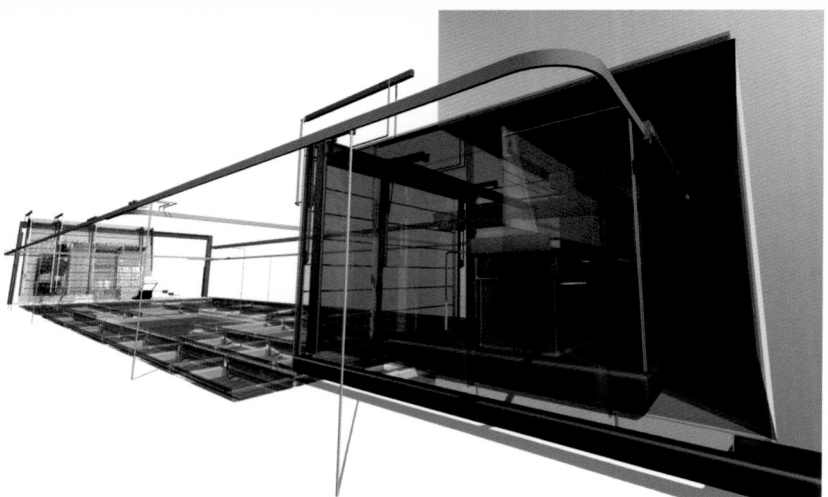

[choreography of the glass garden from winter to summer]

confusing for the poor flowers,' said the man in the hat as he pressed a button on what looked remarkably like the remote control of a TV. Quietly hissing, the glass carpet closed up and the spectrum of reflected and refracted colour, which was really quite marvellous to behold, began to vanish leaving Alicia and the little man in a quiet colourless place. 'T Carter at your service, Miss,' said the man, taking off his hat and bowing several times. 'Inventor Extraordinaire, creator of the world-renowned alarm-clock-bed that tips you out of slumber at your appointed hour.'

'That sounds just what I need!' said Alicia. 'I always have the most terrible trouble getting out of bed in the…'

'And I have dreamed up and shaped ideas far more wondrous since!' broke in T Carter.

'Ah. I would love to hear more, Mr Carter,' began Alicia politely. 'But I really must be…'

'It's so refreshing to met an inquisitive mind eager to learn from its betters,' interjected the little man. 'This remarkable abode yonder, for example,' exclaimed, T Carter, waving his arms around theatrically towards what looked like a glass hut.

'…going,' finished Alicia, who really did need to get home for elevenses.

'Going? Going? Why, you've only just arrived!' cried T Carter.

Alicia, a little crestfallen but glad she did not have to wait till autumn to leave, sat down in silence.

'I rent that place on the other side of the garden,' continued the funny little man, waving to a typical Victorian semi-detached house, '…to a cat and its family of four persons.' Very strange persons. Very strange indeed, if you catch my drift,' he said, nudging Alicia with a bony elbow and winking a squinted eye at her.

Alicia thought to herself privately that the man she was speaking to was quite the oddest person she had ever met (save perhaps the two infantile twins that had endlessly harangued each other at Sittingbourne) and that people who lived in glass huts should not throw stones.

'They seem to think that I rent this stately home from them,' he added, indicating the tiny glass edifice large enough to and indeed containing only a bathtub. 'And to cap it all off, they insist on mispronouncing my name as Caretaker!'

Alicia was convinced that this man was very deluded indeed, although the garden was rather astounding.

'This, here,' said T Carter, indicating a brightly-lit glass rampart, 'is my seedling wall. The plants inside live off my breath and, in return, they produce oxygen for me. And those flowers you were…"talking to",' sniggered T Carter, waving two fingers of each hand insultingly in the air, 'are my latest invention – a floral clock! The flowers tell me the time by opening and closing their petals.'

'That's not an invention!' exclaimed Alicia indignantly. 'The flowers open and close according to the hour regardless. And they did so speak to me! Besides, I've already read about the floral clock in one of the books at home!' accused Alicia.

'Yes, yes. Well, you said you had to be off, didn't you?' said T Carter quickly, ushering her out of the hut. 'Elevenses, wasn't it? Goodbye. Do call again!' And with that, Alicia found herself bundled rather unceremoniously out of LookingGlassHouse and back into her bedroom.

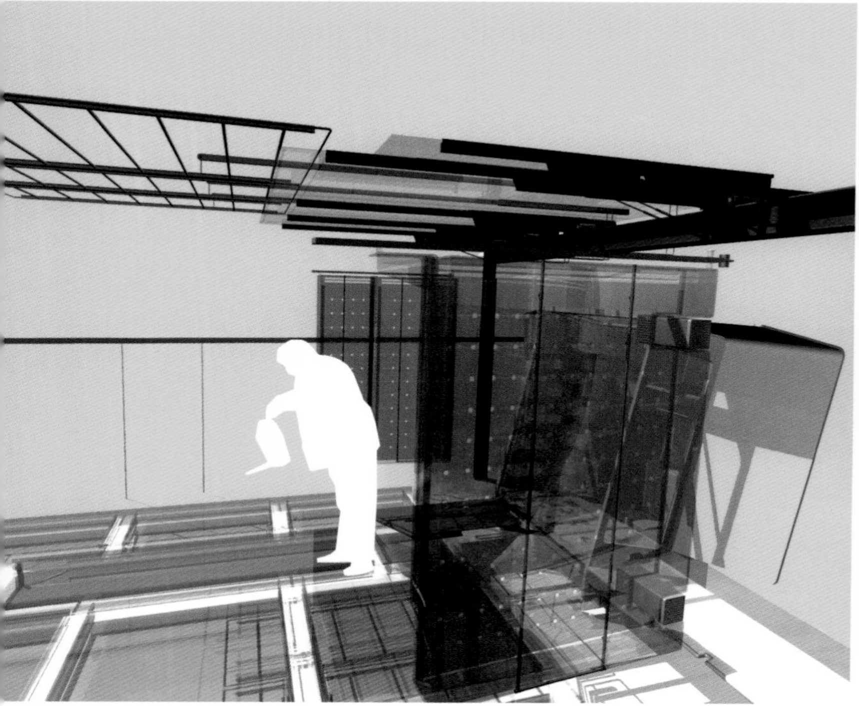

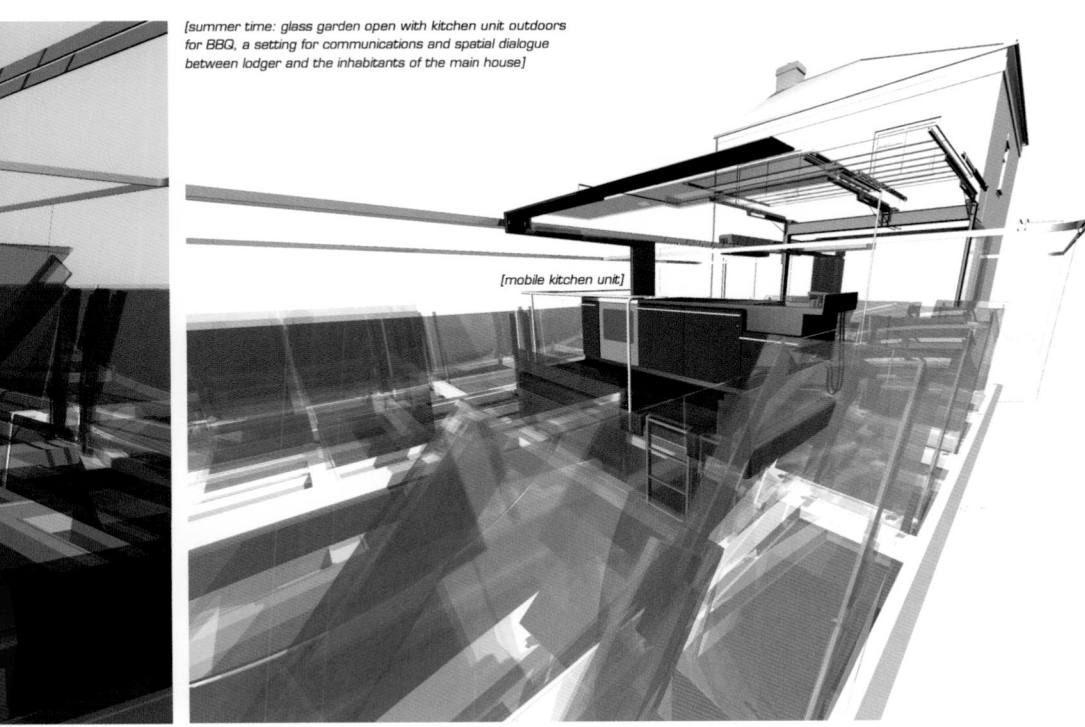

[summer time: glass garden open with kitchen unit outdoors
for BBQ, a setting for communications and spatial dialogue
between lodger and the inhabitants of the main house]

[mobile kitchen unit]

12 may **spring**

(Looking)Glass House

[through the looking glass garden]

MIRRORED TEXT

'I wonder what time it is,' said Lu-Tze, who was walking ahead.

Everything is a test. Lobsang glanced around at the flowerbed.

'A quarter past nine,' he said.

'Oh? And how do you know that?'

'The field marigold is open, the red sandwort is opening, the purple bindweed is closed, and the yellow goat's beard is closing,' said Lobsang.

'You worked out the floral clock all by yourself?'

'Yes. It's obvious.'

'Really? What time is it when the white waterlily opens?'

'Six in the morning.'

- Terry Pratchett, The Thief of Time

Theophilus Carter, supposed inspiration for Lewis Carroll's Mad Hatter, was a furniture dealer who habitually wore a top hat and invented an 'alarm clock bed'.

noon ∎∎3

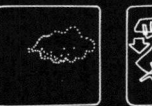

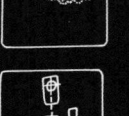
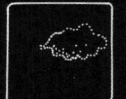
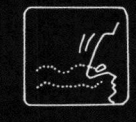
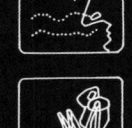
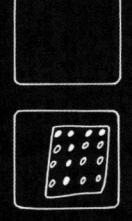

CHAPTER 3:
IN WHICH ALICIA IS VISITED BY A GARDEN AND SUCCUMBS TO A BOUT OF LIGHTHEADEDNESS

S taring dreamily out of the kitchen window down onto the street below, Alicia remarked, 'I so wish we had a garden'. Wishes, in Alicia's experience, had a habit of not coming true, so she was quite amazed as a garden pulled up in front of the house, lazily stretched itself out across the street, and rose up on its three spindly legs until it reached the level of Alicia's sparkling eyes. Her Uncle Charles had once told her that the price of having your wish granted was getting what you once wished for. At the time, Alicia had nodded politely, but was privately thinking that that wasn't much of a price at all. So without further ado, she hitched up her skirt and clambered out of the window into the waiting foliage.

'How peculiar!' exclaimed Alicia. 'All the plants are trapped inside little glass cages. The air out here smells very sweet indeed, and the plants certainly look very healthy, but how on earth can they breathe? And there's no soil, but the whole world knows that plants need soil to get their daily fill of nutrients.'

'COO! Aeroponics,' said a caterpillar from inside one of the glass cages next to her. 'COO! Plants breathe see-oh-two'

Alicia rubbed her eyes and opened them again. The multicoloured caterpillar was still there, sitting on a spiky green plant within a transparent bubble and smoking a miniature hookah.

'And who might you be?' asked the Caterpillar. Its voice was languid, sleepy, and somewhat distorted by the bubble.

'My name is Alicia ... Mister Caterpillar,' unsure of the correct form of address for polypodal invertebrates. Indeed, she was starting to question her own sanity and whether it was appropriate to engage an insect in conversation at all. The smoke was starting to make her dizzy.

'Oh dear!' exclaimed caterpillar looked up from his hookah. 'Oh dear, no. You must get down at once! Only Marcias, Gregs, Jans, Peters, Carols, Mikes, Cindys or Bobbies can sit here. Alices must sit over there, next to the barbecue. Alicia is long for Alice, isn't it?' the caterpillar asked sternly.

'Yes. I suppose it is,' said Alicia, feeling quite drowsy.

'It's Alice's job to tend the barbecue,' said the caterpillar.

'But there is no smoke to cook with, and no food to cook! Besides, I wouldn't know where to begin.'

'You must!' shrieked the caterpillar. 'You're Alice!' By this time, Alicia was not quite sure whether she was Alice, Alicia, or herself for that matter, although she suspected the last two were one and the same. 'Alices do all the cooking, the ironing, the cleaning and the gardening in the household!' Alicia climbed over to the seat by the barbeque, which seemed to placate the caterpillar somewhat.

'This is ridiculous!' thought Alicia. 'I haven't made up imaginary object and animals since I was

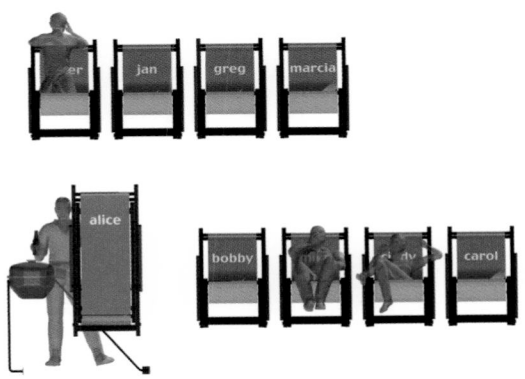

[Deckchairs on a mobile frame traverse the length of the garden. The nine deckchairs make reference to the quintessential all-American happy family from the 70's TV series "The Brady Bunch"]

Plant BillBoard

[garden delivered to your front door]

[Billboard advocating the lifestyle of the happy family while concealing the illicit substances that makes such harmony appear possible.]

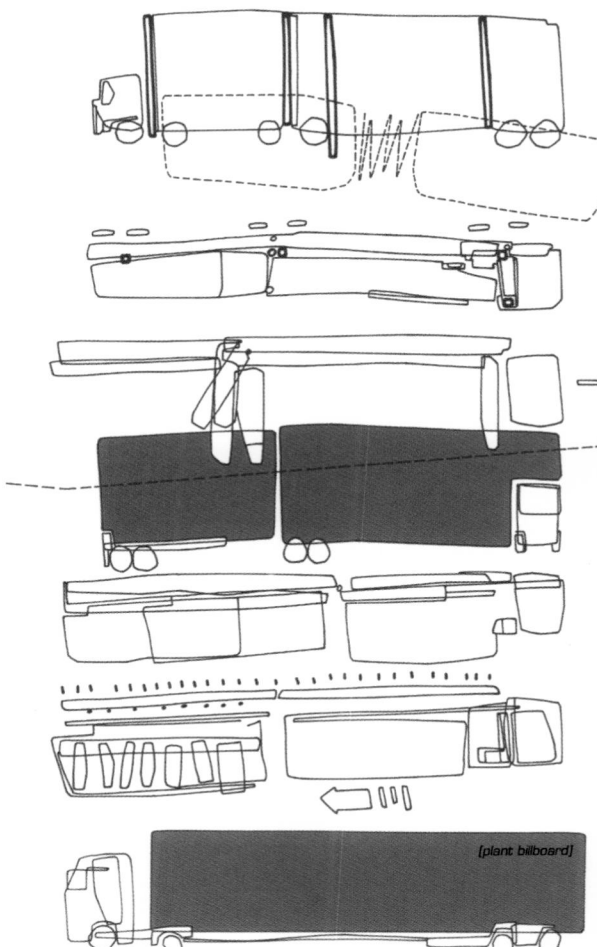

[plant billboard]

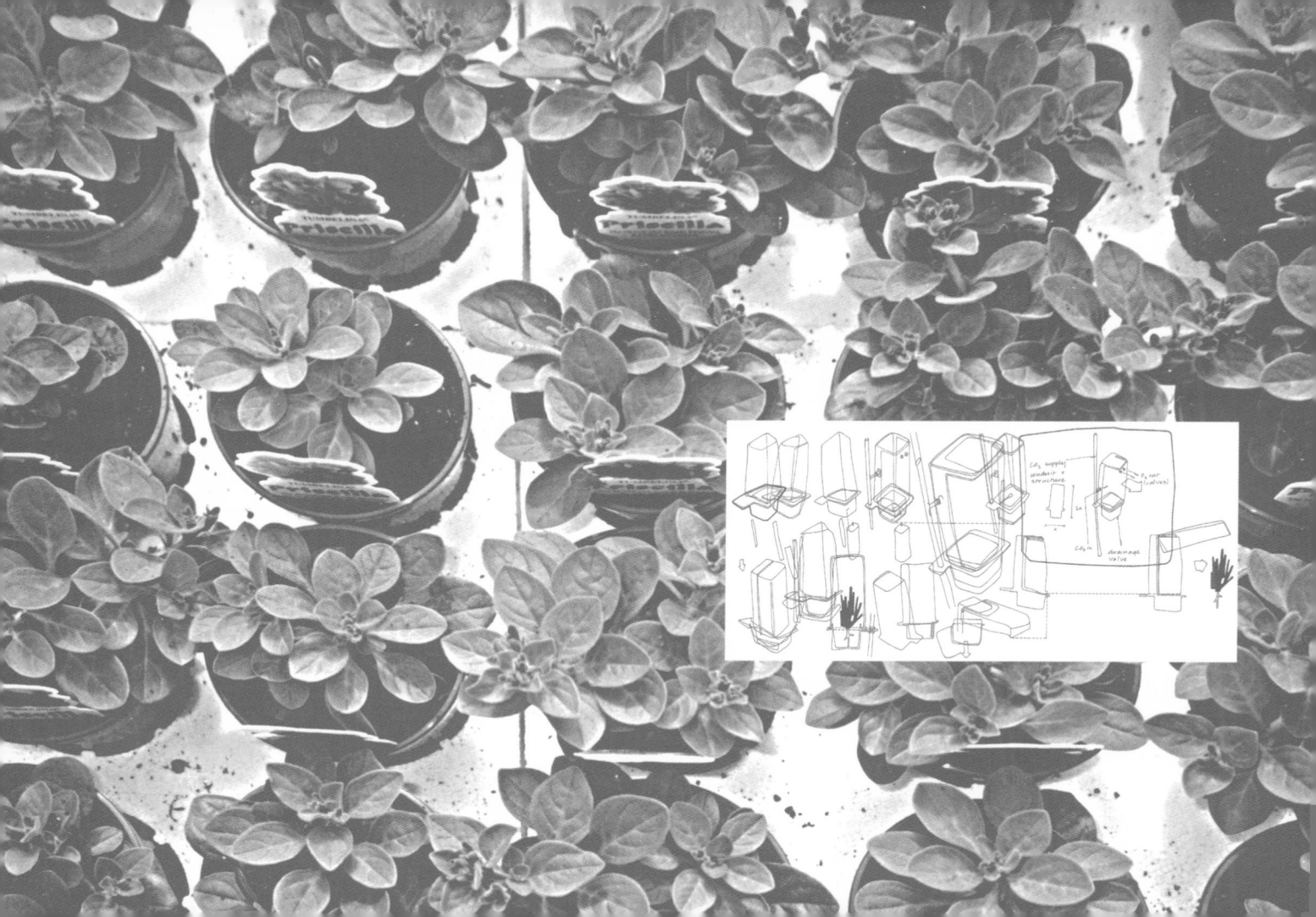

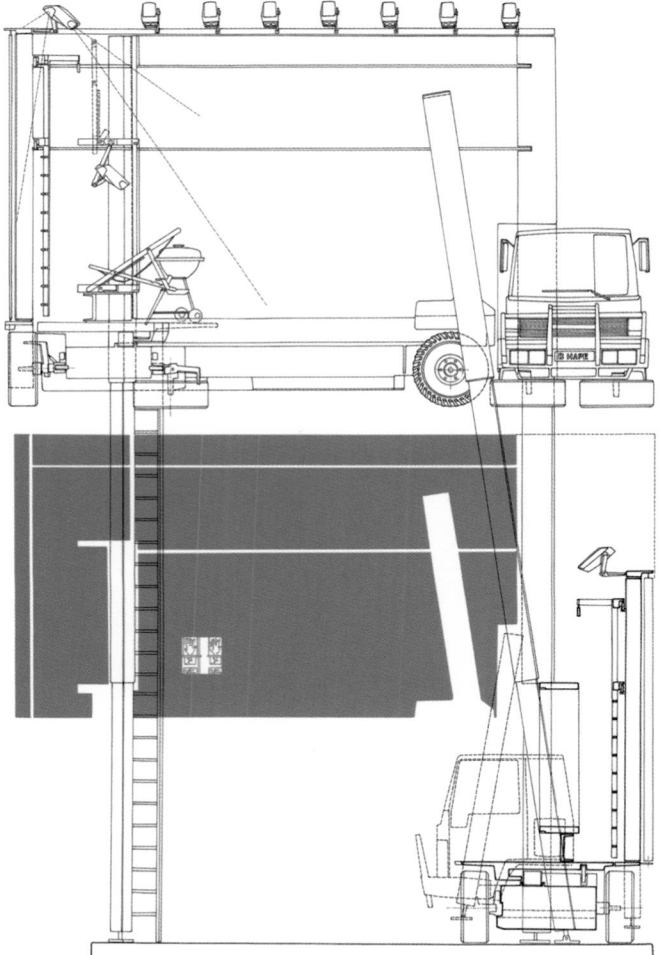

a little girl.' Away from the caterpillar's watchful eye, Alicia took out the little green book she had borrowed from the library. It opened up on the following page:

The hanging gardens of wanton harmony are not gardens at all.

'I thought this was too good to be true,' said Alicia wistfully. Eager to find out what she had landed herself in, she read on:

Simultaneously an advertisement and realisation of a transitory moment, it is a picture-postcard of happier times and sunnier climes. An extended family of nine perch showcased in an oasis of green, chatting amicably or snoozing in the sun with the barbecue wafting scents of wellbeing to all and sundry. But like any advertisement or postcard, the veil of substance is paper-thin and easily sundered.

The heart of the home where the family may gather and interact socially has gone through many incarnations, from the heart(h) to the dining table to the television set. Taking this trend to its logical conclusion, the hanging gardens of wanton harmony lack a focal point

[The garden is open to the elements, flooded by light from bi-directional luminairies that light the plants while bathing the family in UV radiation for that mid-winter tan.]

altogether. Privacy, security and comfort, those cornerstones of the home are all absent, save only in the most superficial, empty terms. There is no roof. There are no curtains. The barbecue is a sham and familial accord comes only from smoking the endless rows of aeroponically-grown dope from the garden.

'My Goodness! What kind of dreadful place have I stumbled upon? This garden is absolutely horrid!' And with that, Alicia picked up the hems of her skirt and crawled back into the discomfort of her new gardenless home.

Pot Soup

1 pint chicken stock
3 tablespoons grass
3 tablespoons lemon juice
1/2 pint water
3 tablespoons chopped
watercress

Combine all ingredients in a
pan and bring to a boil over
medium heat. Place in a
refrigerator for two to three
hours and serve chilled.
Garnish with watercress.

Pork and Beans

200g minced pork
150g lentils
10g marijuana
4 rashers of streaky bacon
50g brown sugar
1/2 teaspoon sea-salt
several chunks of pineapple

Mix together in a casserole
dish, cover top with pineapple and bacon and bake at
350°C for about 45 minutes
or until golden brown.
Serves six approx.

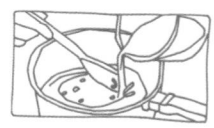
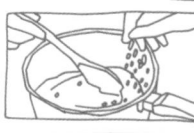
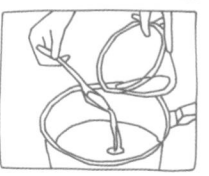

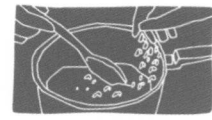

The Meat Ball

1 lb. hamburger
200g chopped onions
1 can mushroom soup
100g breadcrumbs
3 tablespoons grass
3 tablespoons relish

Combine the ingredients and
shape into meatballs. Brown
in frying pan and drain.
Place in a casserole dish
with soup and 150ml water.
Cover and cook over low
heat for about 30 minutes.
Serves four.

Spaghetti Sauce

400g tomato passata
2 tablespoons olive oil
100g finely chopped onions
10g chopped marijuana
pepper
150ml water
1 clove of garlic, minced
1 bay leaf
1 teaspoon thyme
1/2 teaspoon sea-salt

Mix in a large pot, cover and
stir frequently for two hours.
Serve over spaghetti.

Pot Loaf

100g finely chopped onions
400g tinned tomatoes
10g chopped marijuana
200g ground beef
1 egg (beaten)
200g breadcrumbs

Combine all ingredients and
shape into a loaf. Bake for
one hour at 400°C. Serves
six approx.

Chilli Bean Pot

400g kidney beans
200g sliced pancetta
2 glasses red wine
4 tablespoons chilli
1 garlic clove
10g chopped grass
200g mushrooms

Soak beans overnight in
water. Cover beans with boiling water in a large pot
and simmer for at least an
hour, adding more water to
keep beans immersed. Add
remaining ingredients and
continue to simmer for
another three hours. Season
to taste. Serves 10 approx.

Apple Pot

4 apples (cored)
200g brown sugar
100ml water
50g cherries
15g chopped grass
2 tablespoons cinnamon

Powder the grass in a blender. Then mix grass with sugar and water. Stuff cores with the resulting paste. Sprinkle apples with cinnamon, and top with a cherry. Bake for 25 minutes at 350°C or until golden brown.

Pot Brownies

200g self-raising flour
3 tablespoons shortening
2 tablespoons honey
1 egg (beaten)
1 tablespoon water
15g grass
pinch of salt
1/4 teaspoon baking powder
200g granulated sugar
2 tablespoons corn syrup
50g cocoa powder
1 teaspoon vanilla essence
100g chopped nuts

Sift the flour, baking powder, and salt together. Mix in the shortening, sugar, honey, syrup, and egg. Then blend in chocolate and other ingredients, mixing well. Spread in an eight-inch pan and bake for 20 minutes at 350°C.

Banana Bread

150g shortening
2 eggs
1 teaspoon lemon juice
3 teaspoons baking powder
250g granulated sugar
200g mashed bananas
300g plain flour
15g chopped marijuana
1/2 teaspoon salt
200g chopped nuts

Mix the shortening and sugar. Add eggs and beat into mixture. Separately mix bananas with lemon juice and add to the first mixture. Sift flour, salt, and baking powder together, then combine all ingredients together. Bake for 1 1/4 hours at 375°C.

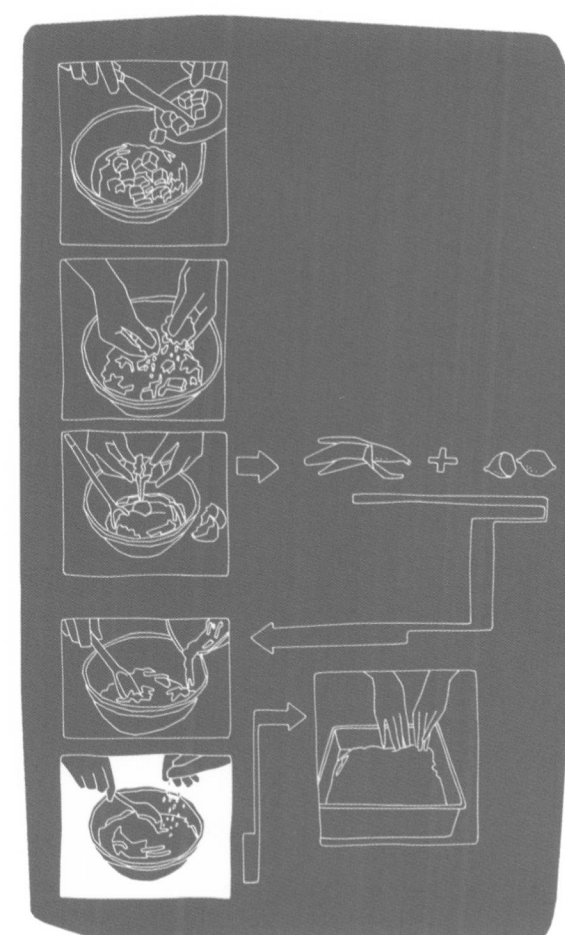

Sesame Seed Cookies

100g ground sesame seeds
1 tablespoon ground almonds
1/4 teaspoon nutmeg
50g honey
1/4 teaspoon cinnamon
1/4 oz grass

Toast the grass until slightly brown and then crush with a mortar and pestle. Mix crushed grass with all other ingredients in a skillet. Place over low heat and add a tablespoon of salted butter. Allow to cook. When cool, roll mixture into little balls and dip them into the sesame seeds.

If you happen to be at a place where pot is being grown, here's one of the greatest recipes you can try. Pick a medium-sized leaf off the marijuana plant and dip it into a cup of drawn butter. Add salt, and eat.

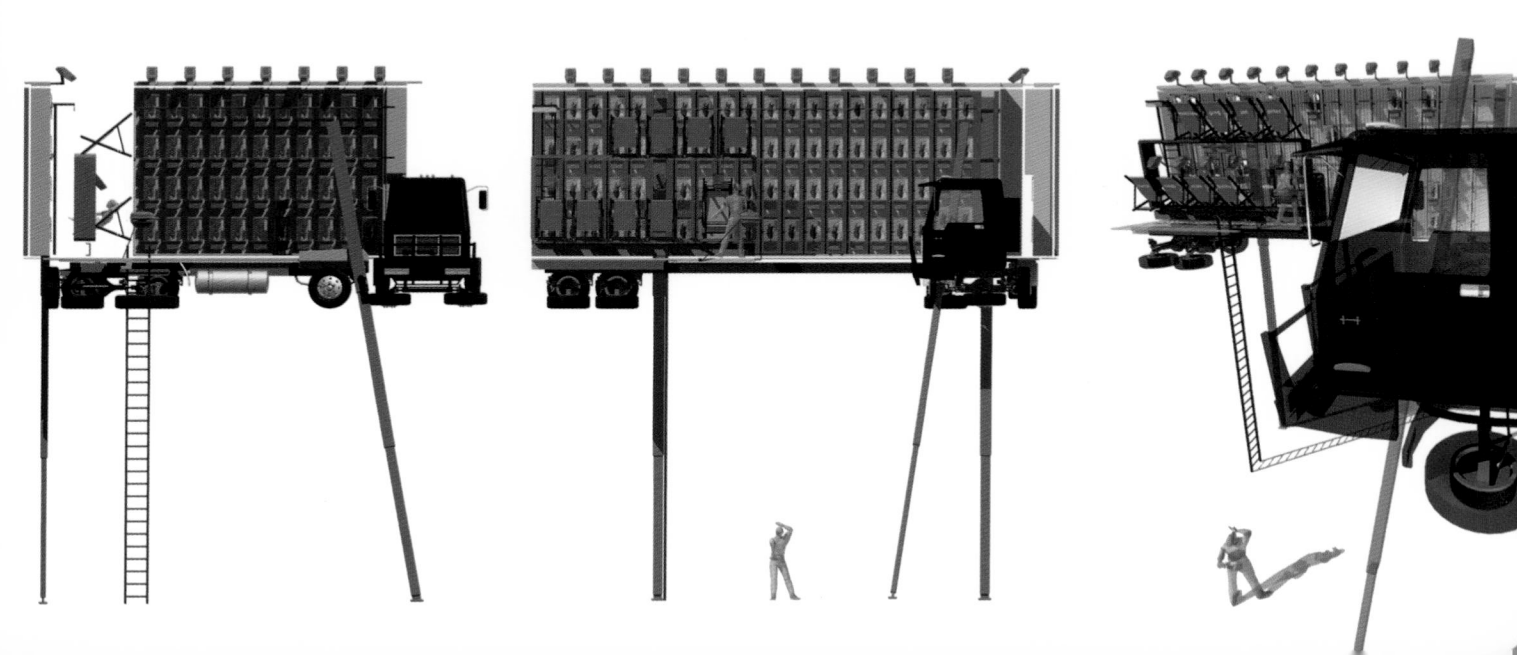

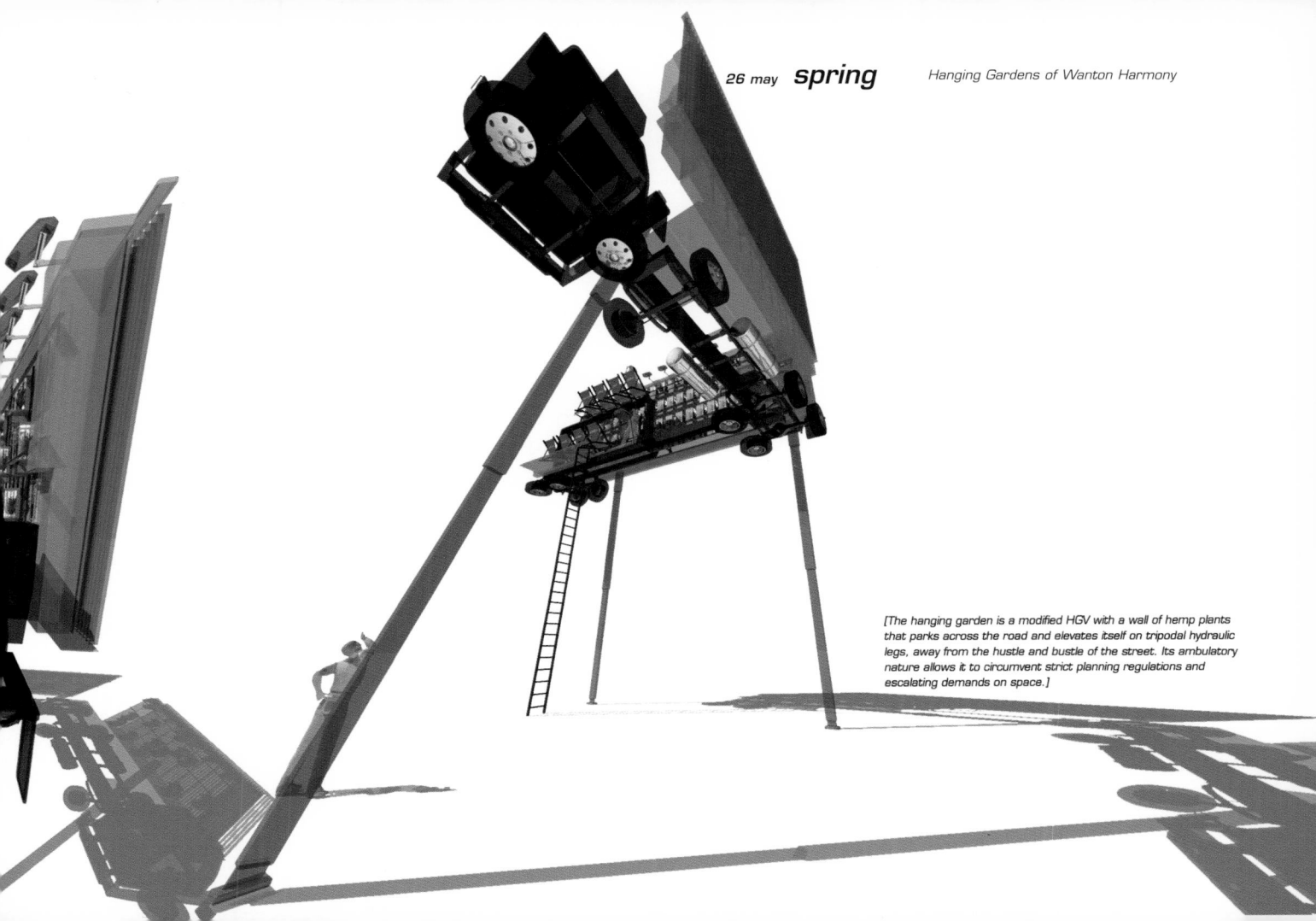

Hanging Gardens of Wanton Harmony

[The hanging garden is a modified HGV with a wall of hemp plants that parks across the road and elevates itself on tripodal hydraulic legs, away from the hustle and bustle of the street. Its ambulatory nature allows it to circumvent strict planning regulations and escalating demands on space.]

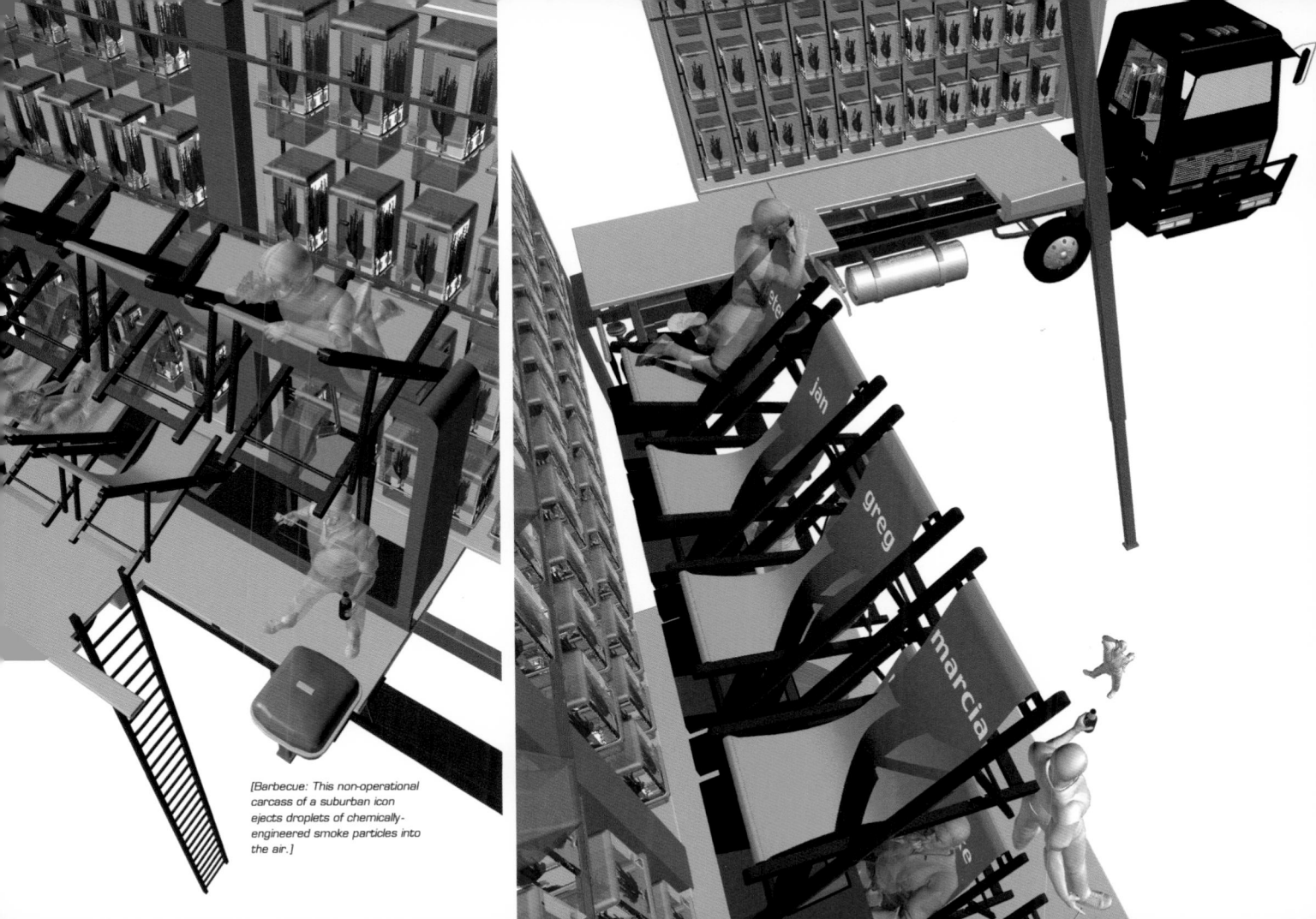

[Barbecue: This non-operational carcass of a suburban icon ejects droplets of chemically-engineered smoke particles into the air.]

[lily of the nile]

[sunflower]

[lemon]

[peaches]

[saxifraga]

[asiatic lillies]

[hydrangea lady katsuko]

[horsetail]

[saxifraga]

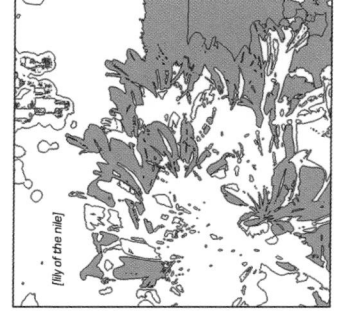

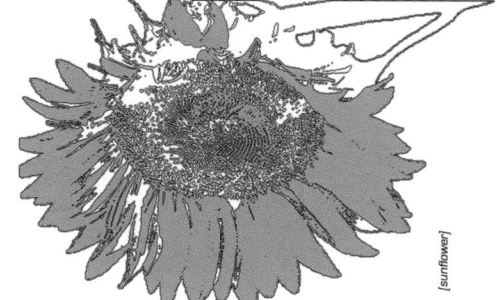

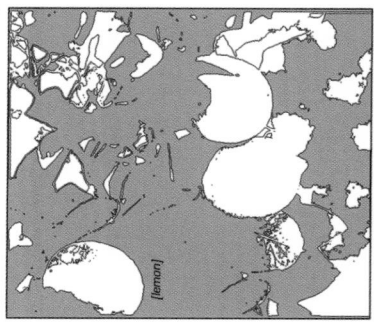

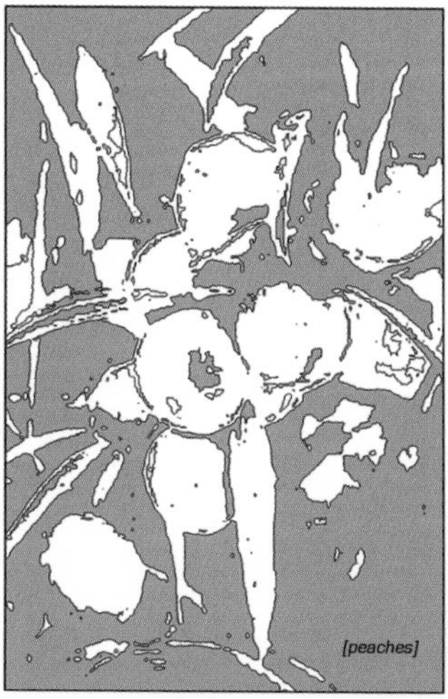

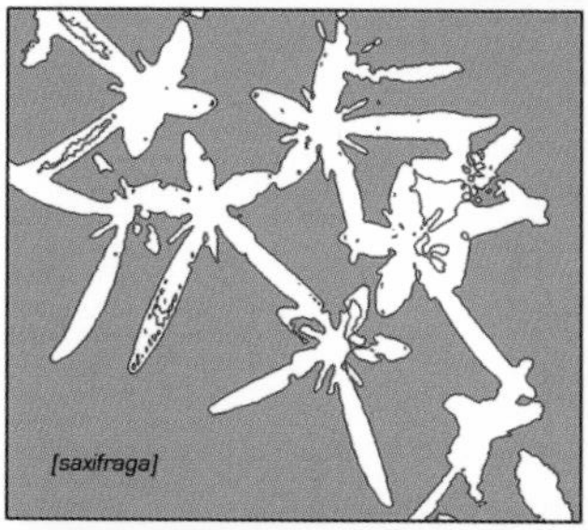

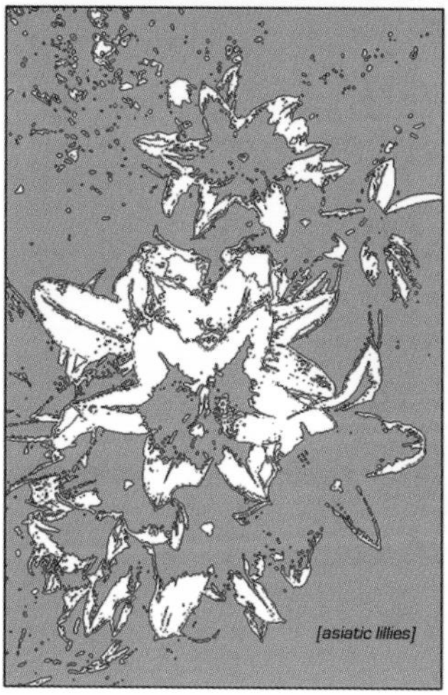

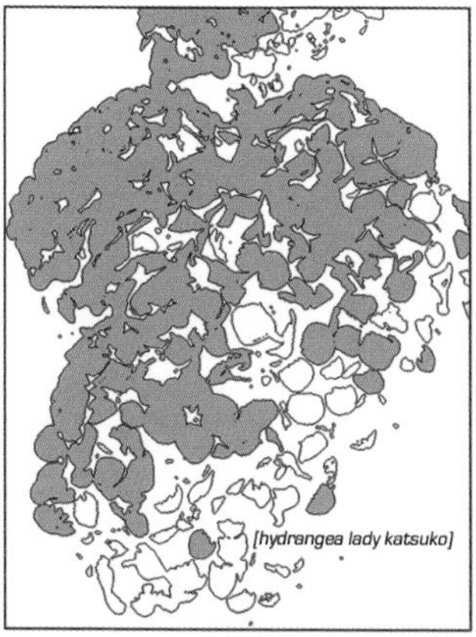

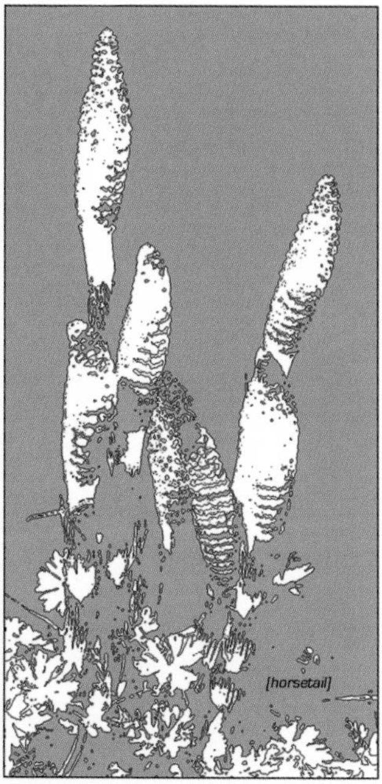

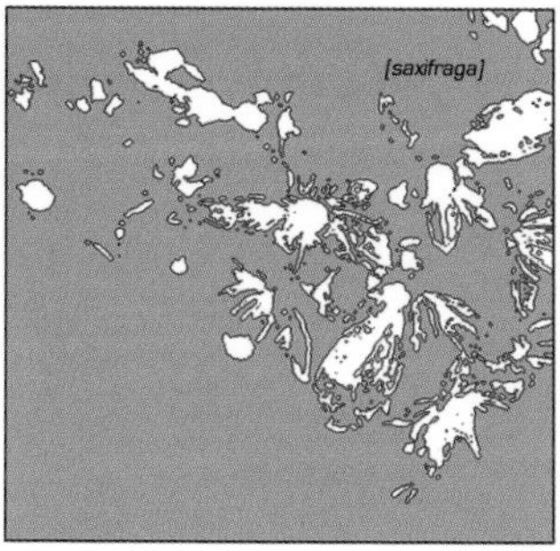

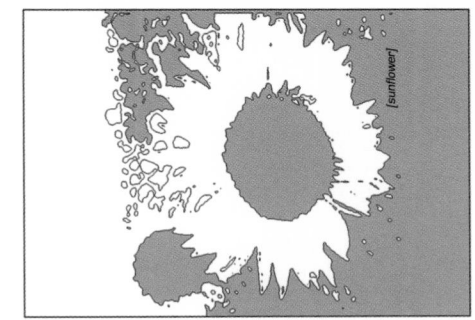

[sunflower]

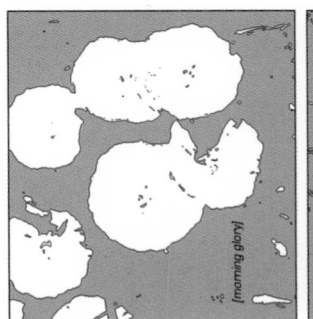

[morning glory]

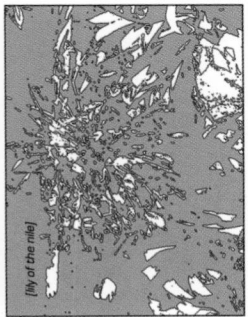

[lily of the nile]

summer

1.30pm 4

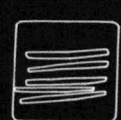

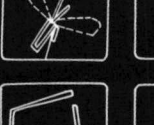

JAN

One afternoon, Alicia was playing hide-and-seek with Edith. As the flat was so scarce of good hiding places, this was, by Alicia's reckoning, the twenty-first time she had secreted herself inside Mother's wardrobe. Nestled next to her were clothes of every hue and texture imaginable. The strange thing was that Mother became somebody quite different depending on what outfit she wore. There was the 'out-for-a-soiree-with-Papa' mother, the 'just-got-out-of-bed-go-away' mother, the 'I'm-an-important-businesswoman' mother and the recent 'painting-the-house-while-Papa-attempts-some-DIY' mother to name but a few. Animals, Alicia knew, could also change their skins to suit their environments like the varying hare, the mosquito fish and the almost-extinct spot-changing leopard. Buildings, though, only managed to change their skins every few decades if they were lucky. That is, until Alicia came across the Green Palace in the book from the library.

Follow the trail and it will lead you to the green palace.

read the small type.

'Trail, trail,' muttered Alicia glancing down at her feet, slippered within two rather worn-looking pink bunnies. Beneath them flashed a pale luminous light. Several paces in front of her was a second light, a third and then umpteen ad infinitum.

'Why it looks as if a little boy has been

CHAPTER 4:
IN WHICH WE LEARN OF A BUILDING THAT CHANGES CLOTHES WITH EACH PASSING SEASON

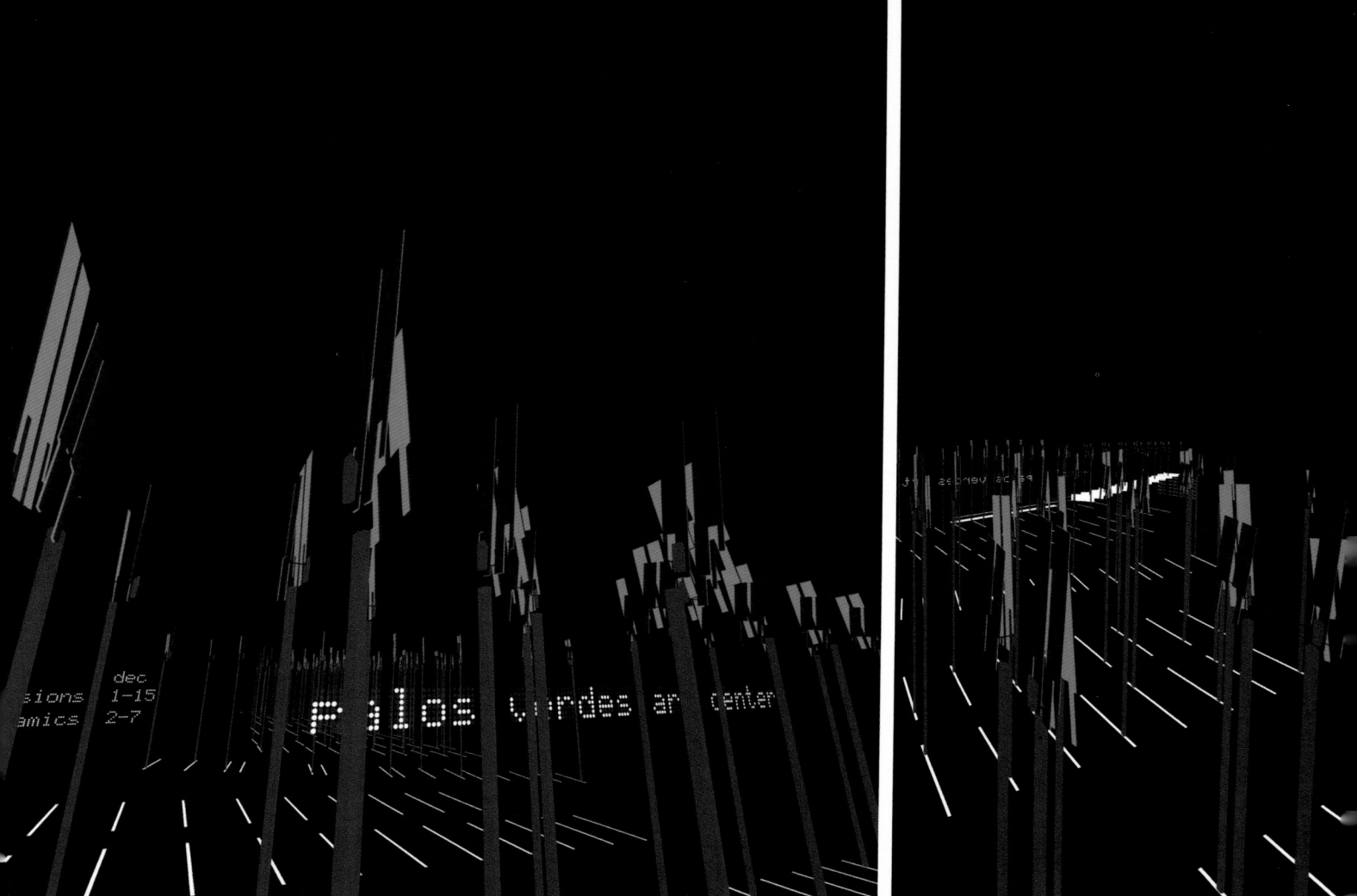

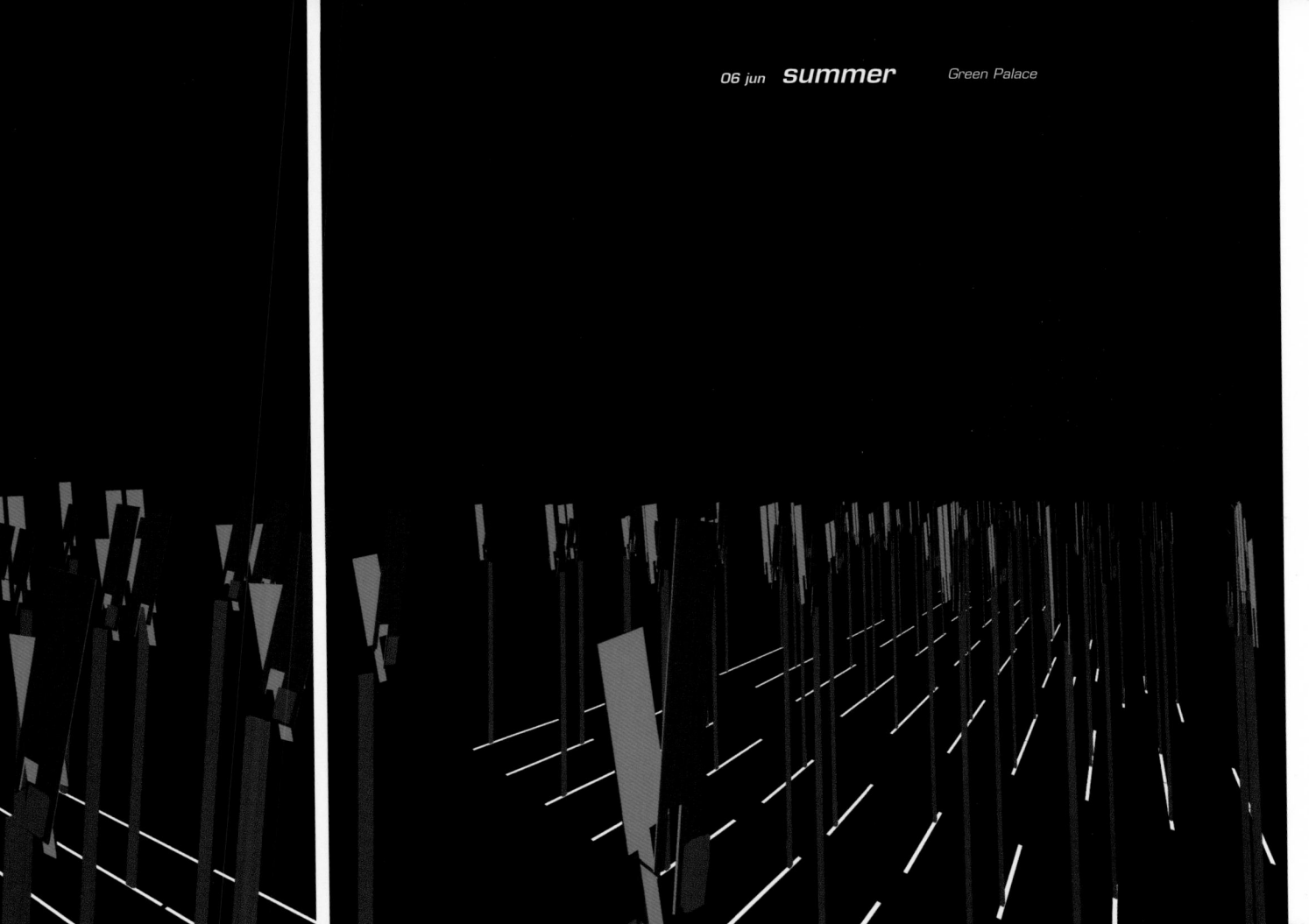

06 jun **summer** *Green Palace*

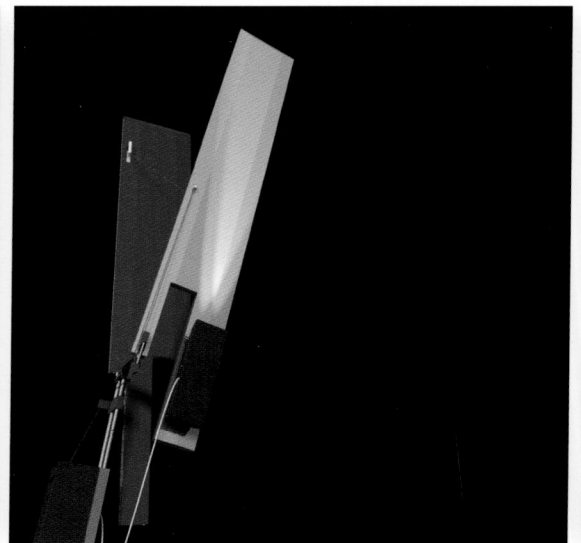

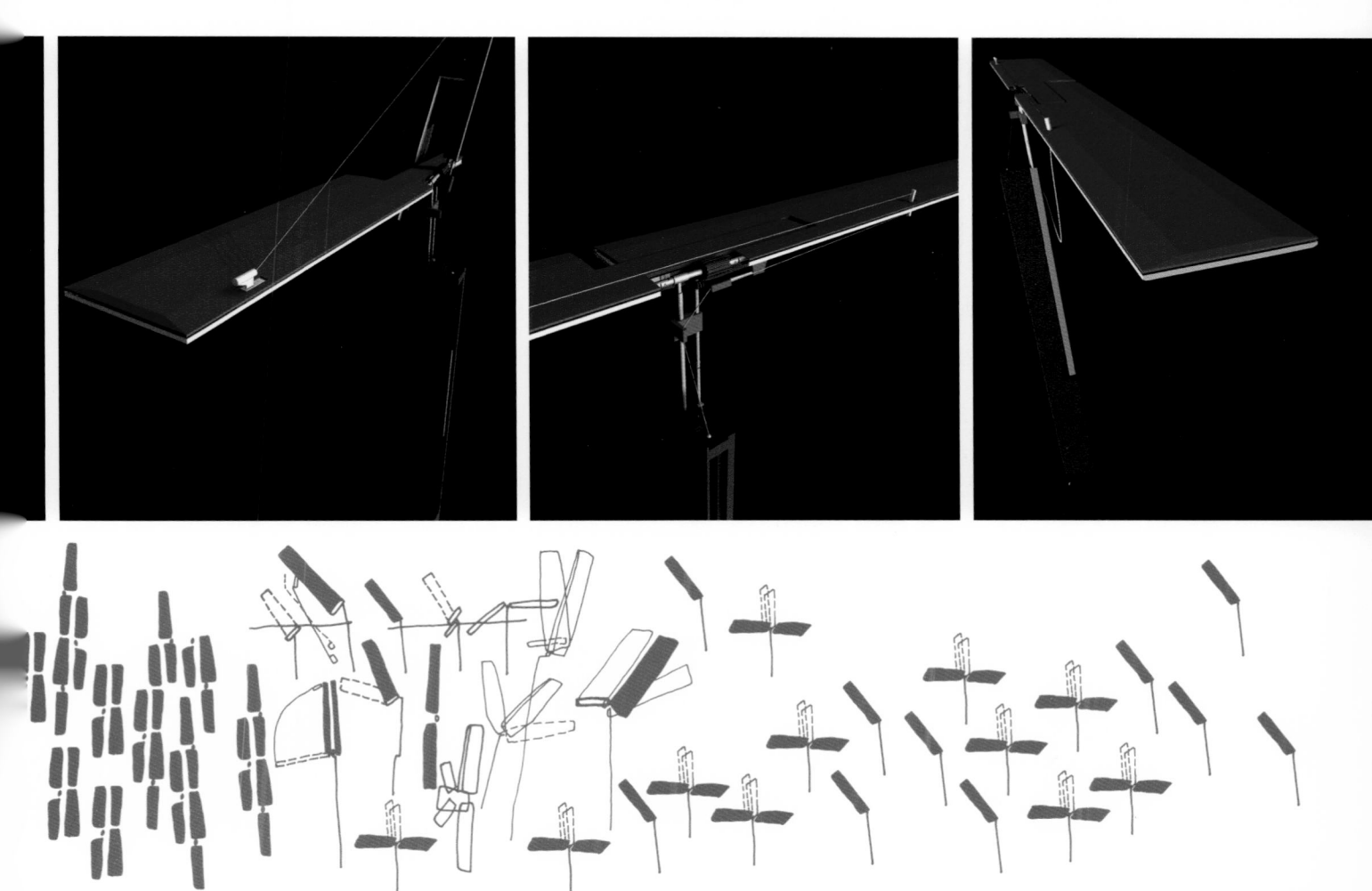

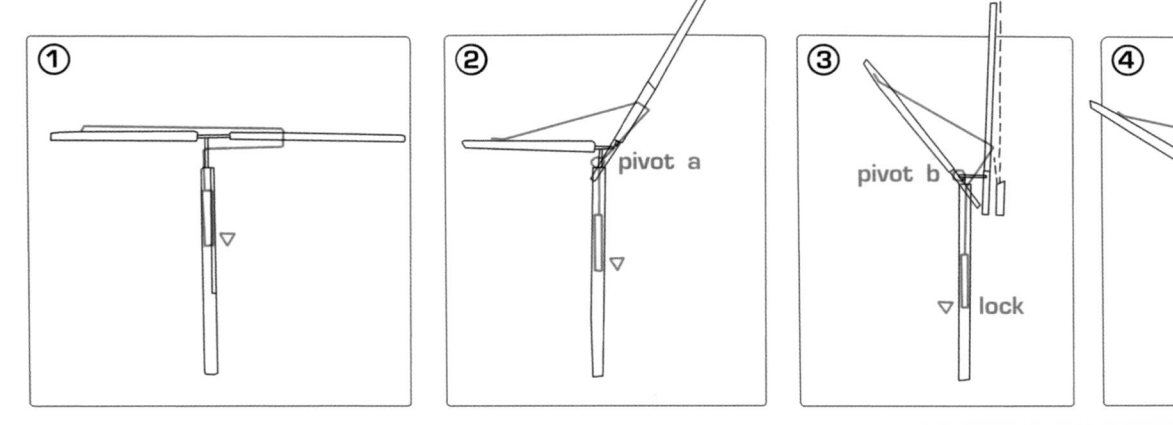

①

② pivot a

③ pivot b   ▽ lock

④ △ release

①a   e⁻   ▽

①b   e⁻   rotate

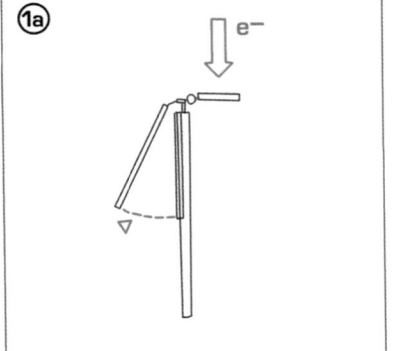

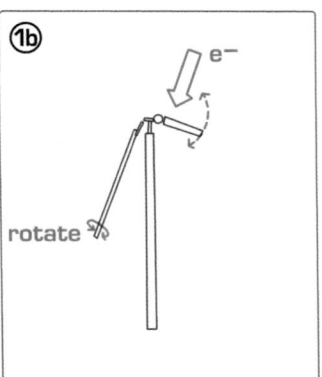

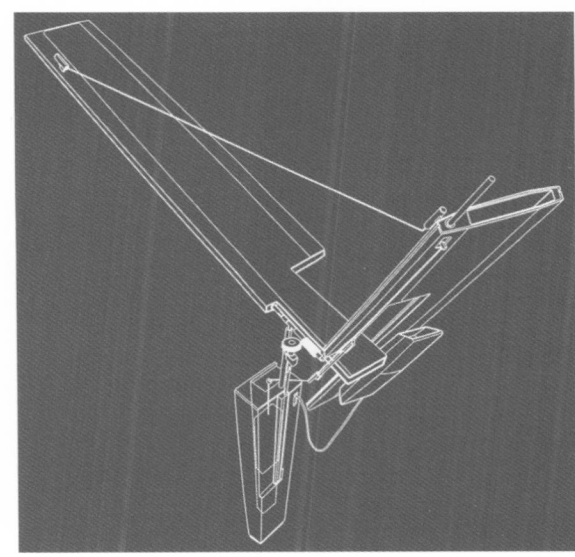

[A forest of slender oversize artificial flowers provide shade within the sit-out areas. Employing a simple counterweight system, each flower may be manipulated to move with the sun, tilting or closing up completely, depending on the whims of the visitor. En masse, they create the effect of walking though a field of undulating petals, shimmering in the wind; small holes in the petals result in a whistling accompaniment. An iridescent red on the exterior and silvered on the underside, the flowers close up at night to reveal the names of sponsors, seen from the road as blades of light.]

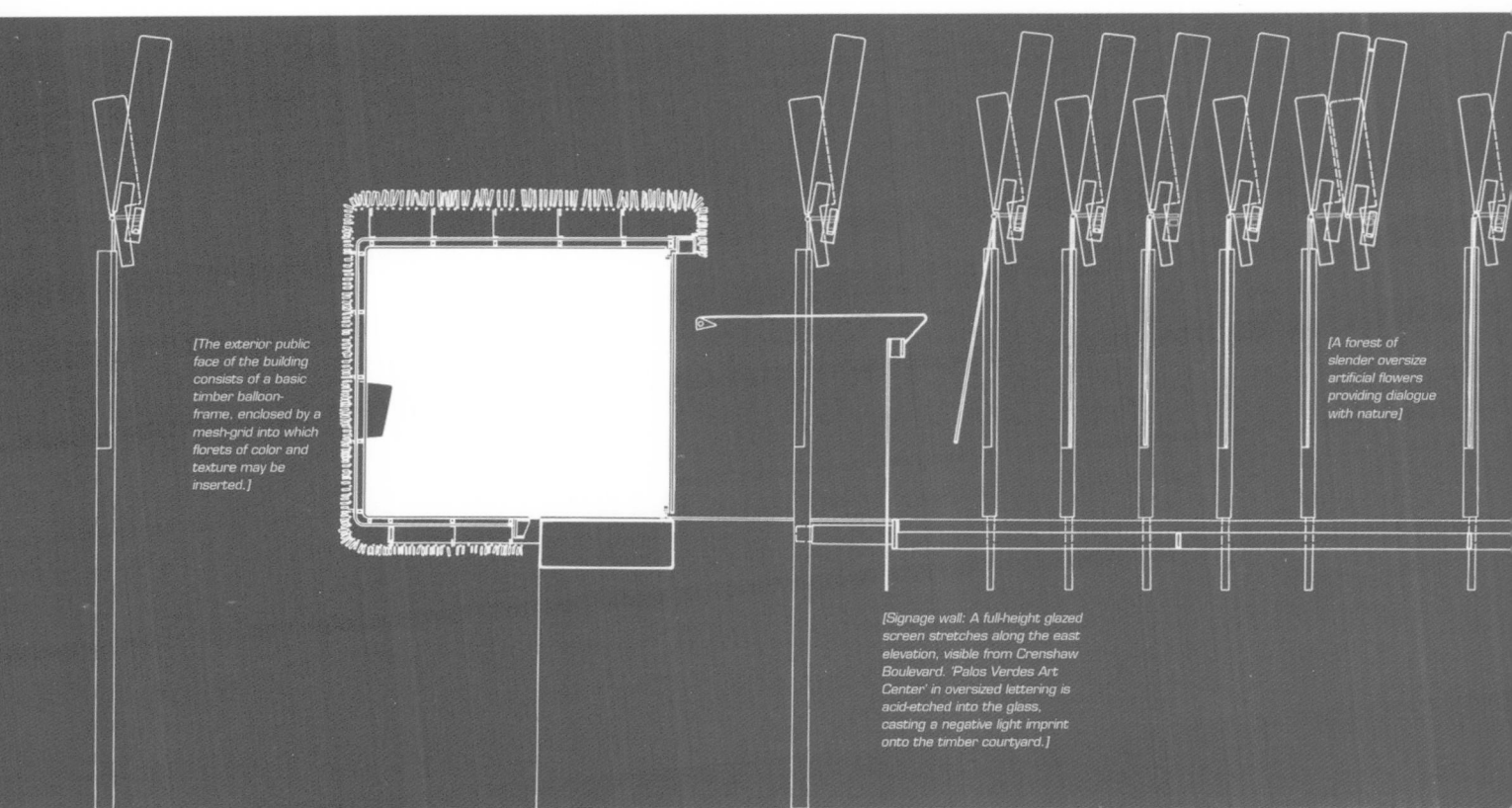

[The exterior public
face of the building
consists of a basic
timber balloon-
frame, enclosed by a
mesh-grid into which
florets of color and
texture may be
inserted.]

[A forest of
slender oversize
artificial flowers
providing dialogue
with nature]

[Signage wall: A full-height glazed
screen stretches along the east
elevation, visible from Crenshaw
Boulevard. 'Palos Verdes Art
Center' in oversized lettering is
acid-etched into the glass,
casting a negative light imprint
onto the timber courtyard.]

[section through central sculpture courtyard]

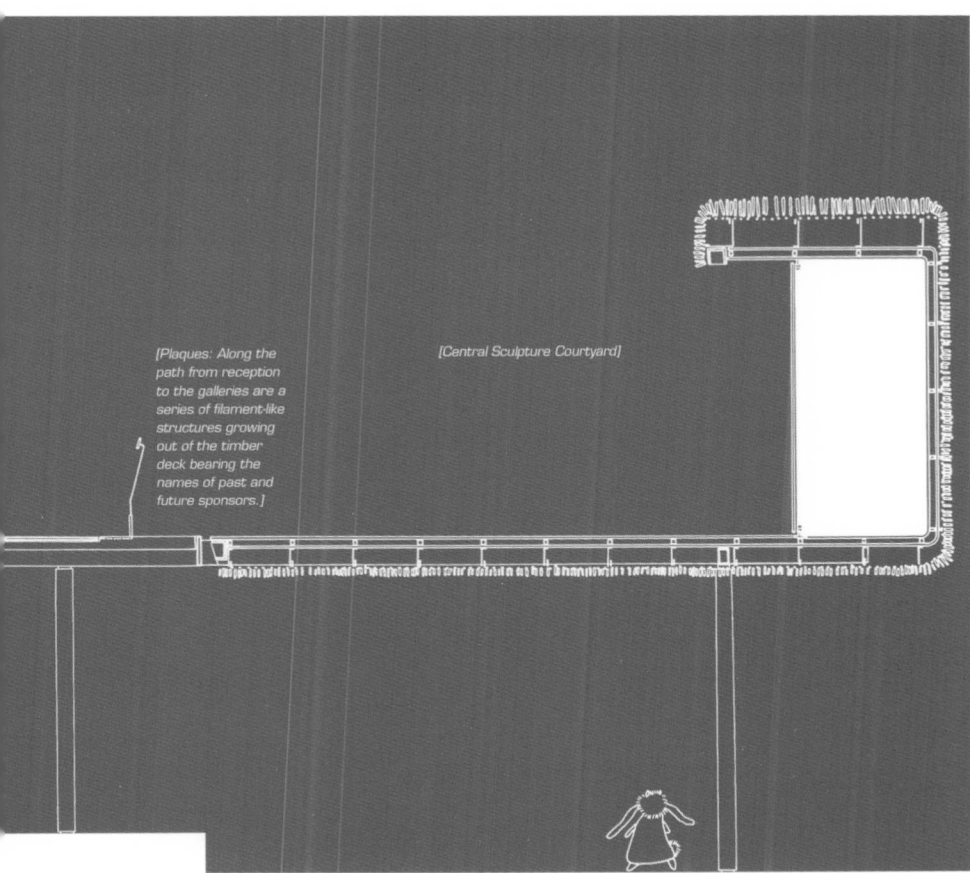

[Plaques: Along the path from reception to the galleries are a series of filament-like structures growing out of the timber deck bearing the names of past and future sponsors.]

[Central Sculpture Courtyard]

dropping crumbs of light behind him so he won't get lost!' thought Alicia fancifully. The crumbs along the path grew more brilliant as she passed through shaded areas and feebler through spaces flooded with daylight. At times, she had to squint in order to recapture the trail. Eventually Alicia arrived in a clearing that was so white and glistening that the way vanished completely and she had to shade her eyes from the glare of the sun. Not far in the distance, however, was a glade and Alicia hastened towards the shelter with relief. To her astonishment, the glade turned out to be a cluster of overgrown flowers rather than a canopy of trees. The sun's rays, dampened through hundreds of giant red petals, coloured everything beneath in a rosy tint while the wind whistled a dulcet air through the leaves and stalks. Pink and disoriented in this Brobdingnagian garden, Alicia felt extremely small.

'These flowers are singularly straight,' observed Alicia, and indeed, the stems were straight as a die (not surprisingly as, unbeknownst to Alicia, they had been extruded from one). She rapped her knuckles on the petiole of the nearest flower and was greeted by a dull ringing sound.

'My goodness! This flower is made of metal!' exclaimed Alicia, and where the flower's receptacle met its stalk, there were an assortment of mechanical cogs, gears and levers. 'I have seen a garden of live flowers before,' said Alicia, 'but never a garden of mechanical ones. What does the book say about it, I wonder?' she asked, leafing to the page on mechanical flowers.

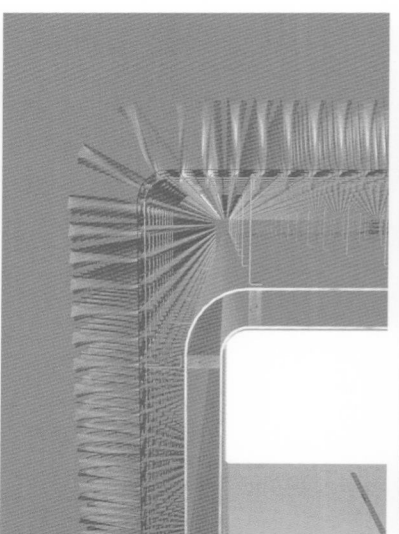

[Relatively simple coloured materials are inserted into the cladding system, giving the building texture and character. The 'dressing of the building' may become a project for visitors and the local community. In their hundreds, the elements would make up large-scale images visible only from a distance like a pointillist painting. The display possibilities are endless, ranging from signage for the arts centre, sponsor logos, or even the American flag. It is envisaged that replacement of the outer skin would be implemented every few years, either as a practical measure, or merely out of a desire for a change of scenery.]

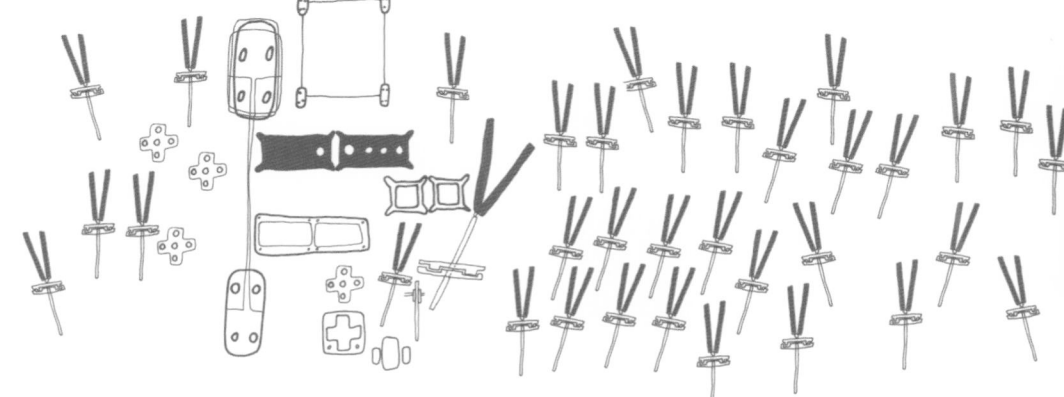

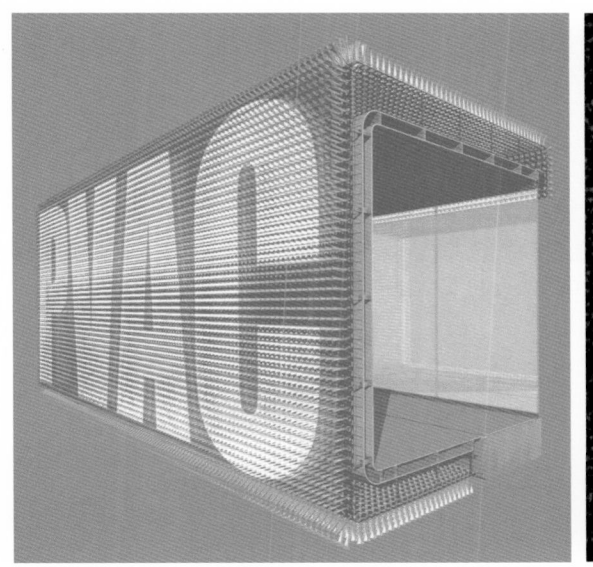  

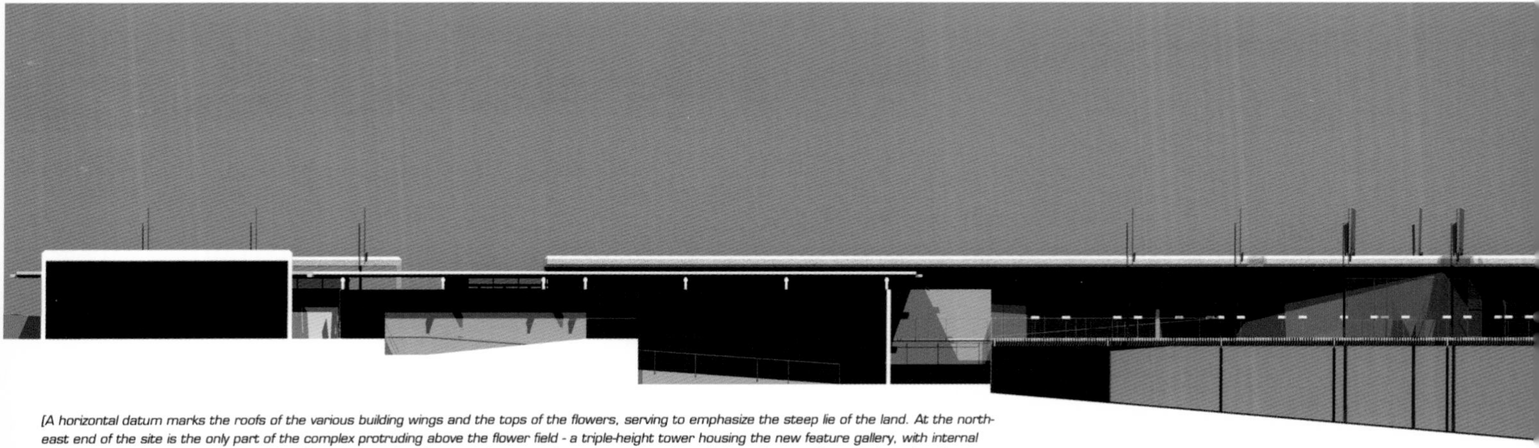

[A horizontal datum marks the roofs of the various building wings and the tops of the flowers, serving to emphasize the steep lie of the land. At the north-east end of the site is the only part of the complex protruding above the flower field - a triple-height tower housing the new feature gallery, with internal viewing balconies asymmetrically positioned to accommodate large paintings seen from afar, and smaller paintings close up. Beneath the gallery lies the auditorium and community space. At the opposite end of the site, the existing main building is renovated to house the Beckstrand, Norris, Stewart and Chacksfield galleries. Internal walls are removed or strengthened to leave four single volume spaces in sequence, the last two being double-height spaces, before returning to the central sculpture court.]

An array of slender shading devices provides relief from the heat in the sit-out areas of the arts centre. Employing a simple counter-weight mechanism, each 'flower' may be manipulated to move with the sun, tilting or closing up according to the whims of the visitor.

The one flower now above Alicia remained stubbornly closed, allowing a trapezium of light to land square on Alicia's face. Alicia squinted and spied something akin to a plumb line or trapped pendulum attached to the flower that was just screaming to be pulled.

"Pull me! Pull me!" it screamed. Next to it, in small letters were the words:

NUDGE HERE

Alicia gave the pendulum the lightest of taps and was rewarded with a delicate choreography of dancing parts that belied the effortless touch that initiated it. Firstly, the pendulum began to rise against its pendulous mass. Then, two vertical silvery blades began to separate, the longer one falling towards the horizontal to reveal an iridescent red upper skin. When it was halfway open, the second shorter petal started to open, as if attached by some invisible cable. With a sigh, the two leaves finally settled above Alicia, blanketing her in shade.

The arbour was most pleasant, and while she was pleased to have the place to herself, she began to wonder why there was no one else about. To assuage her curiosity, she approached one of the low-slung buildings and peered through a glass passageway.

'Everyone is inside!' said Alicia. 'And on such a lovely fine day!' The room was filled with people of old ages. Some of them were sitting in front of easels and painting pictures of fruit and other uninteresting objects, but most of them, including all the children, were hard at work making tiny flowers out of coloured paper. On the whiteboard, somebody had drawn a series of instructions as to how these flowerets should be made. There were literally thousands of them. Perhaps even millions. What could they possibly be for? Yet again, the book came to her rescue:

The exterior public face of the building consists of a basic timber balloon frame, enclosed by a mesh-grid into which florets of colour and texture may be inserted. The 'dressing' of the building is a biannual event for the community — participants of all ages are invited to contribute the elements that make up the cladding and consequently the overall appearance of the building according to a pre-determined scheme. In its unclad state, the mesh acts as a canvas, capturing the shadows of the trees and flowers, either real or synthetic, like a gelatin print.

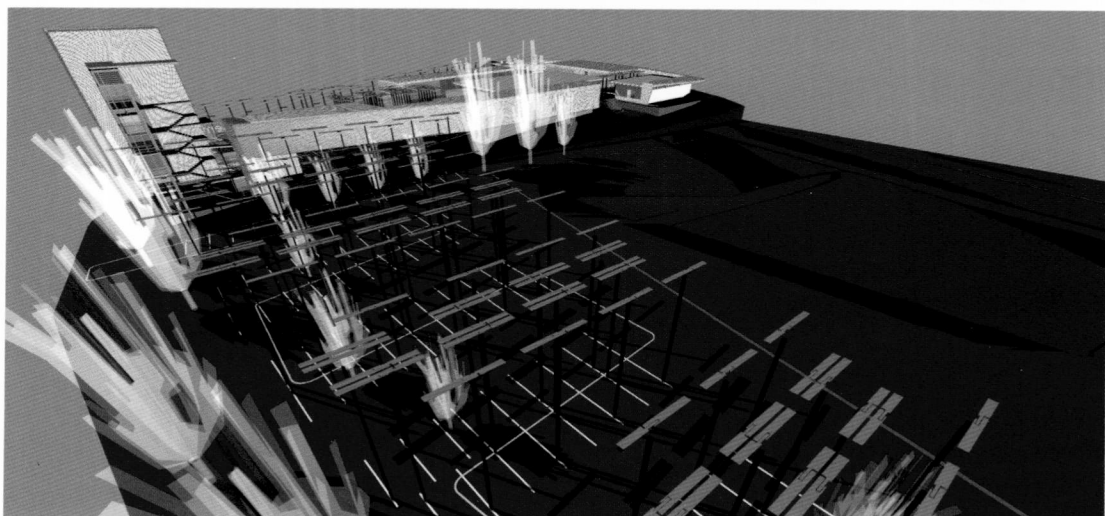

[A gargantuan hedge made up of tiny fragments of art. A trail of light that leads to a garden of delights. A forest of slender mechanical flowers. These are the elements that transform and unify the existing arts complex into a spatially challenging whole. Fairytale motifs and games of scale figure throughout the scheme, comprising a gallery core and courtyard surrounded by administration, classroom and service wings.]

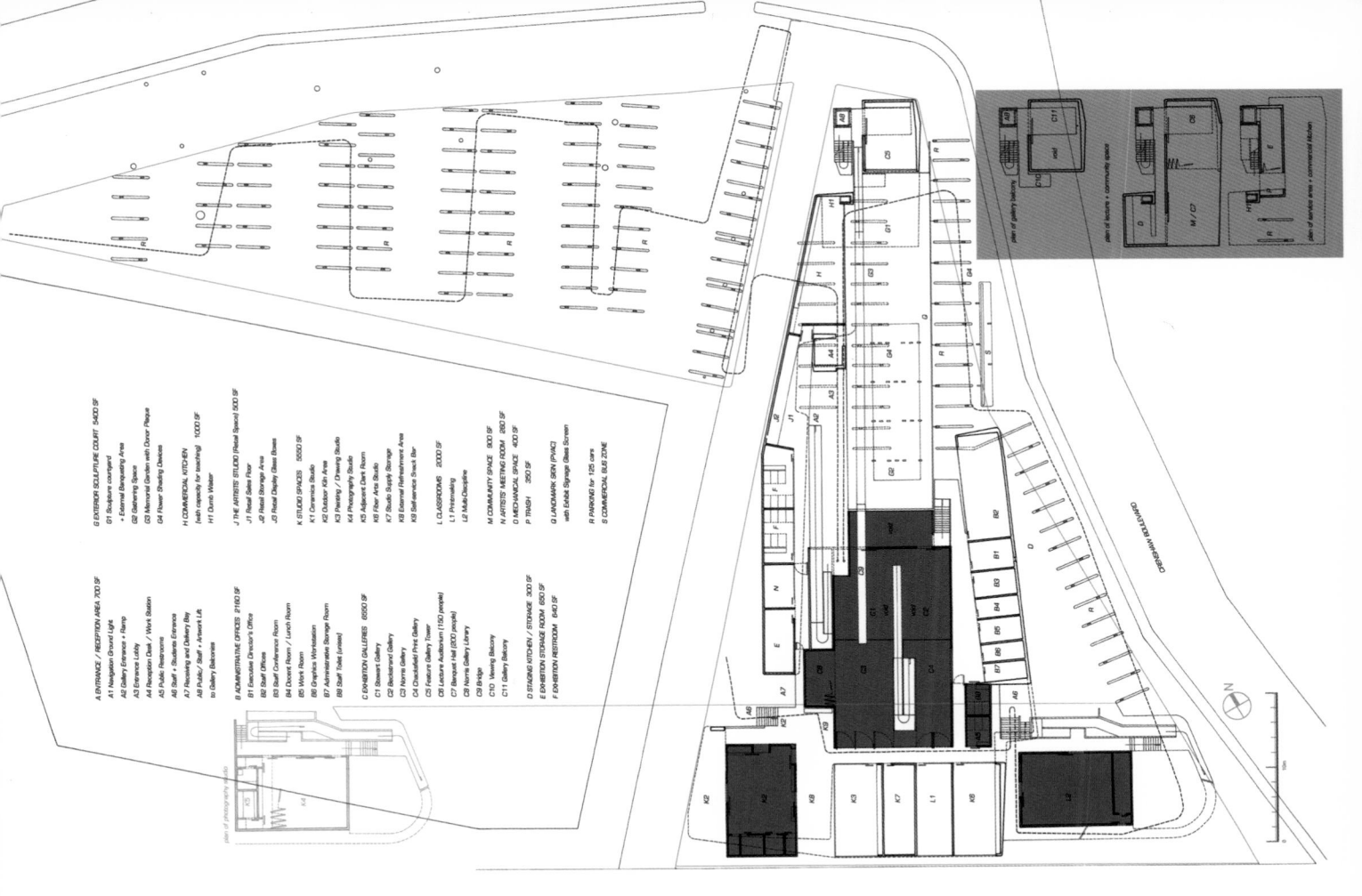

A ENTRANCE / RECEPTION AREA 700 SF
A1 Navigation Ground Light
A2 Gallery Entrance + Ramp
A3 Entrance Lobby
A4 Reception Desk / Work Station
A5 Public Restrooms
A6 Staff + Students Entrance
A7 Receiving and Delivery Bay
A8 Public / Staff + Artwork Lift
to Gallery Balconies

B ADMINISTRATIVE OFFICES 2160 SF
B1 Executive Director's Office
B2 Staff Offices
B3 Staff Conference Room
B4 Docent Room / Lunch Room
B5 Work Room
B6 Graphics Workstation
B7 Administrative Storage Room
B8 Staff Toilet (unisex)

C EXHIBITION GALLERIES 6500 SF
C1 Bowart Gallery
C2 Beckamont Gallery
C3 Norris Gallery
C4 Crocksfield Print Gallery
C5 Feature Gallery Tower
C6 Lecture Auditorium (150 people)
C7 Banquet Hall (300 people)
C8 Norris Gallery Library
C9 Bridge
C10 Viewing Balcony
C11 Gallery Balcony

D STAGING KITCHEN / STORAGE ROOM 650 SF
E EXHIBITION STORAGE ROOM 300 SF
F EXHIBITION RESTROOM 640 SF

G EXTERIOR SCULPTURE COURT 5400 SF
G1 Sculpture courtyard
+ External Banqueting Area
G2 Gathering Space
G3 Memorial Garden with Donor Plaque
G4 Flower Shading Devices

H COMMERCIAL KITCHEN 1000 SF
(with capacity for teaching)
H1 Dumb Waiter

J THE ARTISTS' STUDIO (Retail Space) 900 SF
J1 Retail Sales Floor
J2 Retail Storage Area
J3 Retail Display Glass Boxes

K STUDIO SPACES 5550 SF
K1 Ceramics Studio
K2 Outdoor Kiln Area
K3 Painting / Drawing Studio
K4 Photography Studio
K5 Adjacent Dark Room
K6 Fiber Arts Studio
K7 Studio Supply Storage
K8 External Refreshment Area
K9 Self-service Snack Bar

L CLASSROOMS 2000 SF
L1 Printmaking
L2 Multi-Discipline

M COMMUNITY SPACE 900 SF
N ARTISTS' MEETING ROOM 280 SF
O MECHANICAL SPACE 400 SF
P TRASH 250 SF

Q LANDMARK SKIN (PVAC)
with Exhibit Signage Glass Screen

R PARKING for 125 cars
S COMMERCIAL BUS ZONE

CRESHAM BOULEVARD

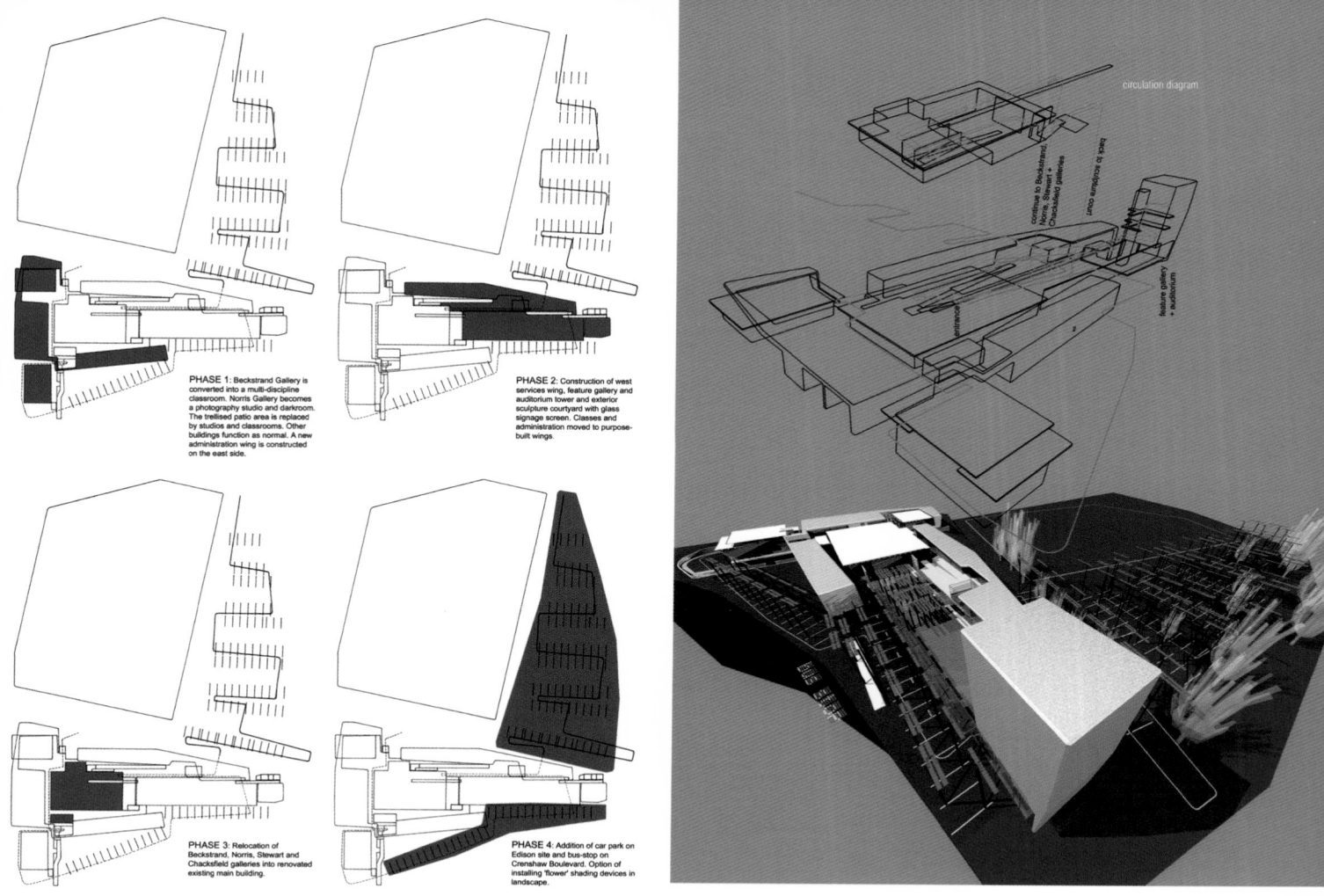

PHASE 1: Beckstrand Gallery is converted into a multi-discipline classroom. Norris Gallery becomes a photography studio and darkroom. The trellised patio area is replaced by studios and classrooms. Other buildings function as normal. A new administration wing is constructed on the east side.

PHASE 2: Construction of west services wing, feature gallery and auditorium tower and exterior sculpture courtyard with glass signage screen. Classes and administration moved to purpose-built wings.

PHASE 3: Relocation of Beckstrand, Norris, Stewart and Chacksfield galleries into renovated existing main building.

PHASE 4: Addition of car park on Edison site and bus-stop on Crenshaw Boulevard. Option of installing 'flower' shading devices in landscape.

circulation diagram

continue to Beckstrand, Norris, Stewart + Chacksfield galleries

back to sculpture court

feature gallery + auditorium

'Help! Help!' Alicia was so startled by the cry that she almost dropped the book. 'Somebody please help!' pleaded a voice from beyond the wall.

Hanging precariously between the parapet of the building and a wobbly ladder was an extremely strange-shaped man. Neither ectomorph nor endomorph, but possibly a mesomorph, the man was decidedly egg-shaped. He also had an admirable collection of bandages and body castes that should have made scaling a ladder quite impossible. Alicia scurried over to the wall and straightened the ladder for the ovoid man to half climb, half-plummet down.

'Thank you so much, Missy. If you ever need help, HD will be at your service!'

It was a silly custom to abbreviate two perfectly good names into initials, thought Alicia, but she took the fragile man's hand and shook it carefully (which was more easily said than done as the arm it was attached to was strung up in a sling).

'I'm just glad to be of assistance. Whatever were you doing, anyway?'

'I'm putting the building back together again,' said the man known as HD. 'The kids can manage re-dressing the building up to yea…aargh high or so,' he said, lifting his arm a metre off the ground and then grimacing in pain as his arm caught in its sling. 'But anything above that and I have to insert these darn little things in myself,' he said, indicating a large bucket of florets on the floor.

'It looks very impressive. What's it going to be?' asked Alicia.

'Something abstract, no doubt. Some artsy-fartsy gobbledegook.'

'Ah,' said Alicia, letting the matter drop. The floral wall rather reminded her of a giant dog, many times her own height that had guarded a glimmering art gallery in the North of Spain. The peculiar thing about this dog was not that it had three heads like Cerberus, the guard dog of Hades, but that it was made entirely of flowers. This had given the dog an aura of amiability, making Alicia doubt its effectiveness as a sentry.

'Er..many thanks for your assistance, Miss,' said HD, interrupting her reverie, 'but I'm afraid I have to clear up here. End of term and all.'

The egg-shaped man hobbled over to one of the tall mechanical flowers and gave the pendulum a tap. Alicia followed its graceful progress in reverse, one blade folding up and lifting the second one after it until they both stood vertical like a tuning fork. As the flower completed its closure, it triggered two others, slightly further afield, and another, and then a few more and more and more until the whole field was enveloped in a wave of kinetic motion. The sighing of the flowers echoed choristers singing a round, the collapsing petals an orchestrated string of falling dominoes. It was time to leave. Alicia waved goodbye and returned to the trail of light. There was a sign ahead. It read:

Alicia followed it into the next garden…

MIRRORED TEXT

Jeff Koons. Puppy is a 43-foot-high, 44-ton West Highland terrier constructed out of stainless steel, swathed in nearly 70,000 petunias, marigolds, begonias, impatiens and lobelias, which are potted in 23 tons of soil and kept alive by an internal irrigation system.

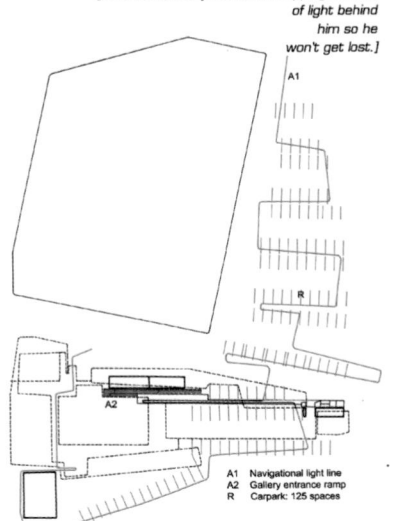

[…as if a little boy has been dropping crumbs of light behind him so he won't get lost.]

A1
A2
R

A1 Navigational light line
A2 Gallery entrance ramp
R   Carpark: 125 spaces

[Rows of half-height rosemary hedges act as mobile partitions to divide up the sculpture court for mixed use. During open-air receptions and banquets, clear acrylic surfaces socket horizontally above the rosemary to form serving tables.]

22 jun **summer**   *Green Palace*

A licia was feeling bored. It was raining cats and dogs outside, and her elder sister Edith was impersonating Adult Edith, her nose deep in some ever-so-dry treatise on architectural history from father's library of ever-so-dry first editions. Alicia made the silent wish that her over-serious sibling's enunciation of the words 'entablature', 'neo-classical' and 'pilaster' would dry out the horrid wet weather so that she could search for disorientated felines and canines in the community garden downstairs. When it soon became clear that the wish would remain ungranted, she sighed and turned her attention to her decrepit toy rabbit...

The new Liddell home could be described as being quite minuscule. While it was not the sort of place where a child could walk through a hidden door into a enchanted wonderland beyond, or even discover long-forgotten treasure in a secret passageway, Alicia did hope to find a few corners she could claim as her own and retreat to when the weather was foul, as it was indeed today. She sorely missed life in the country where she had been allowed to cavort in the mud and rain; here in the city, strange notions of urban decorum had prevailed over her parents; raincoats, umbrellas and staying inside had become the order of the day. It was with this thought that Alicia resolved to bring the countryside to 95 Greencroft Gardens.

Alicia's parents viewed their daughter's efforts to transform their home with good humour and possibly a tinge of guilt at transplanting the family to a concrete jungle. Unbeknownst to them at the time, however, Alicia's initially conservative plan of

CHAPTER 5:
AN INTERLUDE IN WHICH WE LEARN A LITTLE MORE ABOUT OUR HEROINE AND HER ASPIRATIONS FOR THE FAMILY HOME

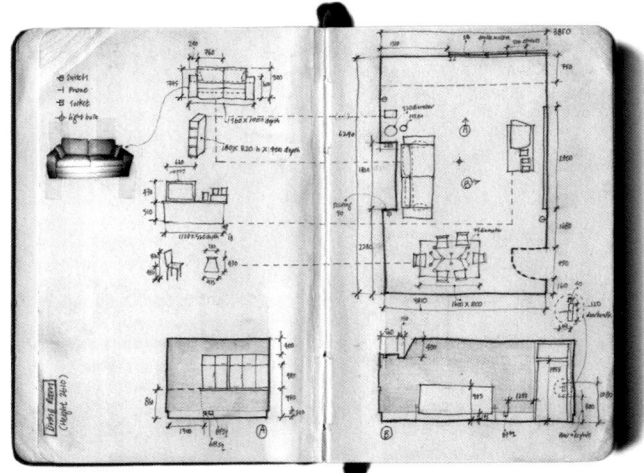

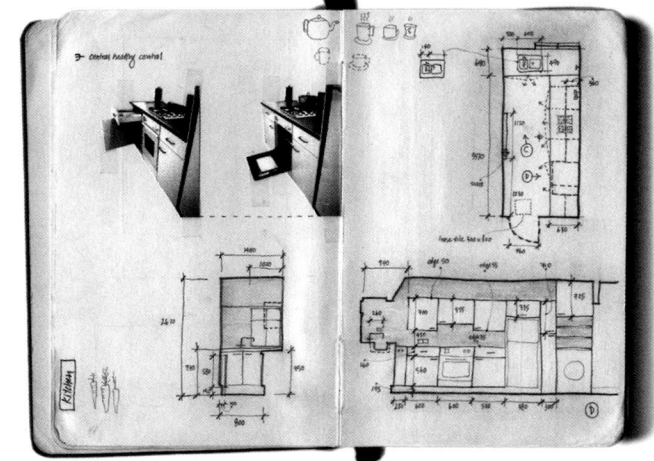

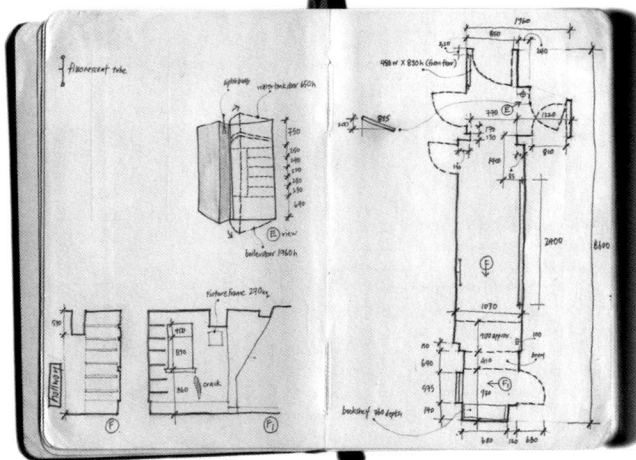

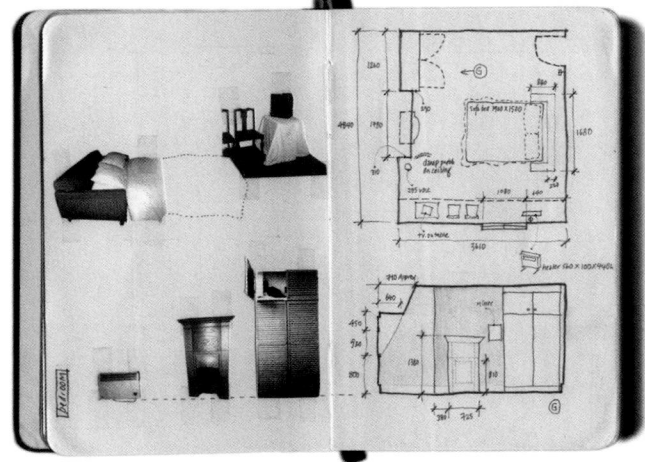

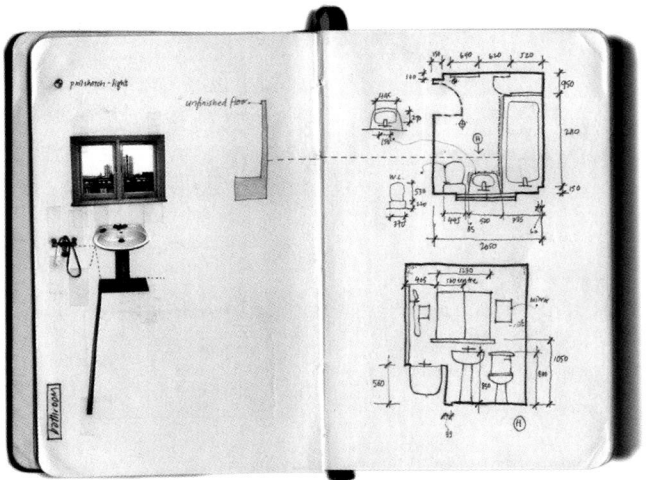

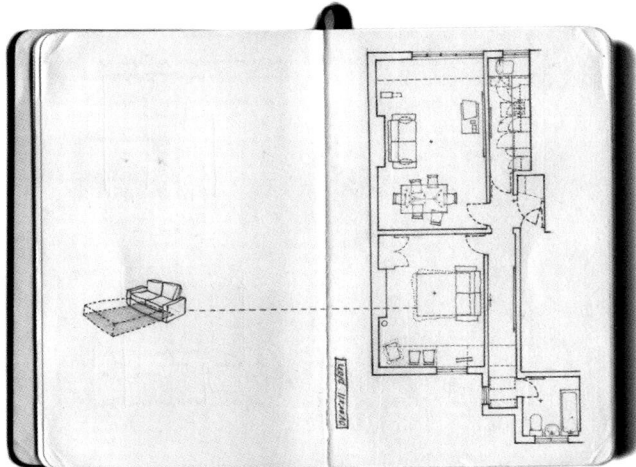

introducing potted plants and window-boxes to the sterile flat would blossom into a fully-fledged interior landscaping project, threatening to swamp the family in foliage and flora. Good humour would turn to mere humour, rapidly degenerate into nervous tolerance and finally settle as unalloyed dread.

And so Alicia set about surveying the flat with a view to restoring a green croft to Greencroft Gardens. In order to scale the apartment up to a suitable size (two-and-a-half times its ordinary dimensions sounded about right), Alicia meticulously combed the five rooms she had identified (the hall, the kitchen, the drawing room, the bedroom and the bathroom) with a magnifying glass. Not an inch of wall or floor was overlooked, not an iota of dust unmolested, as she studiously noted down every detail in her little black notebook with a sharp 4H pencil. She decided to draw in pencil so that with the aid of an eraser, the drawing would evolve into a living organism symbiotically with the flat.

[Alicia's survey of the Liddell home]

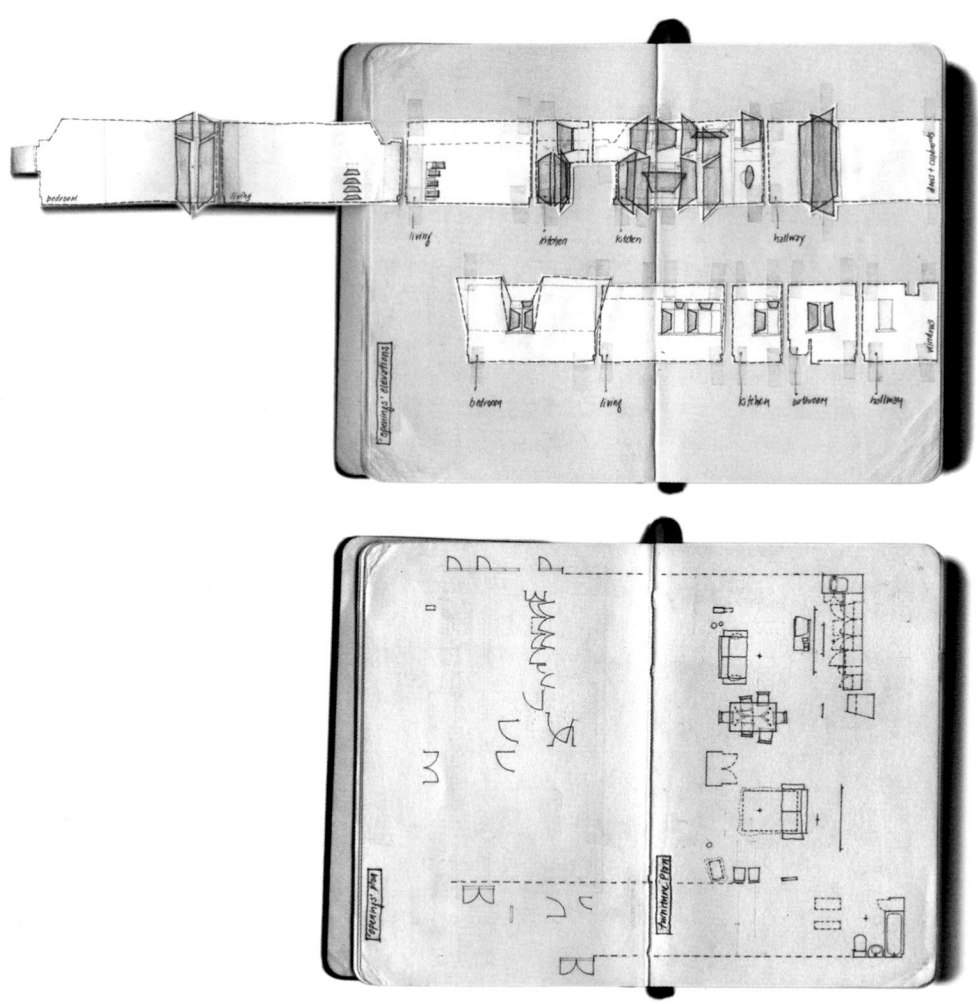

 [bathroom]

 [hallway] [bedroom]

 [living room] [kitchen]

[wardrobe]　　　　[drawer]　　　[kitchen door]　[boiler door]　　[front door]　　　　　　　　　　　　　　　　[bathroom cabinet]

[kitchen cabinets]   [washing machine]

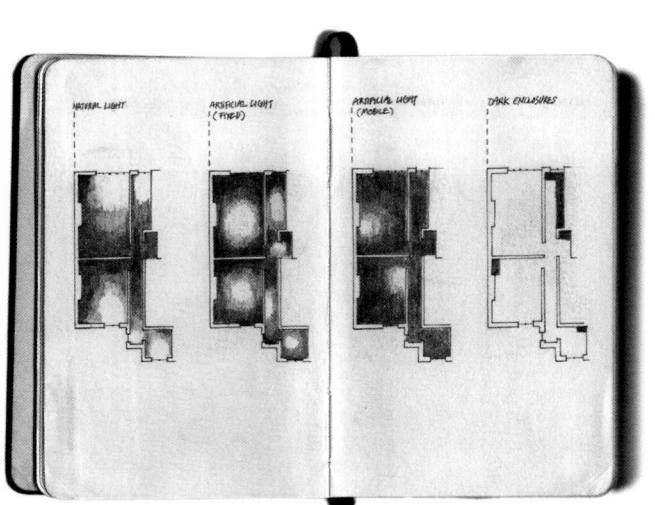

NATURAL LIGHT   ARTIFICIAL LIGHT   ARTIFICIAL LIGHT   DARK ENCLOSURES
                 (FIXED)   (MOBILE)

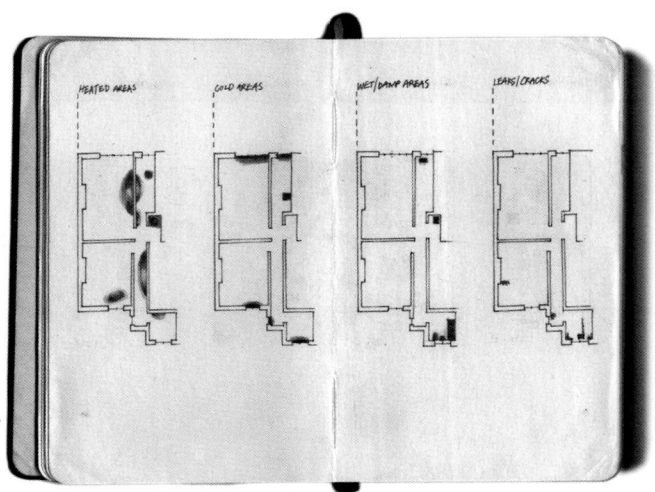

HEATED AREAS   COLD AREAS   WET/DAMP AREAS   LEAKS/CRACKS

Finding a clear space in the drawing room between unpacked boxes of bric-a-brac, Alicia began projecting her jottings into plan form, circumscribing areas of light and dark, moist and dry, warm and cold, with sure confident lines, feeling the bite of lead into vellum. All the while, she rummaged through her botanical knowledge for plants that thrived in light and dark, dry and moist or cold and warm conditions. 'Mushrooms grow in dark moist areas,' noted Alicia, 'and can live on old coffee grounds. 'Moss can grow on virtually anything, and I know just the place to find some.'

Underneath her drawing, she wrote herself a list of things to do -

1. Grow a portable moss rug to carry from room to room to have indoor picnics.
2. Create miniature green worlds invisible to the naked eye (inspired by the Chinese ideal of cultivating a garden no larger than a mustard seed)
3. Grow a living coat from grass to wear.
4. Construct a strawberry chandelier so strawberries can be picked and eaten at the dinner table.
5. Plant a chive path around the rim of the bathtub.
6. Cultivate a corridor of mushrooms.

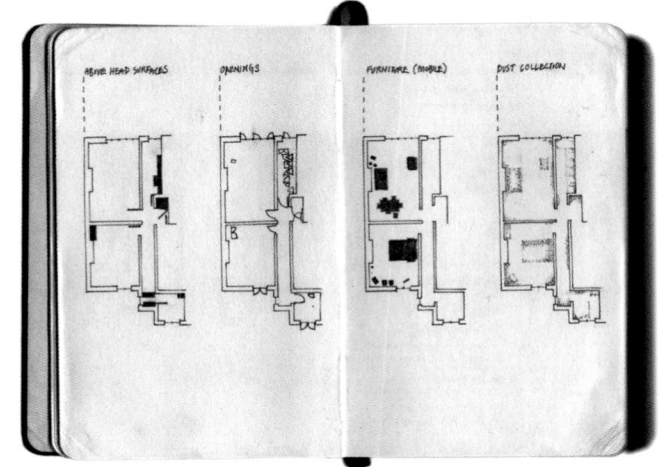

water

pineapple tree in jam jar

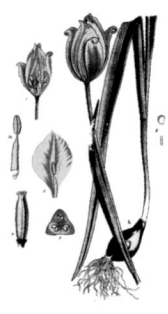

[petticoat moss]

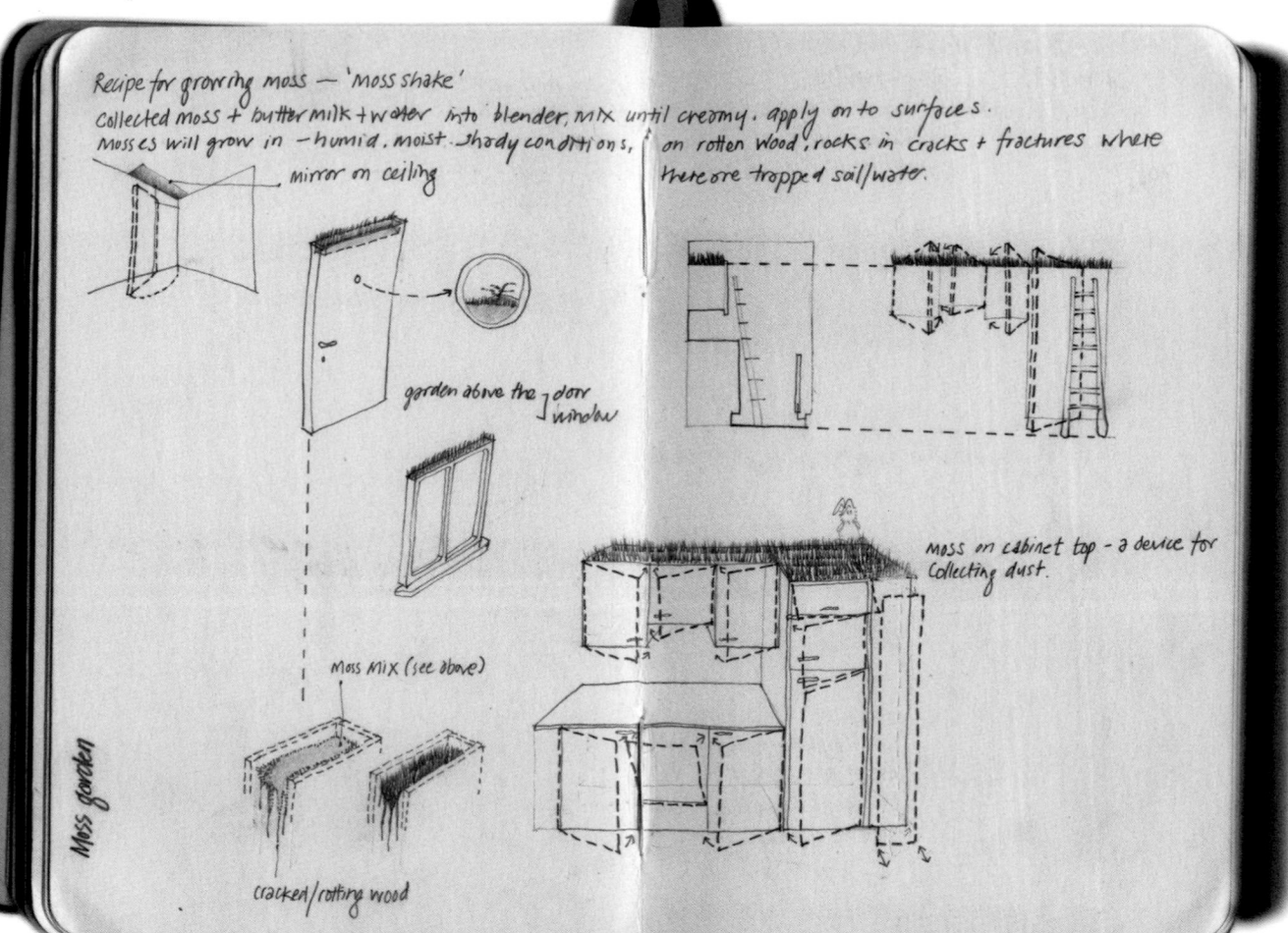

Recipe for growing moss — 'moss shake'
Collected moss + butter milk + water into blender, mix until creamy. apply on to surfaces.
Mosses will grow in — humid. moist. shady conditions, on rotten wood, rocks in cracks + fractures where
there are trapped soil/water.

mirror on ceiling

garden above the door
window

moss on cabinet top - a device for
collecting dust.

moss mix (see above)

cracked/rotting wood

Moss garden

Alicia's early greening experiments heavily featured mosses and grass. The moss she sourced off of a brick wall several houses down and whizzed up in a blender with some buttermilk and water (without Mother's knowledge), and slathered on every surface available. Her parents, naturally enough, were not particularly enamoured with slimy malodorous growths on the kitchen worktop and hallway carpet. With the benefit of a few half-hearted rebukes from Mother and Father behind her, Alicia's skill at hiding her gardens grew in tandem with her parent's mounting dismay and exasperation. Her new strategy was to secret(e) her slime mixture on tops of cupboards, door leaves and window transoms where the wood had begun to rot, and she periodically climbed a ladder to surreptitiously add a few drops of water and examine them under her magnifying glass. Later, she would come to the conclusion that the shock of discovery engendered a disproportionate zeal in her parents' harangues, somewhat cancelling out any inherent benefits of secrecy.

Moss was small, but not quite small enough to achieve Alicia's dream of a miniature world invisible to the naked eye. She did, however, need a magnifying lens to make out the colonies of gossamer thread roots and leaves, that were more closely packed than sardines in a tin can. The most delightful thing about the moss was that they responded to her attentions, visibly swelling in size and confidence when she watered them, although they shrank like violets when she neglected them.

THE COAT THAT LIVED

The idea of an organic grass coat was not one that Alicia could lay claim to – she had seen it in a folio edition of work by two sensational artists, and knew the moment her eyes laid on it that she had to own one. Alicia's favourite colour was blue and the thought of a jacket made of blue-grass almost made her swoon with anticipation. Rye grass, on the other hand, grew twice as quickly. In the end, she convinced herself of her powers of persuasion. She would cajole the blue-grass coat into growing twice as fast by smuggling it outside for a walk in the sun every day, taking no heed of the disdainful looks she would attract. She knew that her ugly duckling would grow into a swan.

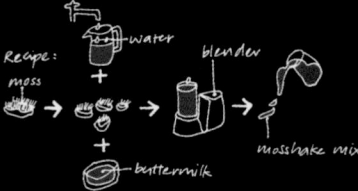

Recipe: moss + buttermilk → blender → masshake mix

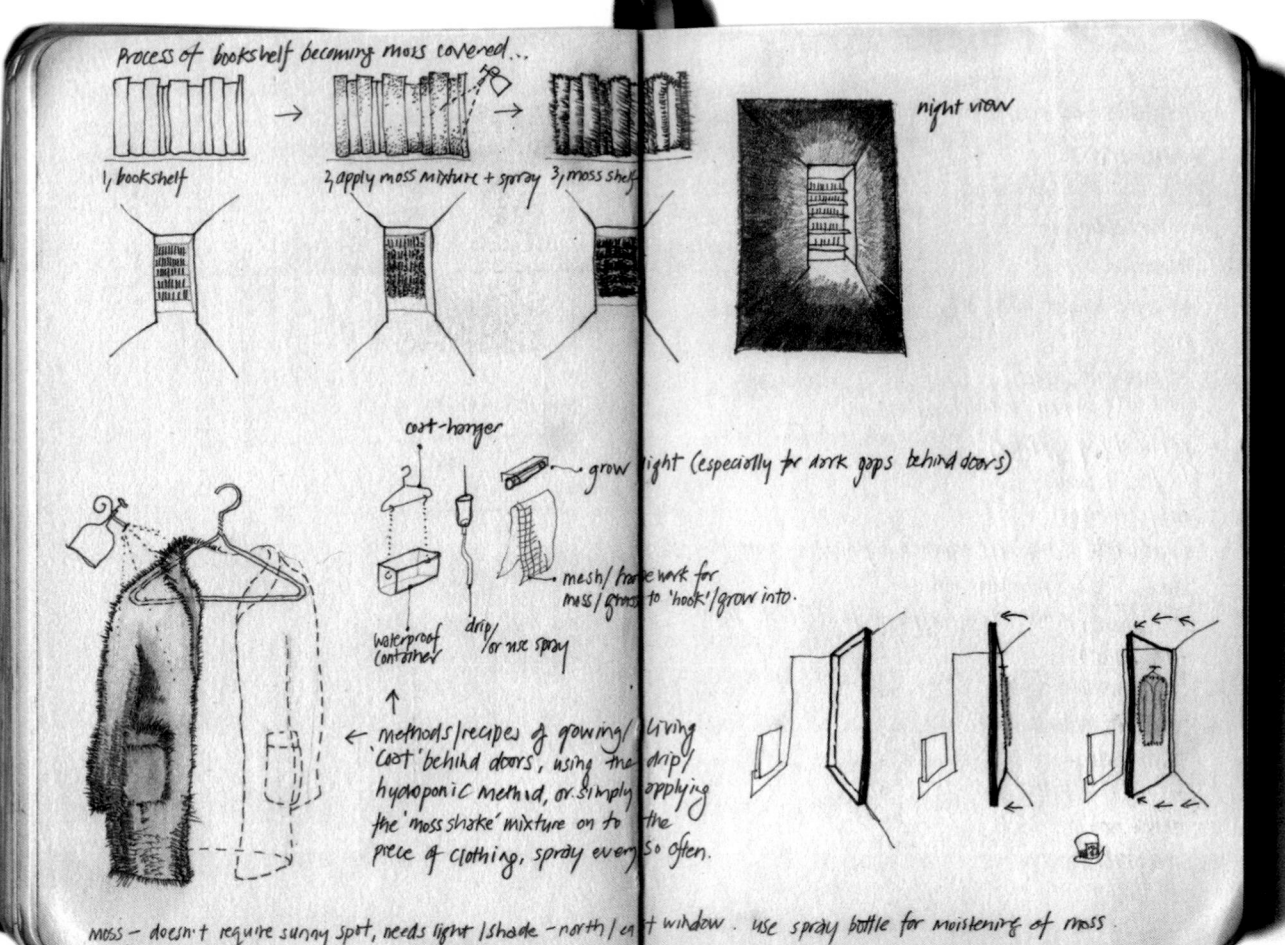

Process of bookshelf becoming moss covered...

1, bookshelf   2, apply moss mixture + spray   3, moss shelf

night view

coat-hanger

grow light (especially for dark gaps behind doors)

mesh/ horse work for moss/ grass to 'hook'/ grow into.

waterproof container

drip/ or use spray

← methods/recipes of growing/ living 'coat' behind doors, using the 'drip' hydroponic method, or simply applying the 'moss shake' mixture on to the piece of clothing, spray every so often.

moss - doesn't require sunny spot, needs light /shade - north/east window. use spray bottle for moistening of moss.

[the coat that lived]

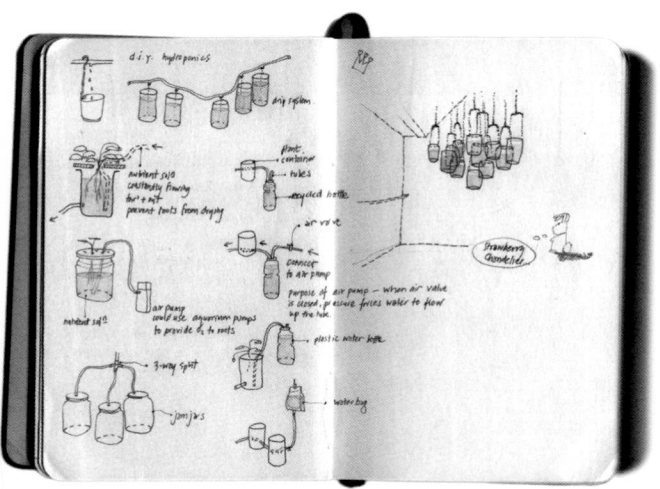

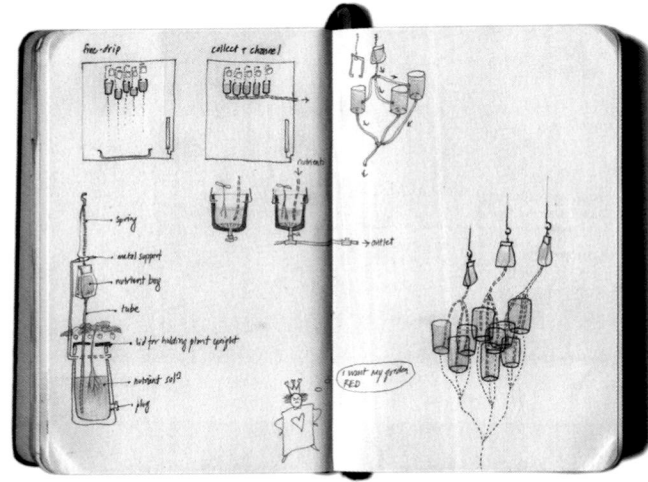

[easy ways of growing hydroponic strawberries indoors]

THE STRAWBERRY CHANDELIER

This was the project that the rest of the family most warmed to. The idea was not that the strawberries would emit light (that would be silly), but that they would emit an aura of strawberriness. Strawberry-light would reflect off the suspended fruit prisms, casting a crimson glow on the ceiling and walls; strawberry-scent would permeate the living room and strawberry-taste would explode on the Liddells' tongues whenever it took their fancy. A pulley system would convey the chandelier from its resting position, high near the south-facing bay windows down to the dining table. The contraption was put together following days of studying Heath Robinson drawings and involved bucket-loads of springs, pulleys, plastic tubing, drip-bags, alpine strawberry (*Fragaria vesca*) seedlings, and an aquarium pump (much to the chagrin of the family goldfish). What was nice about the alpine strawberry, Alicia thought when she was choosing strawberry species, was that it would also help whiten her teeth.

[cezan]

[temptress]

[alpine]

[fresca]

[alpine]

[elan]

[strawberry chandelier]

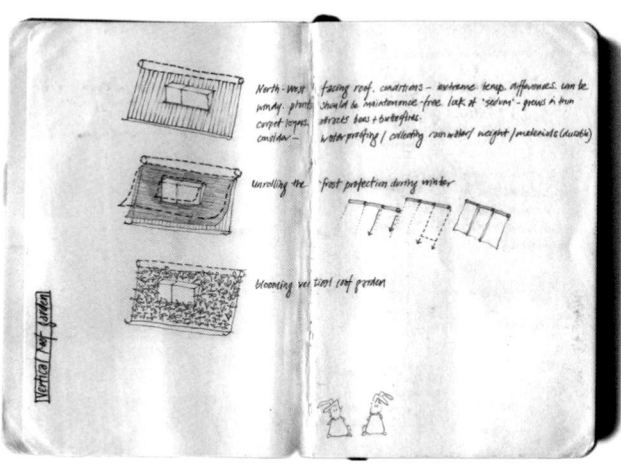

North-west facing roof, conditions - extreme temp. differences, can be windy, plants should be maintenance-free, lack of "screen" grows in two carpet layers, consider: - waterproofing / collecting rainwater / weight / materials (durable)

attract bees + butterflies

Vertical Roof Garden

unrolling the - first protection during winter

blooming vertical roof garden

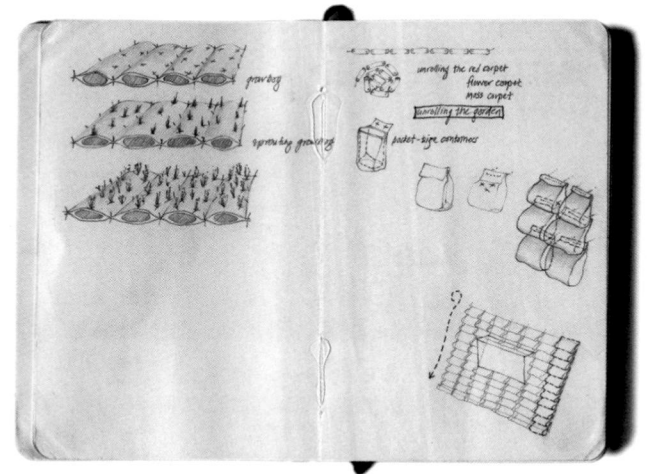

growbag

growbag growing

pocket-size containers

unrolling the red carpet
flower carpet
moss carpet

unrolling the garden

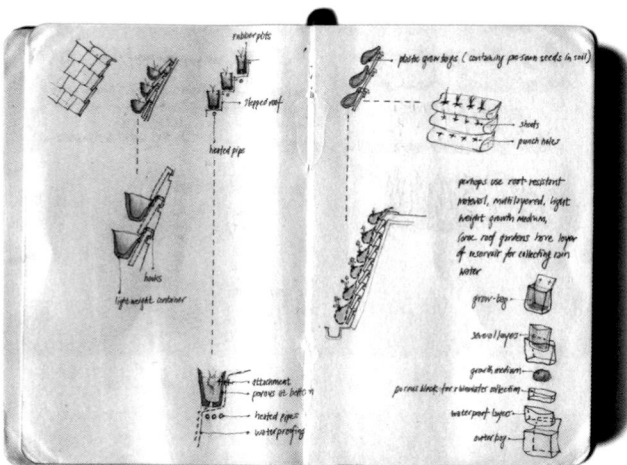

rubber pots

stepped roof

heated pipe

hooks

lightweight container

attachment
porous at bottom
heated pipes
waterproofing

plastic grow bags (containing poison seeds in soil)

shoots
punch holes

perhaps use root-resistant material, multilayered, lightweight growth medium, (one roof gardens have a layer of reservoir for collecting rain water

grow-bag

several layers

growth medium

porous block for rainwater collection

waterproof layers

water bag

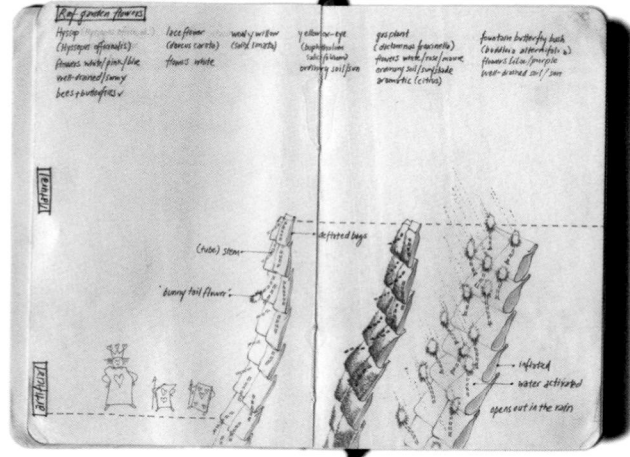

Roof garden flowers

Hysop (Hyssopus officinalis):
(Hyssopus officinalis)
flowers white/pink/blue
well-drained/sunny
bees + butterflies ✓

lace flower
(Daucus carota):
flowers white

woolly willow
(Salix lanata)

yellow-eye
(Euphorbium
salicifolium)
prettily sunflower

gas plant
(Dictamnus fraxinella)
flowers white/rose/mauve
average soil/sun/shade
aromatic (citrus)

fountain butterfly bush
(Buddleia alternifolia)
flowers lilac/purple
well-drained soil/sun

stem
(turn) stem

'bunny tail flowers'

deflated bags

inflated
water activated
opens out in the rain

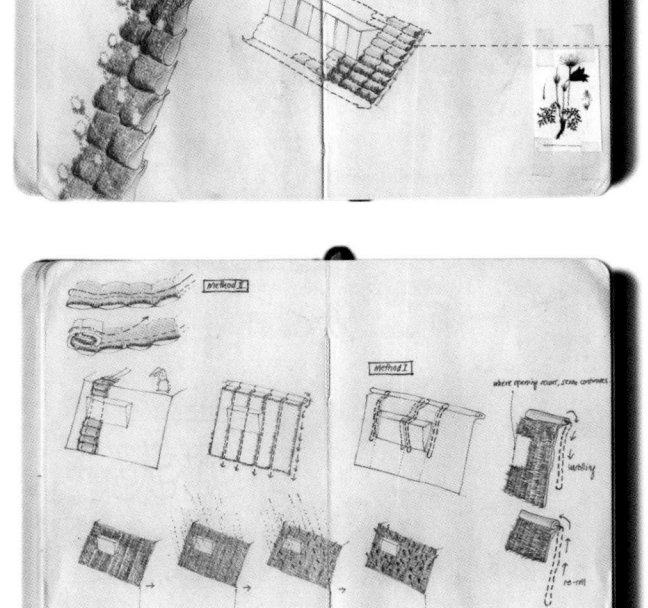

VERTICAL ROOF GARDEN

Against his better judgement, Alicia's father had agreed to 'mount an expedition' up the roof of the house to install a quilt of grow-bags that Alicia had stitched together to unroll over the roof. In order to win over her father, she had marshalled a well-constructed argument, citing the ancient hanging gardens of Babylon as a precedent and had waxed lyrical on storm water management, energy efficiency and aesthetic benefit. What Alicia had neglected to tell her father was her underlying agenda to rear a rooftop nest of rabbits. The deal would be this — the rabbits would be provided with a field of burnet roses (their favourite food) in return for keeping the plants neat and trim. Luckily, she did confide in her sister Edith before implementing her plan, who had asked Alicia (with a face as straight as a poker) whether she would be willing to bear scores of rabbits falling to their deaths on her young conscience. In the end, Alicia resigned herself to crowning the house with a mass of bunny-tail windflowers (*Pulsatilla vulgaris*) to console herself.

optical roof garden now   the house with a range of tr   and ventilare

[growing chives in the bathroom]

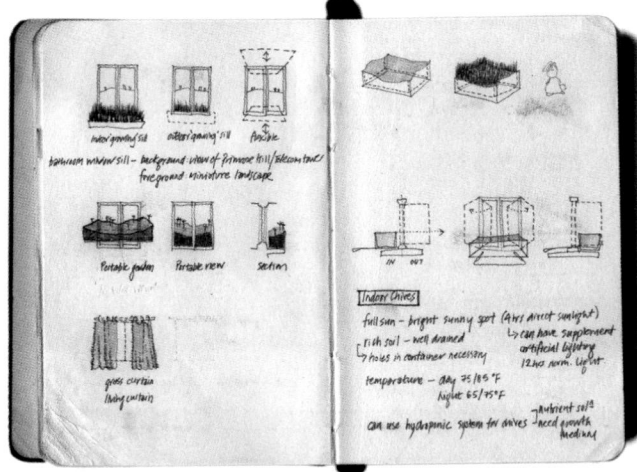

[hall of mushrooms]

[phonebook]

THE HALL OF MUSHROOMS

All good experiments begin with research, and Alicia did her homework on the best ways to grow mushrooms. Yes, mushrooms could grow on old coffee grounds, but coffee-flavoured mushrooms did not really appeal to her. Word-flavoured mushrooms, however, sounded more stimulating for both mind and body. Father had reacted quite hysterically when she had asked if she could borrow his books on classical architecture as a growth substrate for her mushrooms, but she had thought better of it anyhow as the mushrooms would probably not survive in such a dry environment. When he had calmed down somewhat, he did make the rather good suggestion of using the old phone directories in the communal hall that none of the other residents had collected.

Next, Alicia had to decide on what type of mushrooms to grow. Redcaps, perhaps? Eye-catching red mushrooms sounded like just the thing to enliven those dull white walls in the hall. In the end, it was not the fact that the mushrooms gave off an unpleasant acrid odour that persuaded her against them. It was not even the fact that they were VIRULENTLY POISONOUS, but that they held magical properties when ingested (which puzzled Alicia somewhat, seeing that they were also VIRULENTLY POISONOUS). Alicia had had enough of magic in her life already, thank you very much. She finally settled on *pleurotus pulmonarius*. The thought of cultivating a hall of grey oysters rather appealed to her. When she passed through it every day, she would be able to conjure up walruses and other sea creatures in her mind's eye without the use of magic.

In case she wanted to repeat the experiment later and possibly improve on it, Alicia wrote down the following instructions in her notebook:

Take one phonebook and soak thoroughly with water (rainwater is best). Wrap in plastic and shrink to fit with a hairdryer. Then, inject a few squirts of mushroom spores using a syringe to provide even coverage. Place in a dark, warm and damp environment and wait for the mushrooms to sprout.

To make the hall sprout with mushrooms, make a small opening in the wall and insert the prepared phonebook into the hollow. Cover with mesh and a thin layer of plaster and paint to make indistinguishable from the surrounding area. Repeat as desired indiscriminately.

Alicia was particularly proud of this last bit. The only mitigating thing about how pig-headedly-slowly plants and fungi grew, Alicia felt, was that her botanical misdemeanours would not be immediately apparent. This enabled her to defer and ration out her tellings-off so that they were at least bearable, and she considered the mushroom hall to be her most ingenious hidden garden scheme. This was her pièce de résistance; for her parents it would be the final straw.

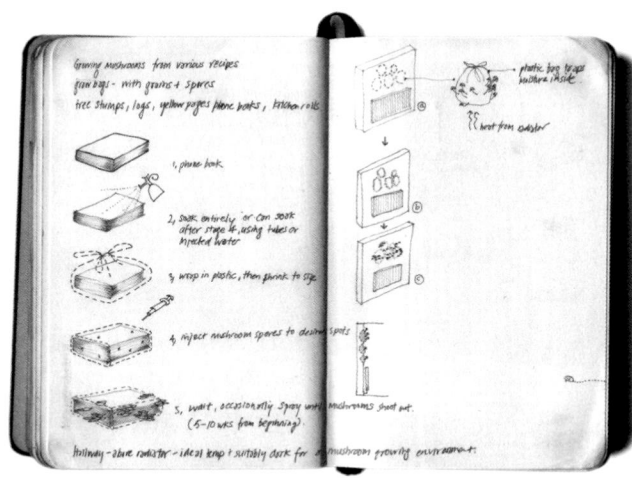

[cultivating grey oysters in the hall]

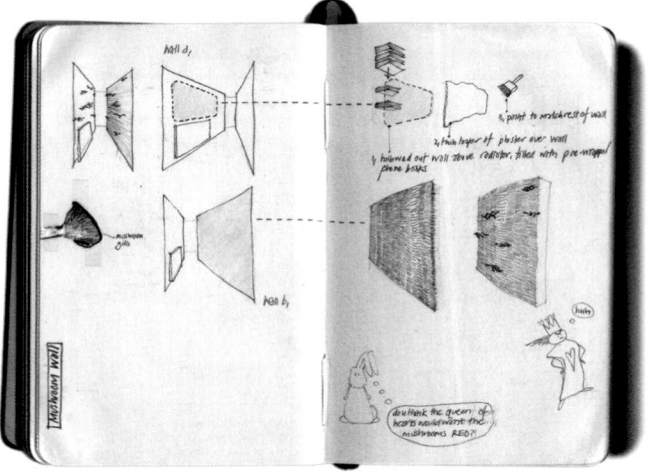

Wall 1

1, hollowed out

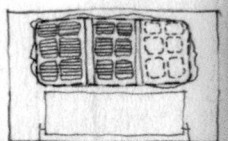

2, filled with wrapped yellow pages *

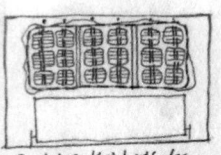

3, tubes thro' bags for water to enter sealed books

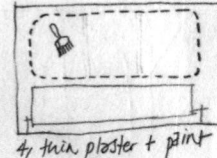

4, thin plaster + paint

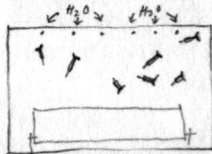

5, soak yellow pages via tube + inject spores at various spots

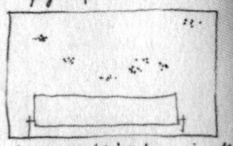

6, spores begin to germinate

7, oyster mushrooms

* yellow pages phone directory

Wall 2

1, hollowed out - complete wall

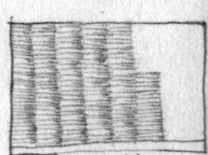

2, entire wall filled with sealed yellow pages

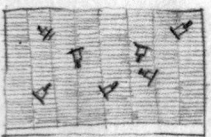

3, inject water to soak book 'bags' thoroughly

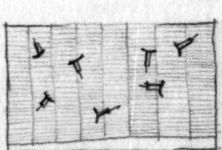

4, syringes to inject spores into pages

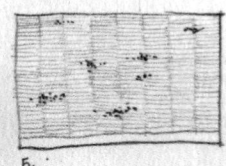

5,

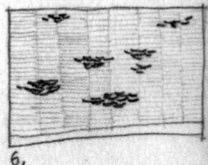

6,

7, plucking time !

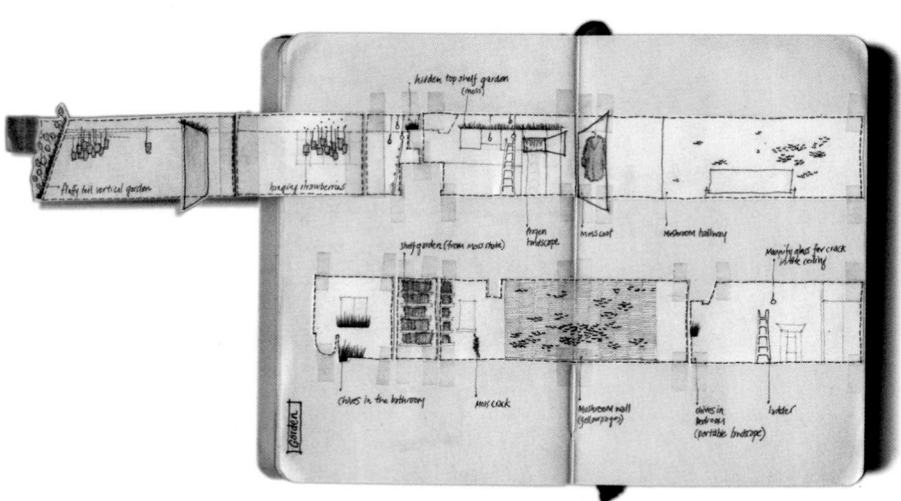

hidden top shelf garden
(moss)

fluffy tail vertical garden

hanging strawberries

shelf garden (from moss room)

frozen landscape

moss coat

mushroom hallway

Magnify glass for crack
width cooling

chives in the bathroom

moss crack

mushroom wall
(yellow pages)

chives in
bedroom
(portable landscape)

ladder

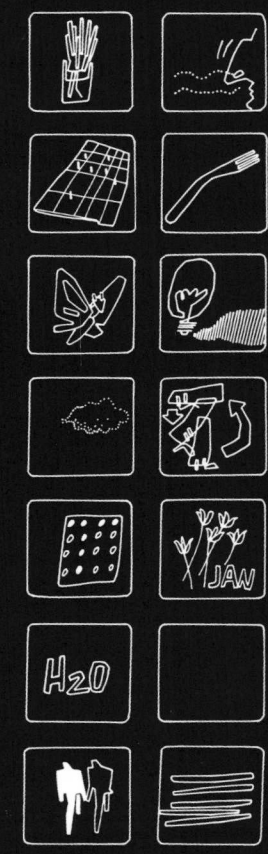

CHAPTER 6:
IN WHICH WE VISIT THE WINDY CITY: A GARDEN FRAGMENTS INTO PIECES AND GATHERS ITSELF BACK TOGETHER AGAIN AND ALICIA ALMOST LOSES HER HEAD

A sudden gust of wind swept Alicia off the path. In a blur, she glimpsed a cacophony of mirrored towers vainly aspiring to scrape the sky. The wind twirled her widdershins through two complete turns and the landscape changed again, settling on a bridge, a meadow and a floating arbour. Alicia felt very small. Although she was almost certain she had not shrunk, she did feel very much like a worm that was crawling through the undergrowth. Peering up past leafy stalks, she could discern plants of every nationality. Palmistes royal from Sainte-Domingue (now Haiti), ironwood trees from Ceylon, peonies from Formosa, flame lilies from Rhodesia, and coral trees from Gran Chaco to name but a few. 'This must be what they call a worm's-eye view,' mused Alicia, digesting the fact that worms had no eyes, or even if they did, that they would have little use for them underground.

This conglomerate floral world was contained overhead in row upon row of lovingly sculpted wooden vessels. Curiously these flower vessels were long and thin, with undersides that tapered at both ends.

The little green book had this to say:

Commemorating the arrival of the Haitian-French explorer, Jean Baptiste Point DuSable in the late 18th Century, the floating park is made up of a thousand boats held aloft by a string of lightweight piers pinned to the water's edge. Each day the boats,

[worm's-eye view]

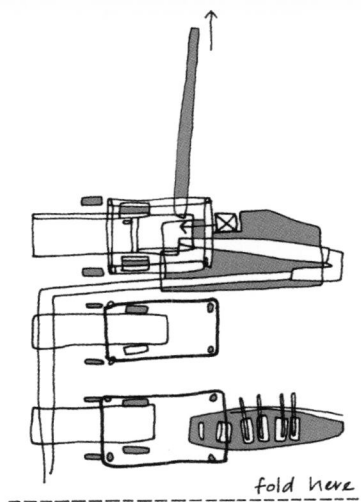

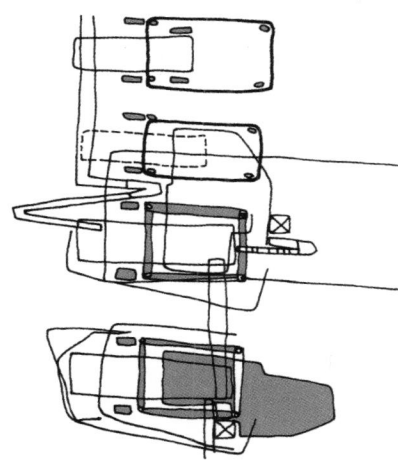

fold here

[plan studies of lightweight pier structure]

loaded with myriad flora, fragment into Lake Michigan to create an ever-changing diversity of ecotypes. Each day, the park is constructed differently in space and time.

Underneath the writing was an etching of a dark-skinned man with a rather severe haircut and the bearded moustache of a musketeer.

'Was this the face that launches a thousand ships each and every day?' wondered Alicia. Craning her neck towards the matrix of boats above, she was jolted by a vivid stab of recognition. Were these the replica boats floating on an imaginary sea that she had seen in the first of the nine gardens? Was that a representation of this boundless garden that shifted and expanded like a droplet of oil and then, in a bizarre display of negative entropy, reconstitute to form an ordered array of vegetation above the meadow?

Alicia put the book down next to a sprawling plant with bright coloured flowers and succulent red berries.

'Pigface!' said an ugly voice from over her shoulder. Alicia turned around and collided with an uncommonly fat woman wearing a red paper party hat.

'I beg your pardon!' said Alicia.

'Indeed you should! Indeed you should! I should say so!' said the woman. 'Who said you could regard my prize pigface?'

Alicia thought that the lady might have judged herself a little harshly, although it had to be said that her visage was quite unfortunate. 'But your face doesn't look like a pig's at all,' she said.

'Uh-oh. Whoops-a-daisy,' purred a new voice from the pea-green boat hovering above Alicia's head. 'You really put your foot in it this time. The flower. The one with the berries. It's called pigface.' Understanding, bewilderment and the plump podgy right hand of the fat lady hit Alicia in one fell swoop.

'What insolence! I have a good mind to have your head off!' the fat lady bawled, storming off in a huff of indignation.

There was a moment of silence. 'That was a close shave,' said the mystery voice from above. 'She really might have had your head off, you know. Oh, and watch out for the fat hen. It's a protected species.' Alicia looked about but could see no sign of poultry, fat or otherwise. She also noted a sign that read:

NO PERSONS ALLOWED ON THE BOATS PRIOR TO EMBARCATION POINT

The owner of the voice was obviously not very trustworthy.

'The fat hen…' said the voice, patiently, is that

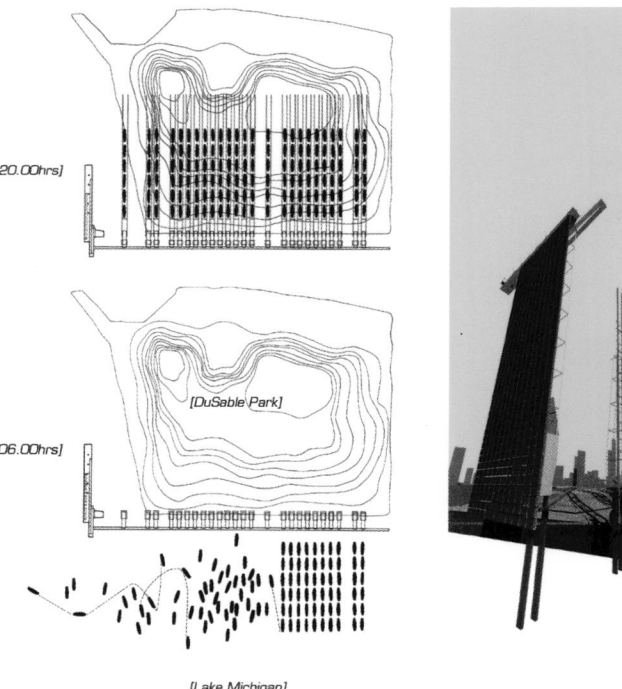

[20.00hrs]

[06.00hrs]

[DuSable Park]

[Lake Michigan]

[Lightweight pier structure: By day, the floating
gardens are deployed onto the lake by
remote-controlled cranes. In the act of releasing
the gardens, the piers lift into their vertical
configuration, revealing the overgrown meadow.
By night, the structures return to their horizontal
positions, collecting and realigning the gardens
into a formal grid.]

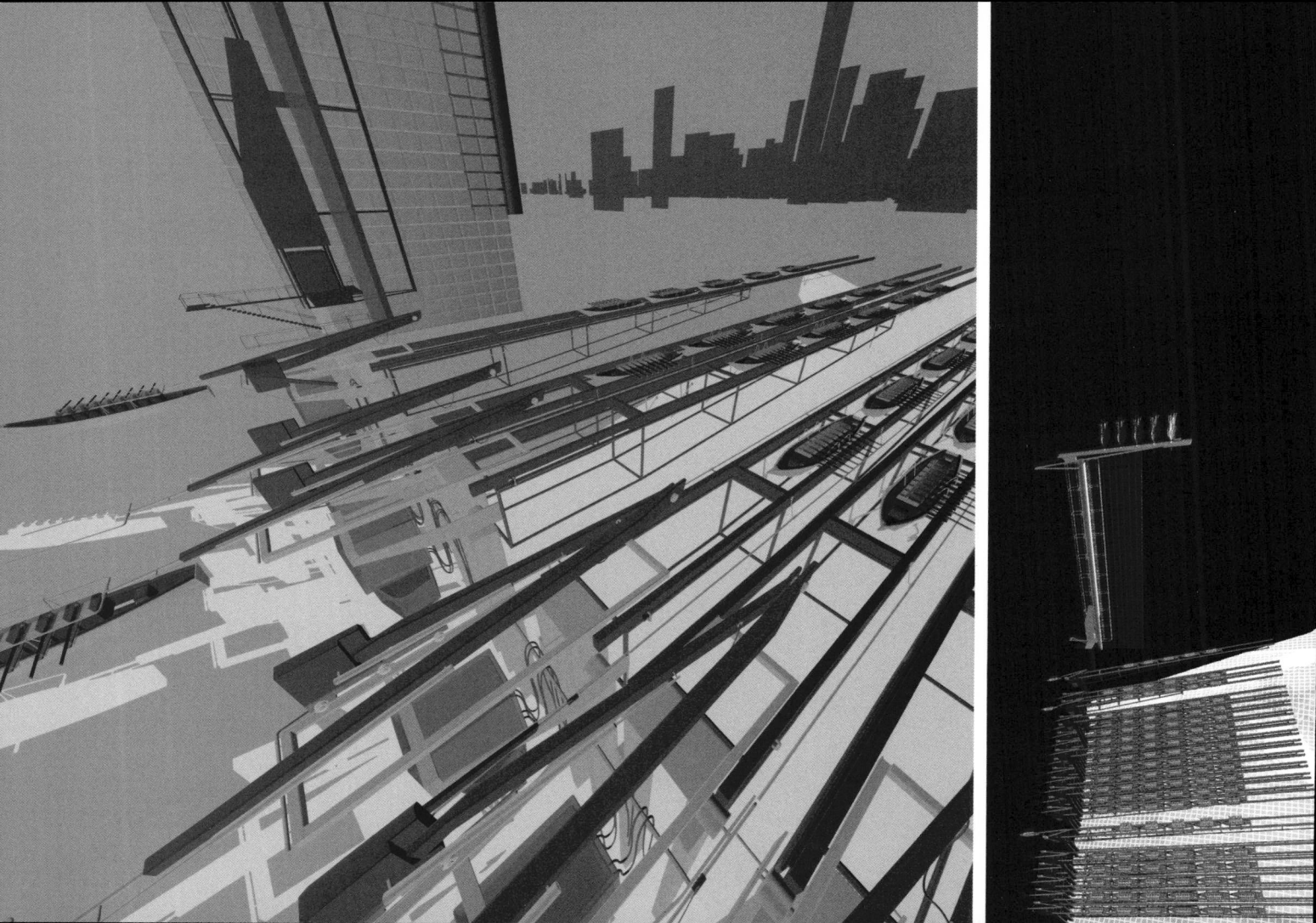

[This community landscape delicately hovers on the edge of an overgrown meadow. It consists of a fleet of floating gardens, a plant nursery skyscraper and a drawbridge linking into Grant Park. The new elements avoid any physical interruption to the meadow: all flora, fauna and romance of the site are preserved.]

small green flower next to your foot. The one with the white scales.'

'Why does it have such a silly name? It looks nothing like a hen at all,' said Alicia.

'How should I know? Do I look like a botanist? (Which Alicia thought was a ridiculous thing for a disembodied voice to say). 'Mind you,' continued the voice, 'it looks no more like pigweed or lamb's quarters which it's also called.'

'The names of flowers are very complicated,' considered Alicia. 'I wonder if they sound the same in the language of flowers. Oak sounds a little like bravery, I suppose. But daffodils and death, and peonies and shame don't go together at all!'

'I don't mind what it's called, as long as it tastes good,' said the voice, strangely muffled. A flurry of half-eaten petals and stems spiralled towards the ground. 'Here, try one,' said the voice, now unencumbered by food. A small green flower head dropped unceremoniously from the boat.

Alicia popped it in her mouth and chewed thoughtfully. 'That's really rather good.'

'Mm-hmm. There's nothing more delicious than lapping up yellow petals fronds from a dandelion on your tongue or crunching into the crisp receptacle of a citrusy hibiscus with your molars. If you close your eyes, you can almost believe you're drinking the colour crimson or supping on distilled light.'

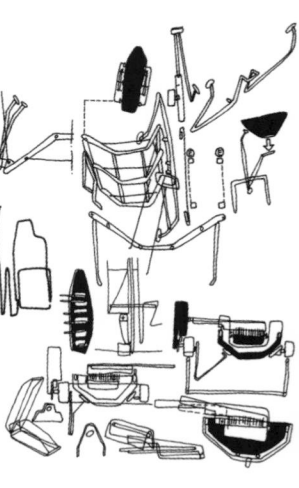

[The boats symbolically celebrate the arrival of the first settler in Chicago: Haitian / French explorer, Jean Baptiste Point DuSable and other subsequent immigrants from various ethnic groups.]

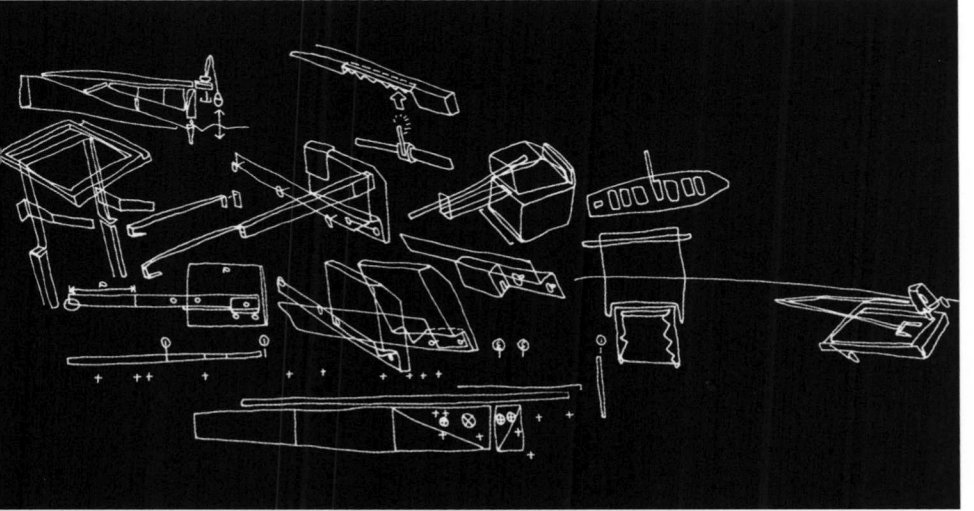

'What other flowers are good to eat?' asked Alicia eagerly.

'Never ones with pesticides,' said the voice, sagely. 'They can make you quite ill. Around here, you should only eat the flowers on the boats, not the ones on the meadow. The ground's contaminated, you see. That's why all the boats are in the air.'

'I see,' said Alicia. 'And how do you know which ones to pick?'

'Ah. You should harvest flowers like you do fruit. Choose the ones with the fullest colour, not the ones that are wilted or look unripe,' said the voice. The boat above began to shift slowly down the meadow. 'Oops! Here we go. You'll have to keep up if you want to find out more! Alicia skipped alongside the boat towards the lake.

'Dandelions are good. Very nutritious. You can dip them in batter and fry them, although I prefer them raw in salads. Snapdragons have a lovely flavour of melon. And sunflowers in their bud stage are as good as artichokes. All roses are edible but if you're going to try some, go for the darker varieties. They're much more flavourso...mind out!'

Alicia ducked as a crane swooped down to pick up the boat in, lifting it high up into the air before depositing it on the water's bobbing surface. As it did so, water began to pour out of the ballast sac attached to the crane.

[The ground is toxic, hence the gardens are elevated above the meadow]

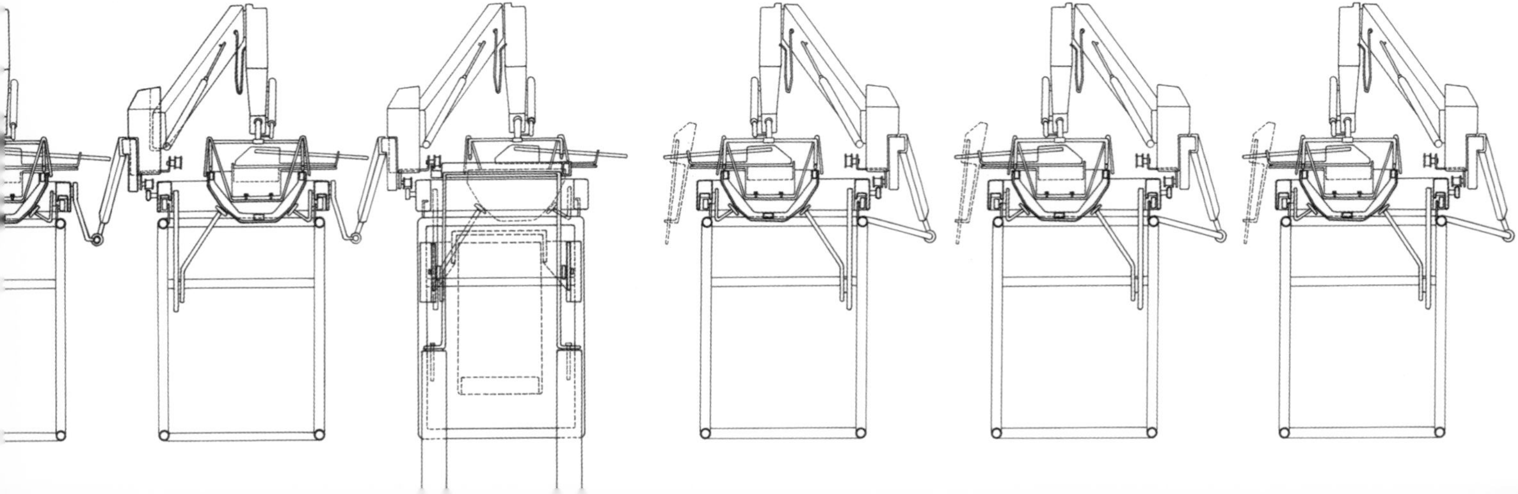

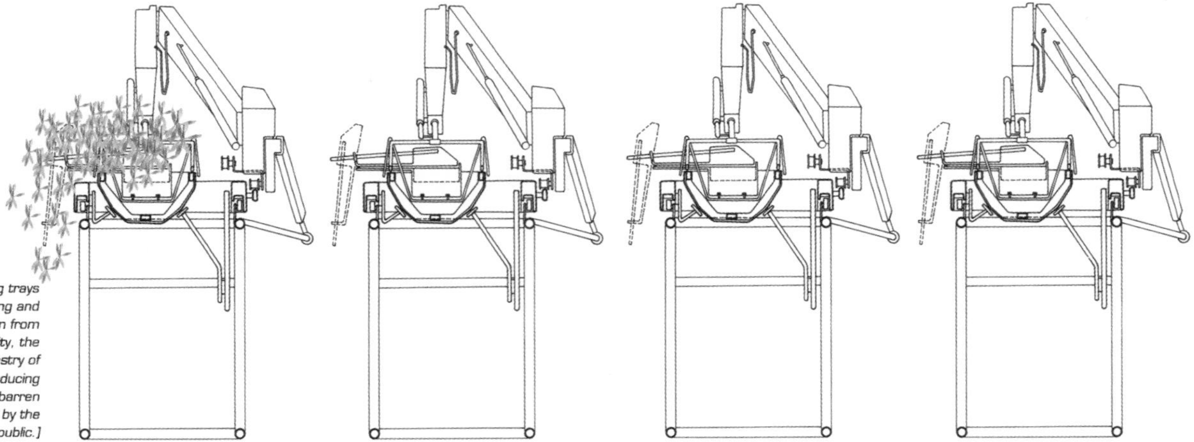

[Boats with integrated planting trays equipped with artificial lighting and plastic covers for protection from frost. Tended by the community, the floating gardens parade a tapestry of non-indigenous flora, introducing alien life and colour to the barren ground and may be rented by the general public.]

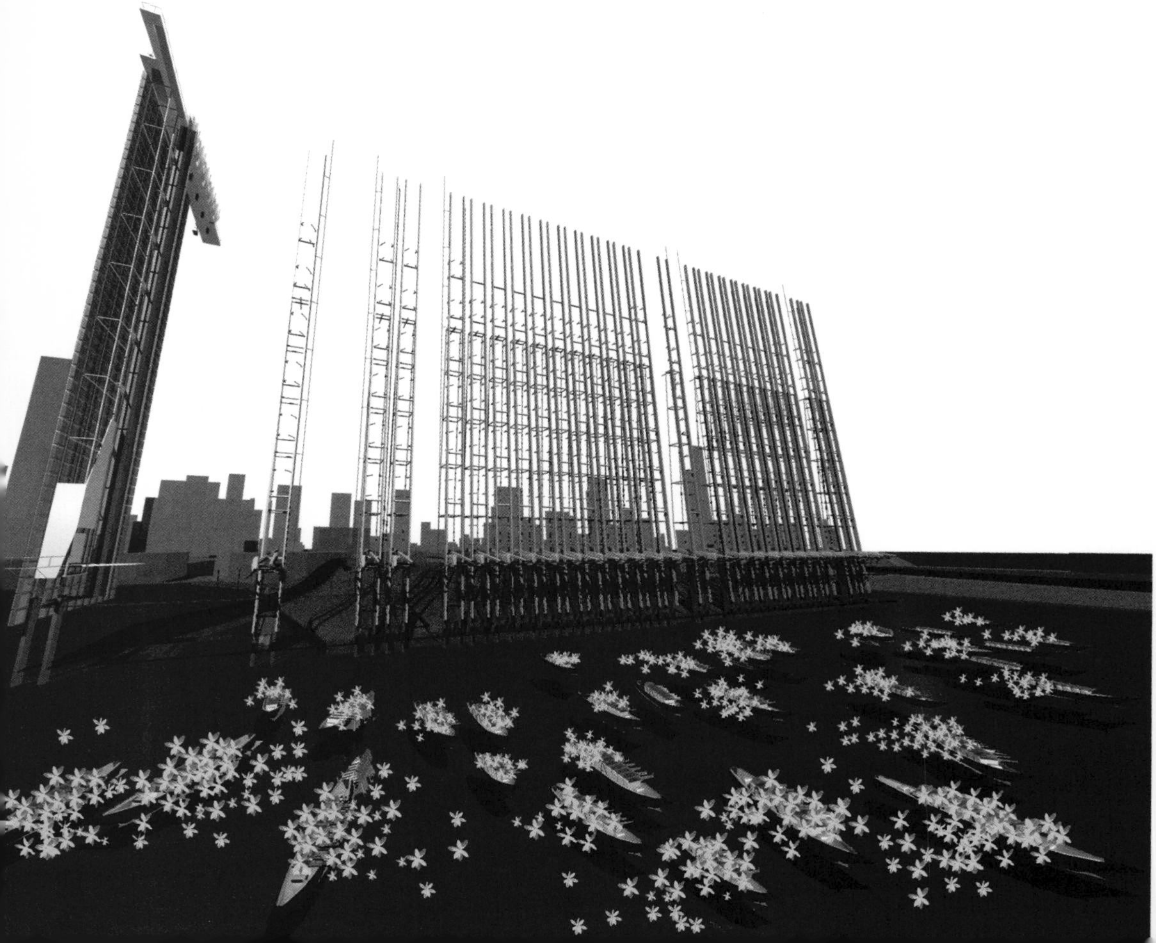

[Nursery skyscraper: This south-facing screen is an inhabitable glass blade mirroring the shimmering high-rise facades of Chicago. As a centre for cultivating non-indigenous flowers, vegetables and rare seedlings, it supplies plants to the floating gardens and the rest of the city. Each seed box is accessed via a vertical harvesting device similar to the window-cleaning systems of neighbouring towers. The nursery is capped by a sky garden planted with hydroponically-grown trees.]

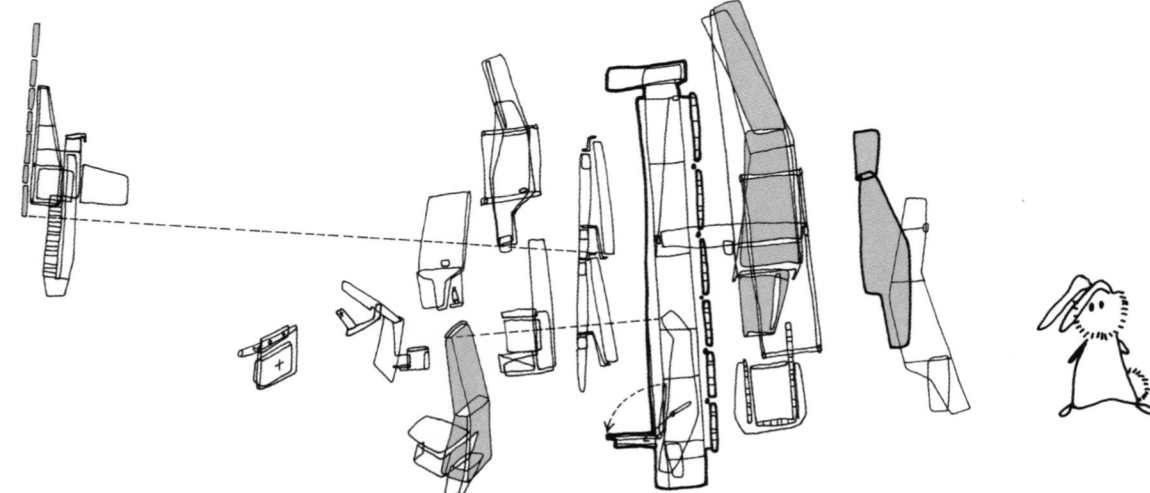

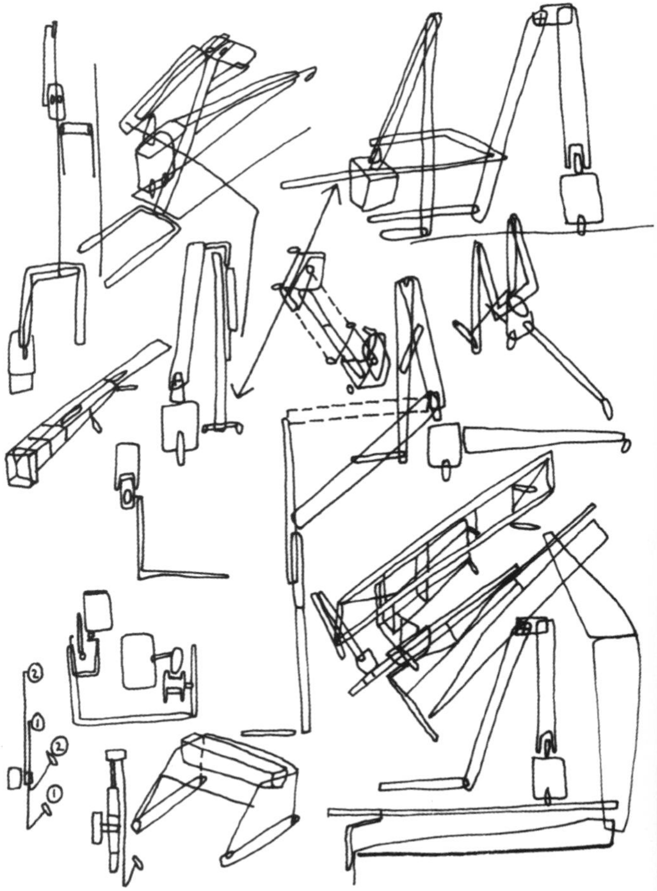

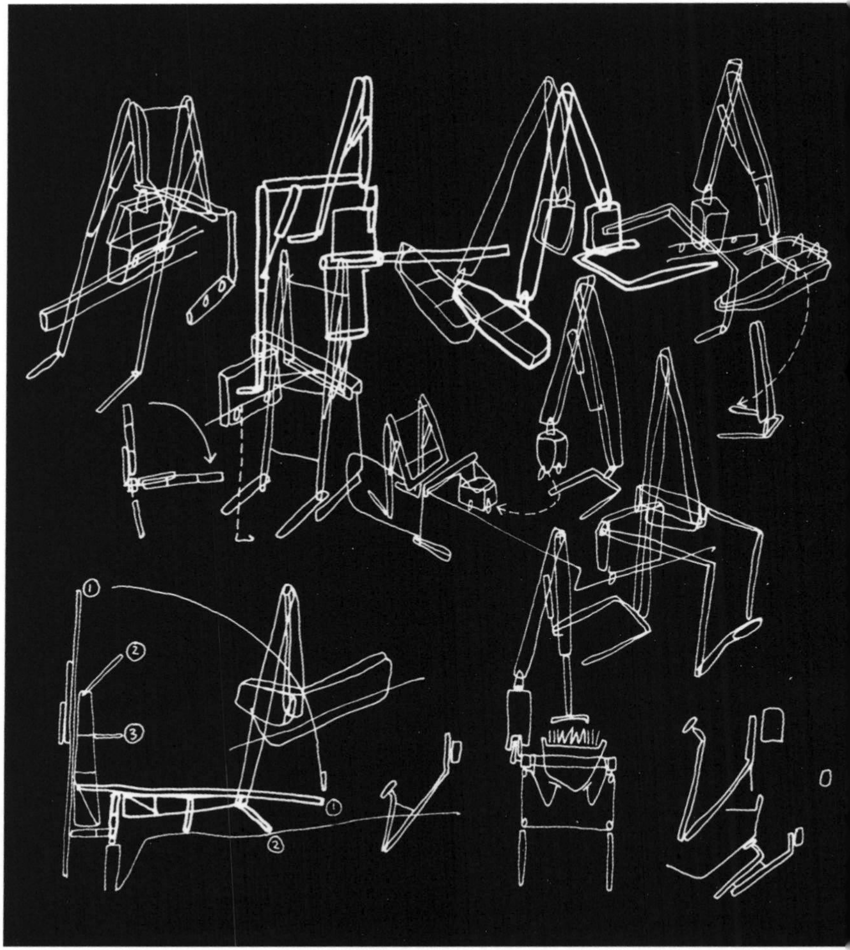

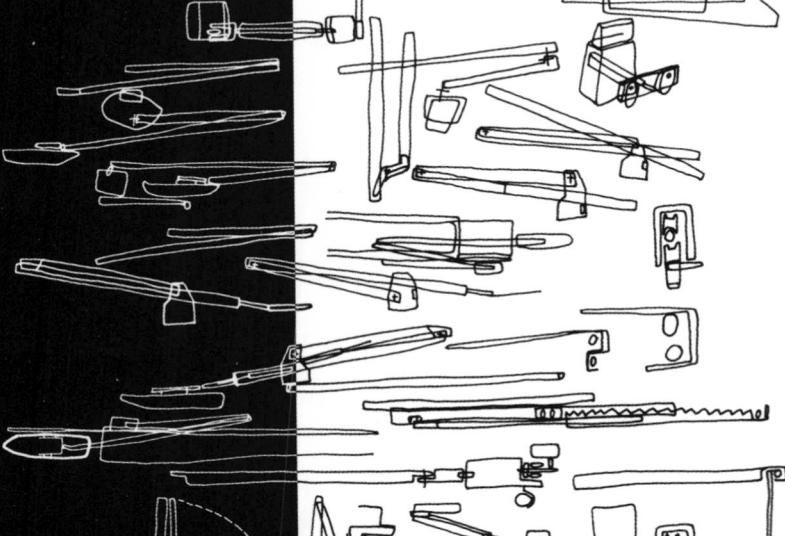

[lightweight pier structure studies]

Park of Sand

A barrage of whoops and yelps came from the punt on the water. 'What boorish behaviour! Give that boat a wide berth,' advised the voice. 'I wouldn't even touch it with my bargepole.'

Alicia studied the planter in the boat more closely.

'What's *in* that boat?' she asked.

'A dog's breakfast is what it is! Dogberry, dogbane, dog fennel, dog rose, dog's mercury, dog's tails, dog's tongues, dog violets, dogwoods.

'It looks like it's gone to the dogs, then,' said Alicia.

'Sometimes,' said the voice wryly, 'you can take a punt too far.'

The boat holding Alicia's companion began to descend, in preparation for launch from the pier. It was crammed to the brim with cat's tails, catmint, catkins and cat's feet. The other thing in the boat was a cat. It appeared to be grinning.

16 *aug* **summer**   *Park of Sand*

[A kitchen at the bottom of the nursery skyscraper can prepare picnic baskets using the local produce. On a clear midsummer's evening with Chicago city as the backdrop, the community can dine in boats, amongst the floating gardens on Lake Michigan.]

Hyacinth Salad

2 gem lettuces
2 ripe peaches
1 handful mint leaves
petals of 3 hyacinth flowers
3 tablespoons olive oil
1 teaspoon lime juice

Shred lettuce and place in a wide salad bowl. Carefully remove petals from the hyacinth flowers. Add to lettuce. Slice each peach into 8 pieces and mix with lettuce. Scatter mint over the top. Toss with extra virgin olive oil and lime juice. Season and serve.

Mushrooms baked with Violets

25g fresh mushrooms
1 handful of violet flowers
2 tablespoons olive oil
8 garlic cloves sliced
salt and pepper

Preheat oven to Gas 7. Tear six pieces of 250mm length baking foil and lightly oil half the sheet. Slice mushrooms and violet flowers. Layer mushroom with violet flowers and garlic. Season and sprinkle with olive oil. Fold and seal the foil edges. Place packets in oven and bake for 15 minutes. Open packets at table and eat hot.

Pilaff Jasmine and Coriander

200g basmati rice
30g butter
1 tablespoon of olive oil
1 chopped onion
2 chopped garlic cloves
half tablespoon cumin seeds
2 cloves
1 teaspoon ground turmeric
500ml water
1 handful of jasmine flowers
2 tablespoons of chopped coriander
salt and pepper

Rinse rice and leave to drain in a sieve. Melt butter with oil in a saucepan. Add onion and fry gently until translucent. Add garlic, cumin seeds, cloves, turmeric and fry gently for 1 minute. Tip in the rice and stir for another minute. Add water and seasoning and bring up to the boil. Reduce heat to very low, cover tightly and leave to cook until all liquid has been absorbed and rice is tender. Tip rice into a wide dish and leave for 10 minutes to dry in its own steam. Stir in jasmine flowers and coriander.

Stir-Fried Chicken with Lilies

2 chicken breasts
1 carrot
2 tablespoons vegetable oil
1 tablespoon chopped fresh root ginger
2 chopped garlic cloves
1 handful chopped lily flowers
1 tablespoon soy sauce
1 teaspoon sesame oil
1 teaspoon corn flour
salt and pepper

Cut chicken breasts into 5mm thick slivers. Marinate chicken with soy sauce, sesame oil and corn flour for at least 10 minutes. Slice carrot into 2mm strips. Heat wok over a high heat until it smokes. Add oil, ginger, garlic and swirl them around. Add chicken and stir-fry for about 3 minutes. Stir in carrots and lily flowers, toss for another 5 minutes. Serve with rice.

Lavender Bunny Shortbread

80g plain flour
80g corn flour
125g softened unsalted butter
50g caster sugar
3 teaspoons fresh lavender flowers

Sift flour with corn flour. Beat butter with sugar until light and creamy. Work in flour and lavender to form a soft dough. Knead briefly and roll out to form a circle about 5mm thick. Cut into bunny shapes with a rabbit cookie cutter. Prick all over with a fork. Bake for 30 minutes until pale brown. Remove from oven and leave to cool. Store in an airtight tin.

Tagliatelle Johnny-Jump-Up

600g fresh tagliatelle
1 handful chopped Johnny-Jump-Up flowers
3 tablespoons olive oil
3 garlic cloves sliced
1 teaspoon crushed fennel seeds
2 dried red chillies
1 tin peeled and chopped plum tomatoes
salt and pepper

Gently heat olive oil in saucepan. Add garlic, fennel seeds, chillies, tomatoes and season. Simmer gently and reduced to a thick sauce. Cook tagliatelle in boiling water until al dente. Drain, add Johnny-Jump-Up flowers and stir in sauce. Serve hot.

Stuffed Zucchini Flowers

18 zucchini flowers
18 basil leaves
250g ricotta
200ml sunflower oil
2 lemons

Remove stamens of flowers.

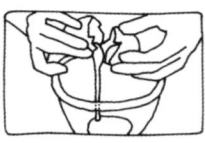
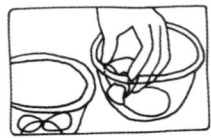

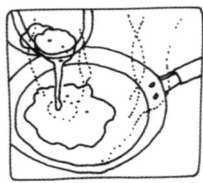

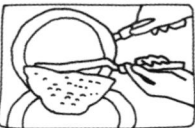

Push 1 tsp seasoned ricotta and 1 basil leaf inside each flower. Dip flowers individually into a basic flour batter. Carefully place flowers into hot sunflower oil. Fry until light brown. Drain on kitchen paper. Serve with lemon.

Rose Petal Omelette

3 eggs yolks
petals of 1 rose
20g butter
1 tablespoon olive oil
salt and pepper
1 rose bud
1 lemon wedge

Gently separate rose petals from stem. Crack eggs into a bowl. Separate egg whites. Whisk egg yolks until foamy. Add butter and season with salt and pepper. Heat olive oil in frying pan. Pour mixture into pan. Reduce heat. Sprinkle rose petals over egg mixture. Gently fold half the moist omelette over. Serve immediately with rose garnish and lemon.

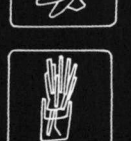

The new flat was still quite empty of chairs, and so Alicia found herself seated on the carpet next to the radiator. This did not much bother her, as she often sat and rolled around on the floor when playing with her cat, Deena. The carpet inherited with the flat was pale green in colour and quite threadbare. There remained, however, certain patches of the carpet that were more voluminous, capturing the shadows of absent furniture in relief as if someone had tried to mow the carpet and been unable to get under the chests and bookcases.

'Alicia? Alicia, where are you, girl?' Mother was looking for her again. 'Honestly, how can you disappear in such a minuscule flat? Ah, there you are Alicia,' said Mother, popping her head around the parlour door. 'Do be a dear and put the kettle on for some tea, would you?'

Alicia sighed and decamped to the kitchenette. In truth, she rather enjoyed the ritual of making tea, inhaling the aroma from the leaves of Earl Grey and watching the air above the spout of the kettle began to shimmer and shake, as if reality itself was uncertain of its existence.

While waiting for the kettle to whistle, Alicia slipped into an improbable world where two of the known four dimensions appeared to be absent. Here was a land that time forgot, or at least momentarily overlooked. The buildings in front of her, the landscape and the dress of its denizens

CHAPTER 7:
IN WHICH ALICIA IS INVITED TO TEA AND DISCOVERS THE ART OF SMELLING PAINTINGS

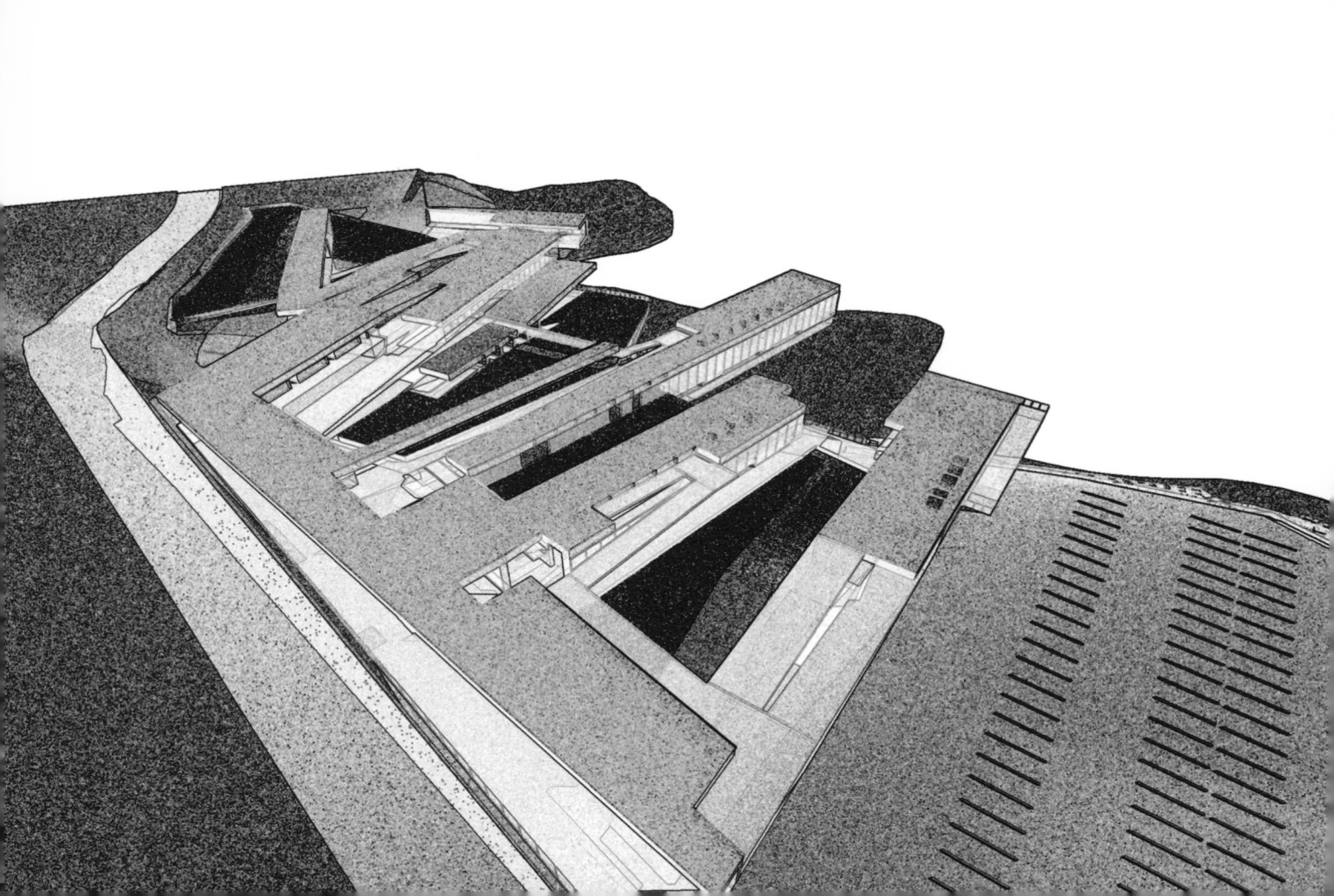

[Walking with nature is the concept for this design. This museum nestles itself within the deep green slopes of the surrounding mountains and lakeside. Reflecting the seasonal nature of Tomihiro Hoshino's work, the route through this single-level building takes you through autumn, winter, spring and autumn galleries.]

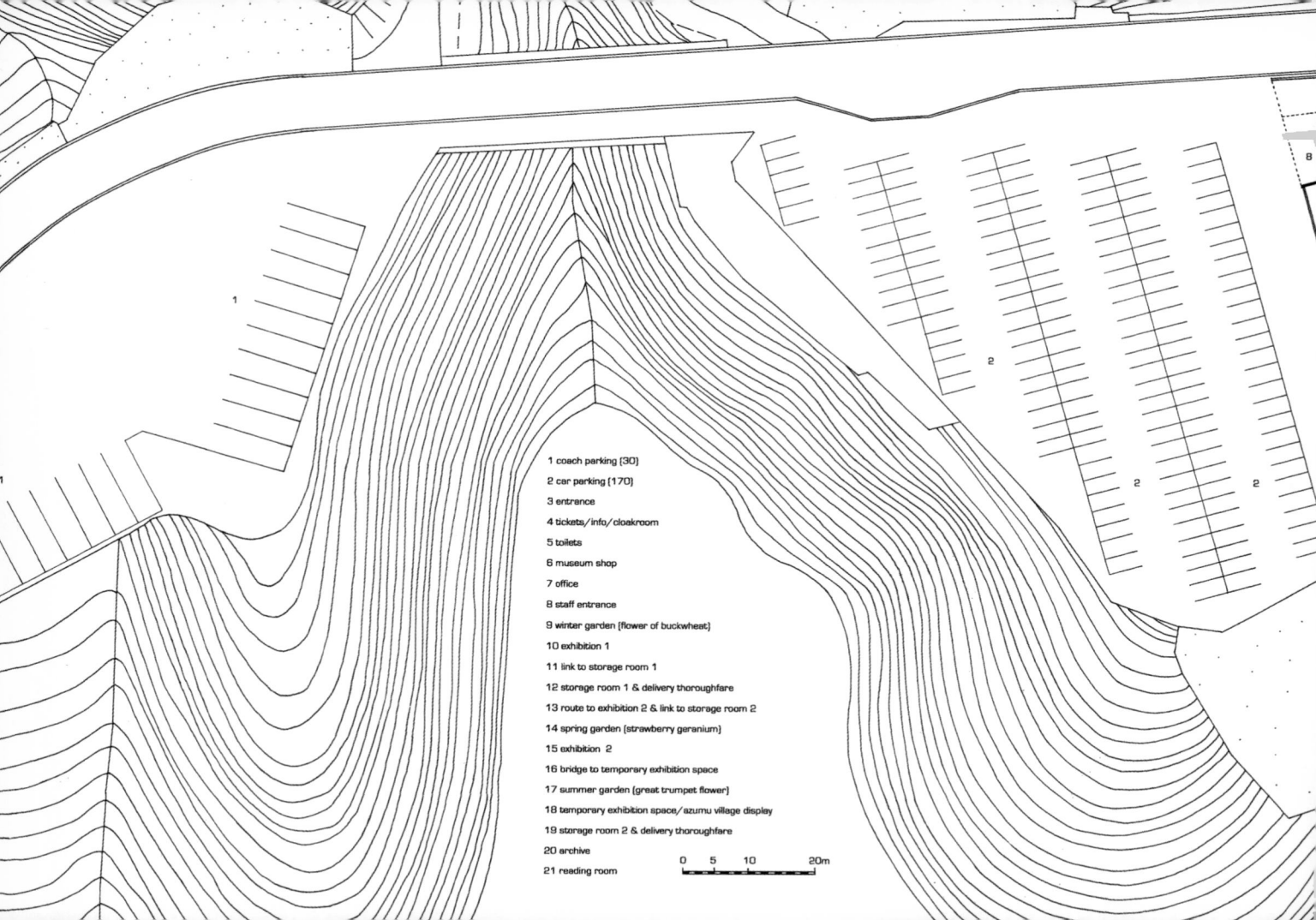

1 coach parking (30)

2 car parking (170)

3 entrance

4 tickets/info/cloakroom

5 toilets

6 museum shop

7 office

8 staff entrance

9 winter garden (flower of buckwheat)

10 exhibition 1

11 link to storage room 1

12 storage room 1 & delivery thoroughfare

13 route to exhibition 2 & link to storage room 2

14 spring garden (strawberry geranium)

15 exhibition 2

16 bridge to temporary exhibition space

17 summer garden (great trumpet flower)

18 temporary exhibition space/szumu village display

19 storage room 2 & delivery thoroughfare

20 archive

21 reading room

0 5 10   20m

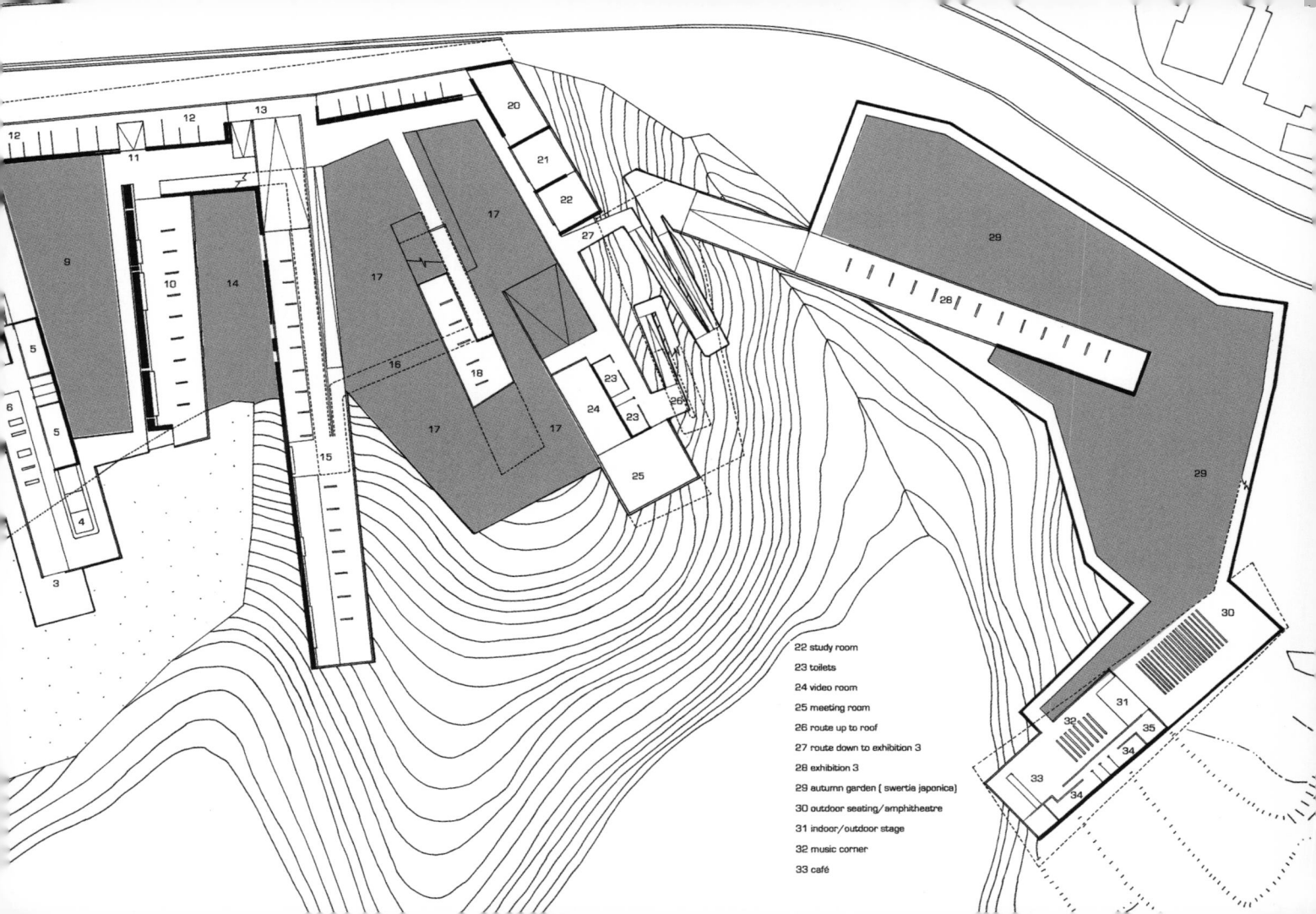

22 study room

23 toilets

24 video room

25 meeting room

26 route up to roof

27 route down to exhibition 3

28 exhibition 3

29 autumn garden [swertia japonica]

30 outdoor seating/amphitheatre

31 indoor/outdoor stage

32 music corner

33 café

1 coach parking (30)
2 car parking (170)
3 entrance
4 tickets/info/cloakroom
5 toilets
6 museum shop
7 office
8 staff entrance
9 winter garden (flower of buckwheat)
10 exhibition 1
11 link to storage room 1
12 storage room 1 & delivery thoroughfare
13 route to exhibition 2 & link to storage room 2
14 spring garden (strawberry geranium)
15 exhibition 2
16 bridge to temporary exhibition space
17 summer garden (great trumpet flower)
18 temporary exhibition space/azumi village display
19 storage room 2 & delivery thoroughfare
20 archive
21 reading room

22 study room
23 toilets
24 video room
25 meeting room
26 route up to roof
27 route down to exhibition 3
28 exhibition 3
29 autumn garden (swertia japonica)
30 outdoor seating/amphitheatre
31 indoor/outdoor stage
32 music corner
33 café

0   5   10   20m

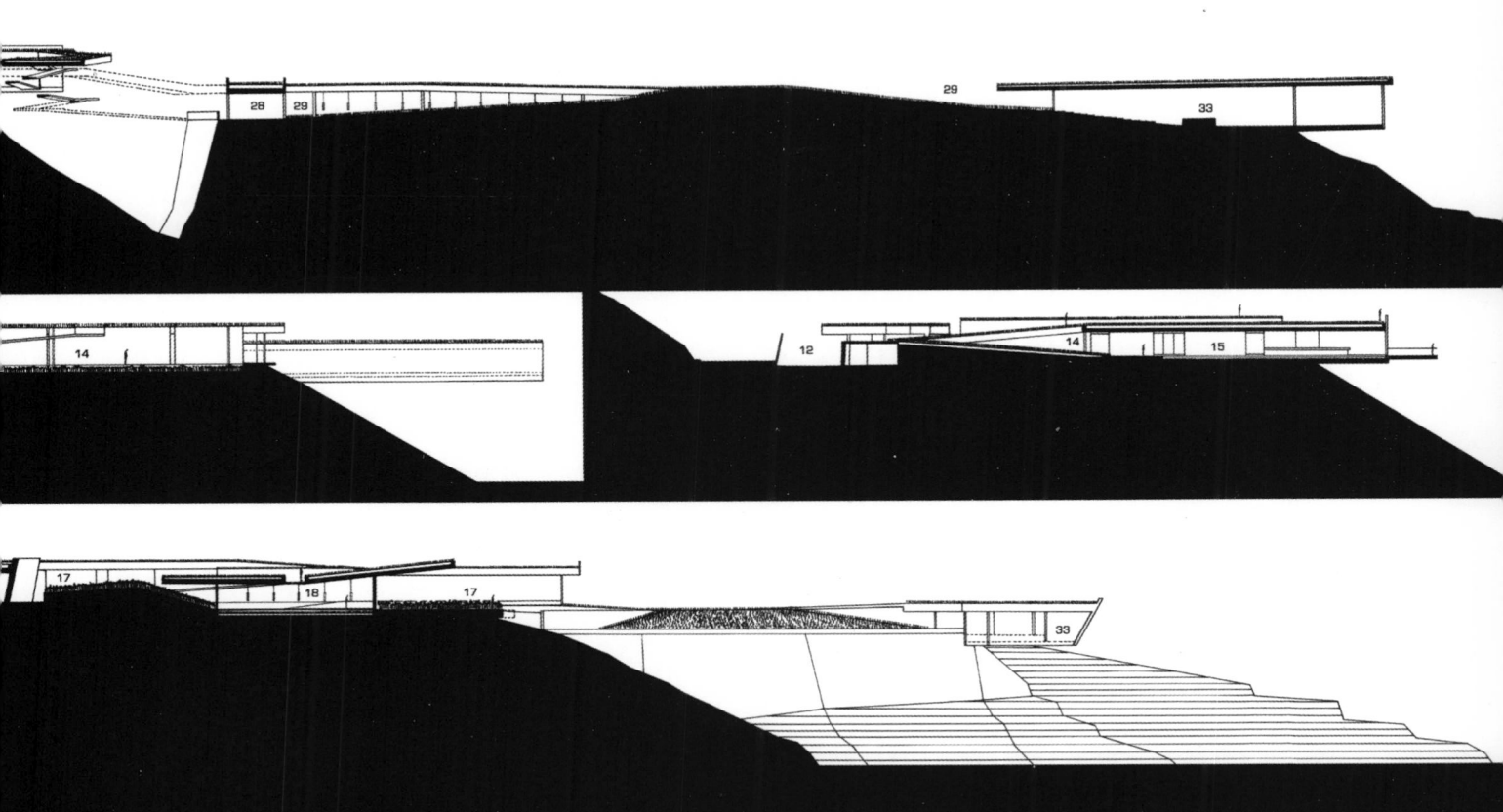

08 sept **summer**   *Gallery of Four Seasons*

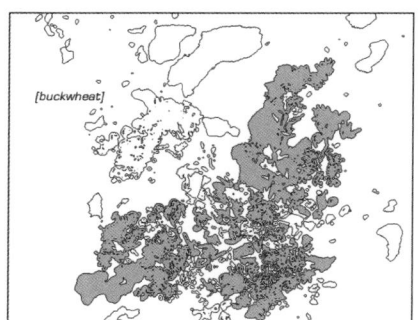

[buckwheat]

[winter garden]

I want My garden RED

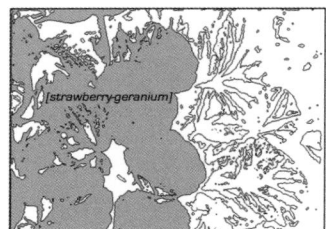

[strawberry-geranium]

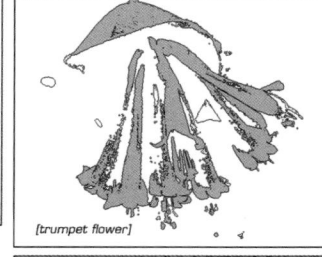

[trumpet flower]

[spring garden]

[lily of the nile]

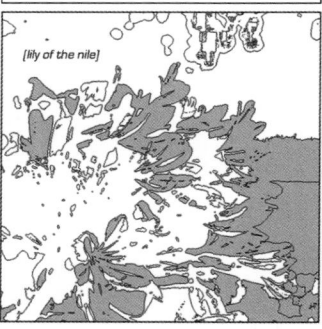

[sunflower]

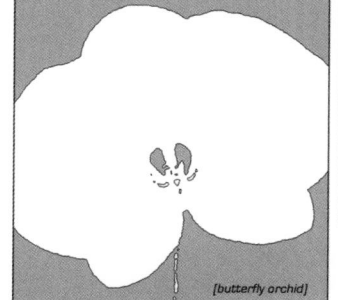

[butterfly orchid]

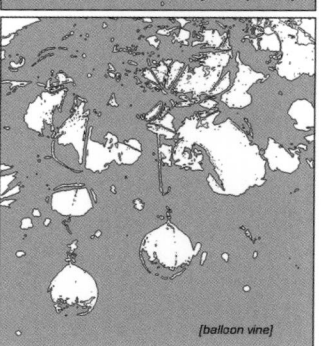

[balloon vine]

[summer garden]

[swertia japonica]

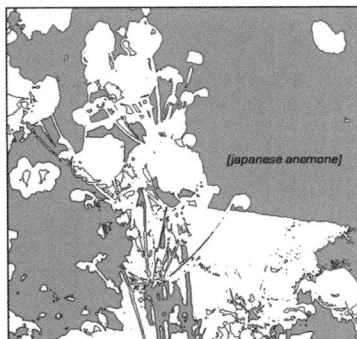

[japanese anemone]

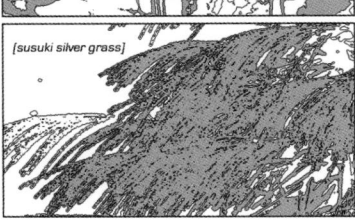

[susuki silver grass]

expected were kimonos, zori and topknots from Edo-period Nippon.

The second dimension that was missing in this tableau was the third one – that is to say that all Alicia surveyed, including Alicia herself, was utterly flat and two-dimensional. Oriental Alicia quickly overcame her shock and dismay. Perspective was, after all, a western invention.

'Please take a seat, Honoured Miss,' said a tremulous serving girl, bowing several times in welcome.

Alicia gave her host a slightly bewildered curtsey and looked around for a chair, but just as in the new family flat, there were none to be found. By the time she had gathered her wits to ask, the serving girl in her kimono and white cotton socks had scampered off. Alicia made herself comfortable on the reed floor. She glanced over at the next mat where a man, also seated on the ground, was surreptitiously pulling a mouse out of his cup by the tail. Noticing Alicia, he hurriedly palmed it into his sleeve and slurped his tea noisily as if nothing out of the ordinary had occurred.

Alicia's host returned bearing a black-lacquered tray and placed it on the floor.

'Excuse me, Ma'am. What is this?' asked Alicia politely.

'Tea. You are in a teahouse, Honoured Miss.' She bowed again and retreated to greet some newly-arrived guests, rabbiting to them in incomprehensible strings of Japanese.

Alicia eyed the bowl of green sludge masquerading as tea rather dubiously. Next to it was an unappetising ball of something resembling green marzipan. Feeling quite unhungry, she slid the offending tray to one side and turned her attention to the man with the concealed mouse. Despite his Asian features, he bore a striking likeness to the redoubtable T Carter Alicia had met at LookingGlassHouse, and she soon convinced herself that this man was the Occidental Carter's Oriental doppelgänger. Sensing Alicia's scrutiny, the Japanese Carter-san returned a frosty stare that abruptly metamorphosed into a look of horror and a strangled croak. He muttered something under his breath, looked pointedly at Alicia's shoes and then, still spluttering, took his hat (an oversize conical affair that looked like a squashed dunce cap) and his leave, sidling off in a strange marionette motion into the surrounding garden.

'How rude!' said Alicia, indignantly. She smoothed down her dress and picked up her book, looking for information to orient herself.

If you have time, take the opportunity of enjoying a cup of green tea while you are at the museum of the celebrated Japanese artist Tomihiro Hoshino.

began the chapter.

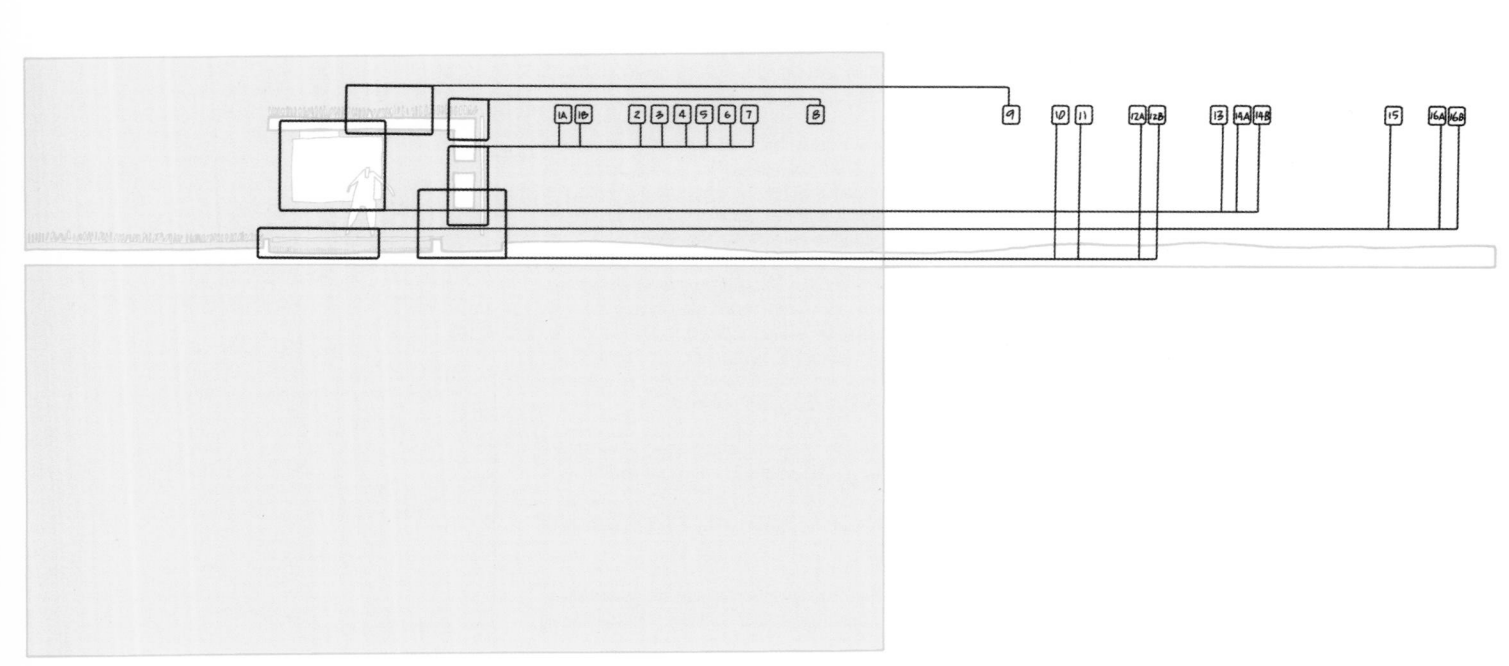

An educational resource for the art of SHI-GA, each gallery space in the complex is a seasonal garden, framing the poetry and paintings of Tomihiro with its real-life subject matter to create an effect the Victorians would have called a grand conjunction. The predominantly visual and text-based nature of Tomihiro's work is juxtaposed with the scent, texture and sounds of the garden.

Not over-enamoured with the tea (even the best guidebooks aren't 100% reliable), Alicia decided to explore the museum buildings. This museum was quite different from any Alicia had ever visited. She could walk through or in or over or between or under it. There were walls, and floors and ceilings, but there were breaches everywhere, as if some *non compos mentis* architect had cut away at the building with a giant saw. Sometimes the walls did not touch the floors, and sometimes the ceilings did not touch the walls, allowing snow and rain and leaves and grass to insinuate their way all over the interior surfaces. But what was in and what was out? If Alicia could walk on the ceiling, would she be walking endlessly in a moebius loop?

There were many things in the museum that caught Alicia's imagination. She found that the umbilical bond between the work and the land that birthed it allowed her to smell, hear and even taste the poems and paintings, which more than made up for losing the third and fourth dimensions in this landscape. Another surprise was that the floor of the gallery was made of grass, only Alicia's two feet floated two feet above it, disconnected by a sandwich of glass. What most transfixed Alicia, however, was a single painting. Unusually, the subject was not a flower, but a girl in a room.

'Why that looks just like me!' she exclaimed pointing at the picture and risking the wrath of the wandering curator. 'She's even wearing that ghastly pinafore dress that Mother made me wear all the time!' Within the painting, Alicia stood in front of a picture, looking somewhat bewildered. The original Alicia squinted hard and discerned yet another Alicia being gazed at by her second self. A wave of giddiness assailed her.

After an hour of telescoping into the image looking for ever-smaller Alicias, a steward ushered her out into one of the seasonal gardens. Surely it was not already closing time? Alicia did not have to wait long, however, before the reason for her removal was made clear.

Little by little, the paintings and poem cabinets began to creep down to the entrance of the gallery, concertinaing to a fraction of their original volume. When the gallery was completely clear, the glass floor folded up in sections like the wing case of an exotic beetle, exposing the mantle of lush, if slightly overgrown, grass. A man stepped into the enclosed ring and began to mow.

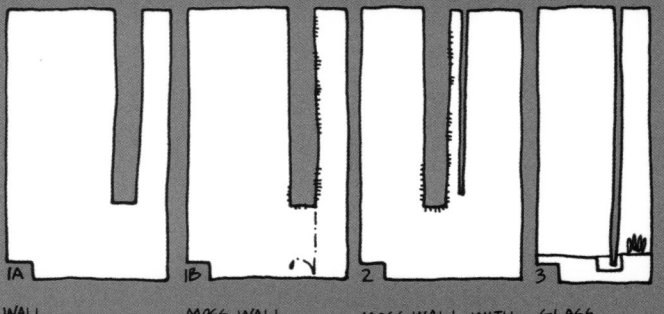

1A   1B   2   3

WALL   MOSS WALL   MOSS WALL WITH GLASS OUTER LAYER   GLASS BOUNDARY

4

NO BOUNDARY INTERNAL GALLERY + EXTERNAL GARDEN MERGE

PICTURE
OF GARDEN

RAIN-BLURRED
PICTURE OF
GARDEN

A little while later, Alicia was taking a stroll through a small valley saturated with trees in early blossom when she came across a group of people drinking wine and singing songs.

'Is it somebody's birthday?' inquired Alicia politely of a genial old lady from the gathering.

'No, no, you are mistaken, Honoured Miss,' the lady answered in exquisite English. This is hanami — that means cherry blossom viewing party. Every spring we come here.'

'But it's almost autumn now!' said Alicia.

'No, no, I'm so sorry you are again mistaken, Honoured Miss. Spring is here. In autumn there are no cherry blossoms to view. Almost autumn is over there.' The lady pointed over the hill.

Alicia was a little cross at being so often mistaken, but as she departed, she could see the blossom-viewers were quite correct. Time in this world stood still. Autumn, covered in falling leaves and mellow mist was gradually coming into view.

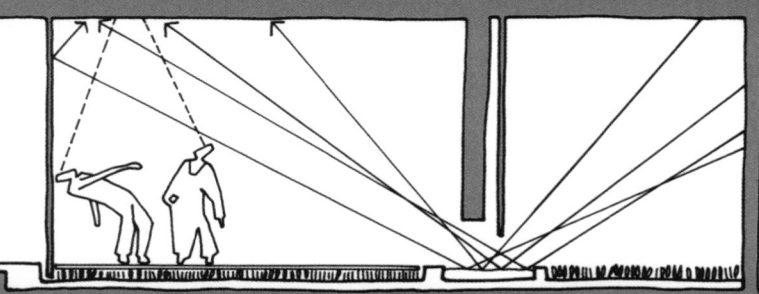

CAUSTICS
IMAGE

6

7

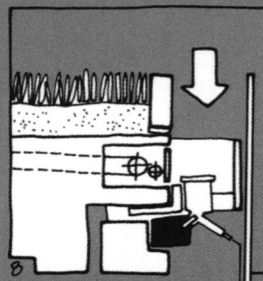

8

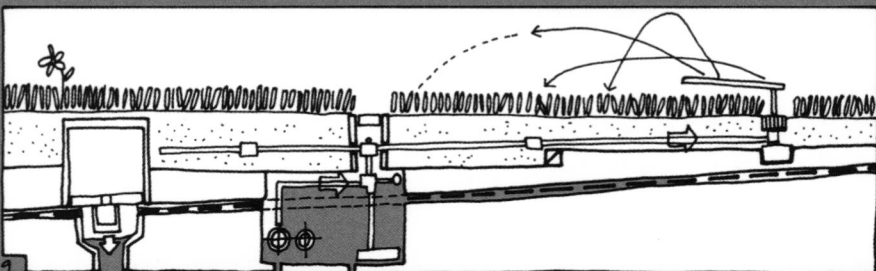

9

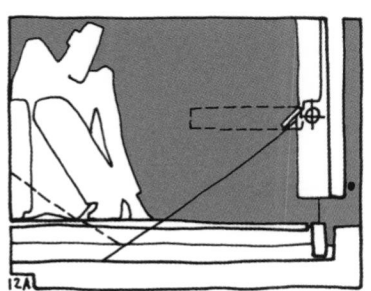

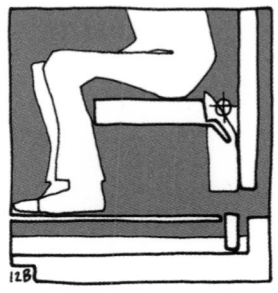

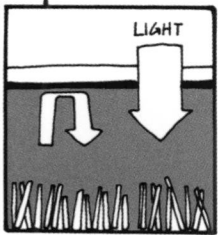

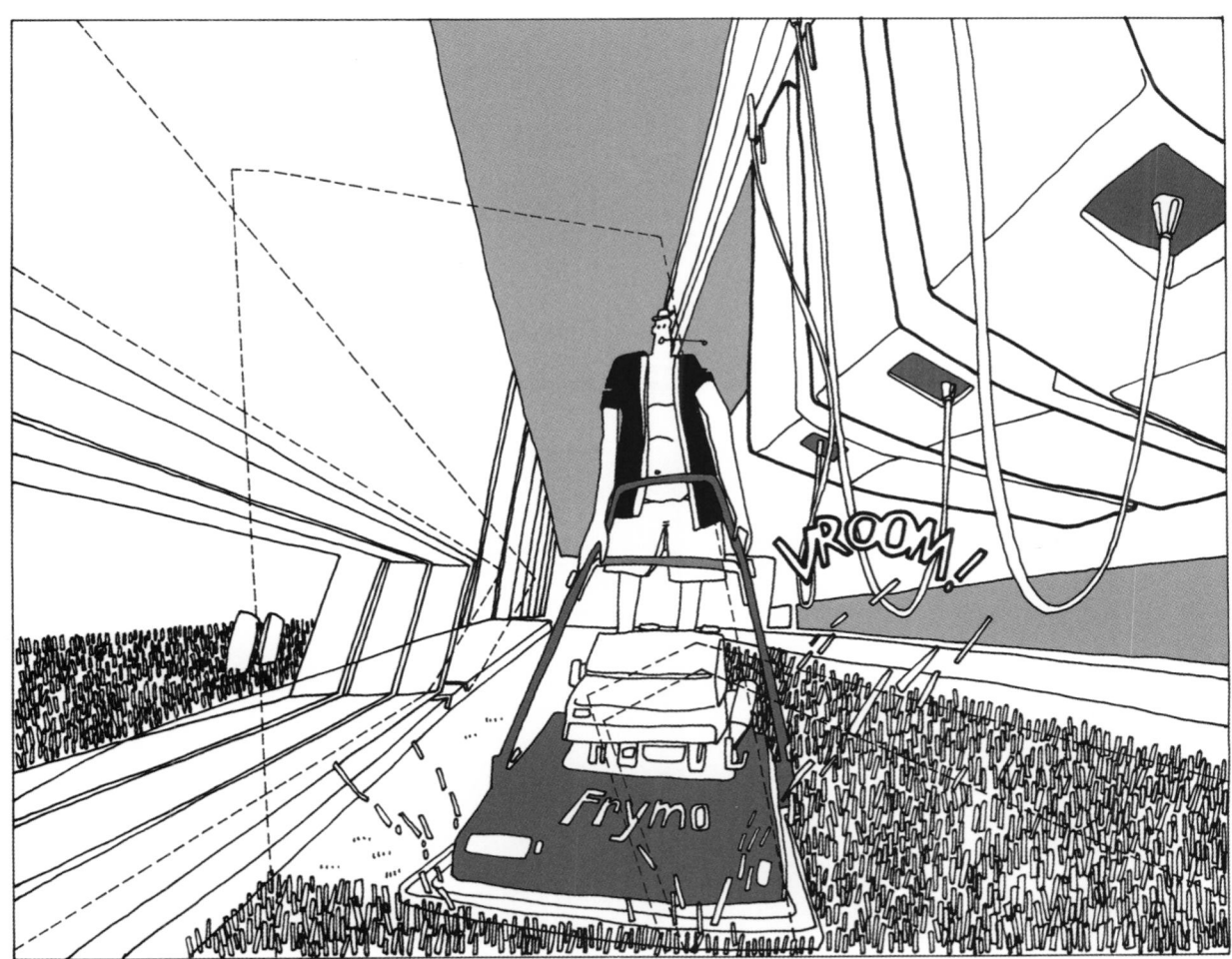

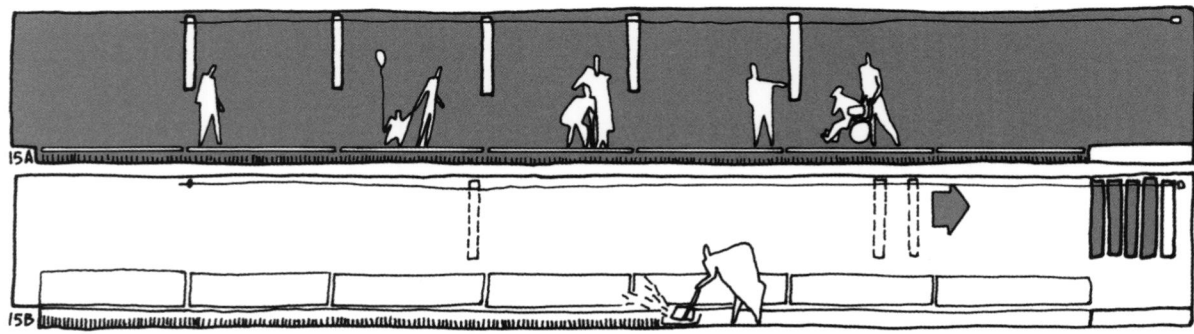

15A

15B

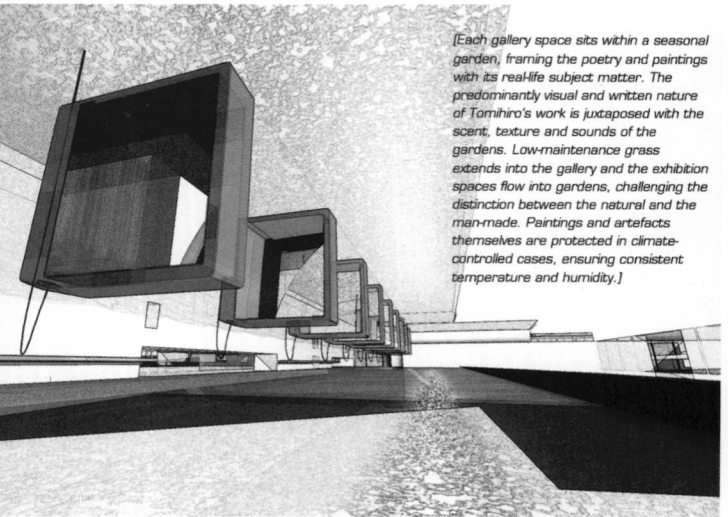

[Each gallery space sits within a seasonal garden, framing the poetry and paintings with its real-life subject matter. The predominantly visual and written nature of Tomihiro's work is juxtaposed with the scent, texture and sounds of the gardens. Low-maintenance grass extends into the gallery and the exhibition spaces flow into gardens, challenging the distinction between the natural and the man-made. Paintings and artefacts themselves are protected in climate-controlled cases, ensuring consistent temperature and humidity.]

22 sept **summer** *Gallery of Four Seasons*

14
[retractable glass floor]

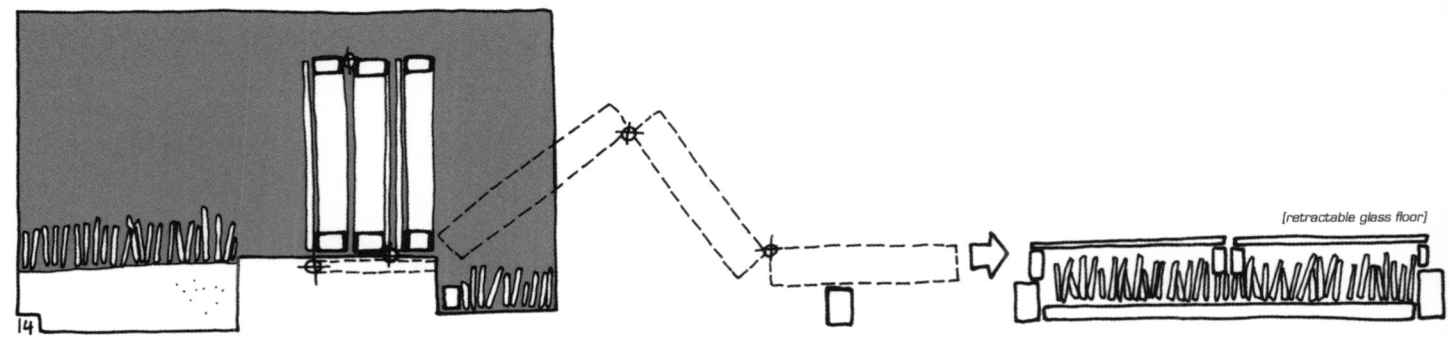

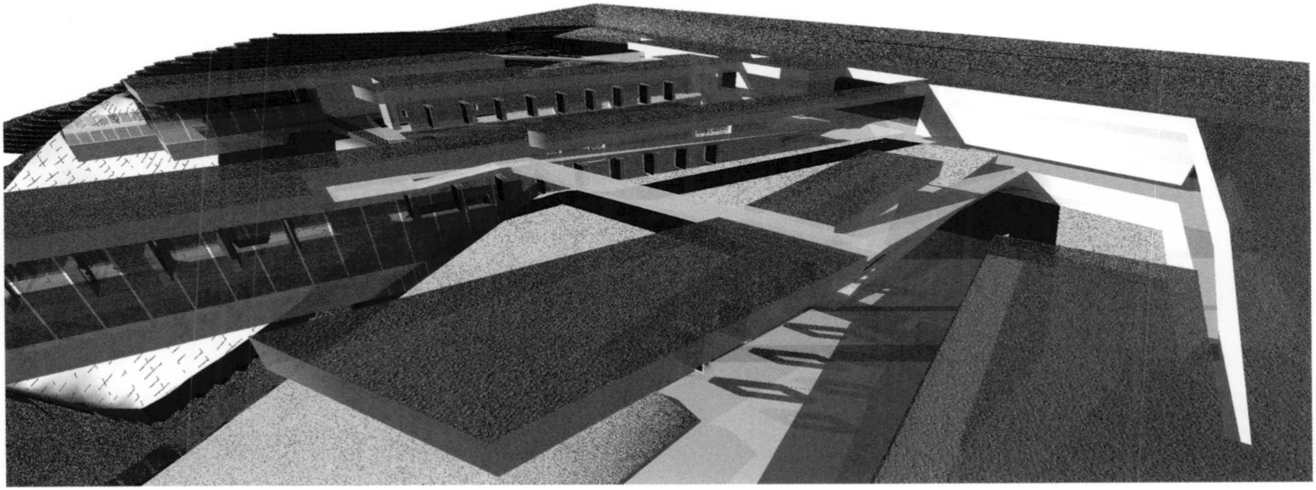

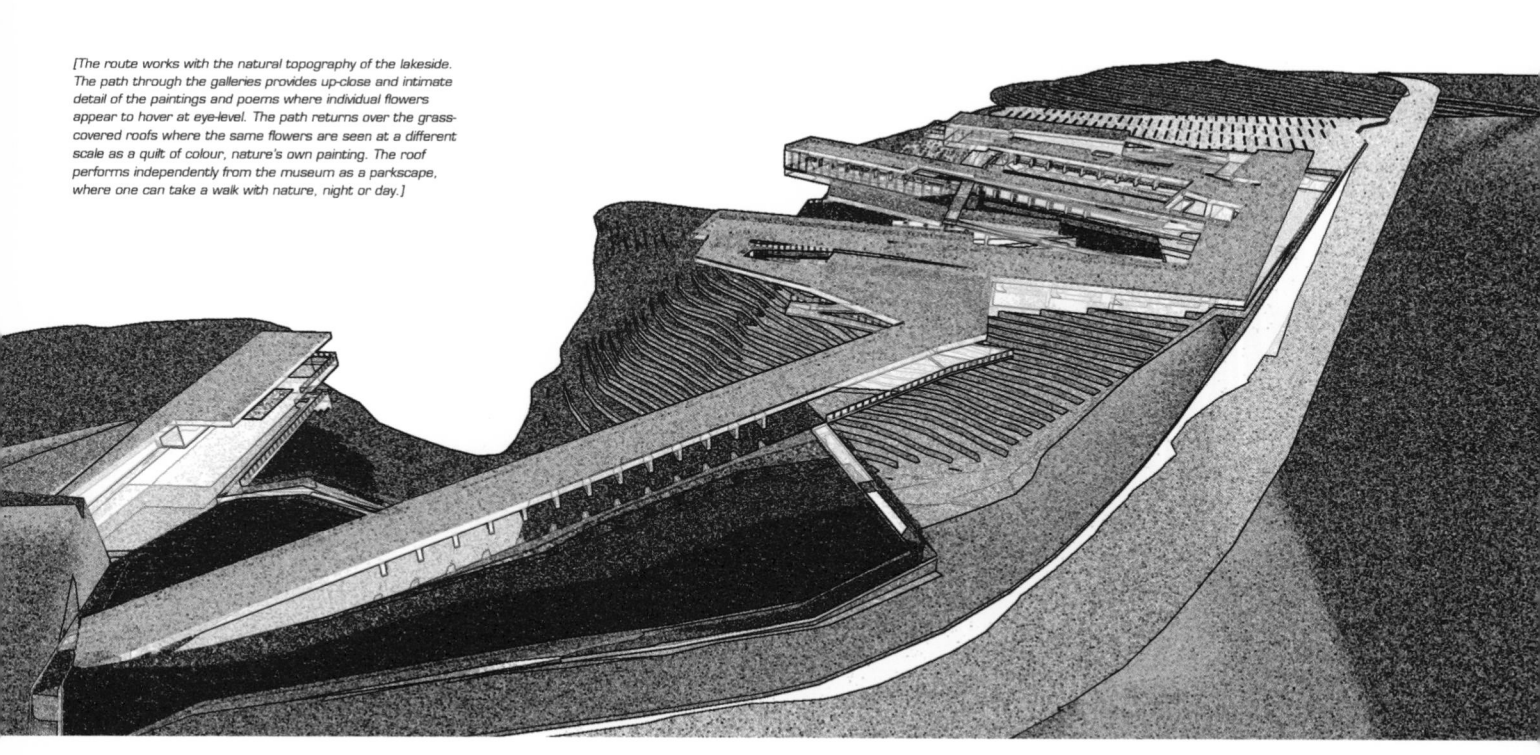

[The route works with the natural topography of the lakeside. The path through the galleries provides up-close and intimate detail of the paintings and poems where individual flowers appear to hover at eye-level. The path returns over the grass-covered roofs where the same flowers are seen at a different scale as a quilt of colour, nature's own painting. The roof performs independently from the museum as a parkscape, where one can take a walk with nature, night or day.]

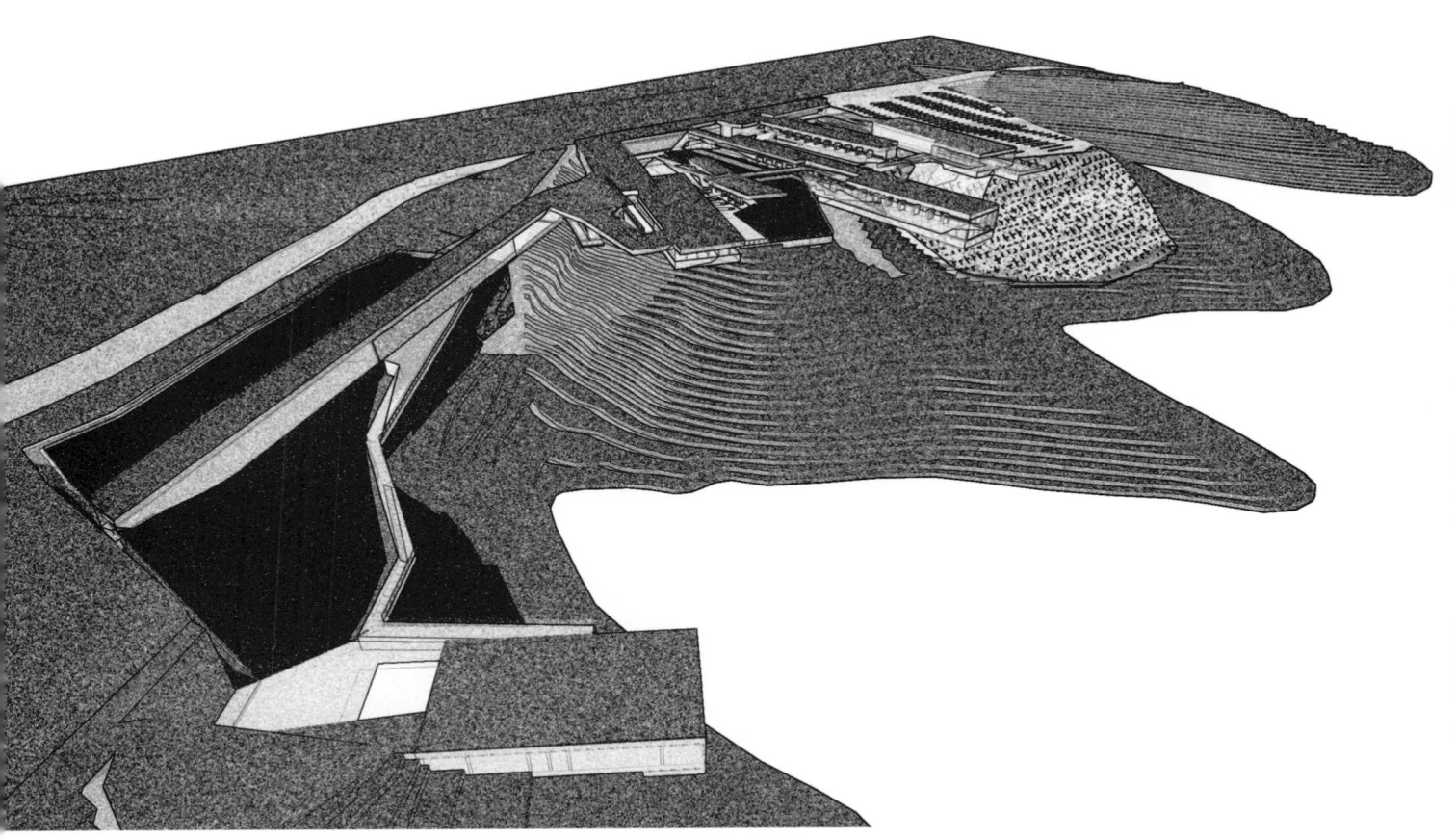

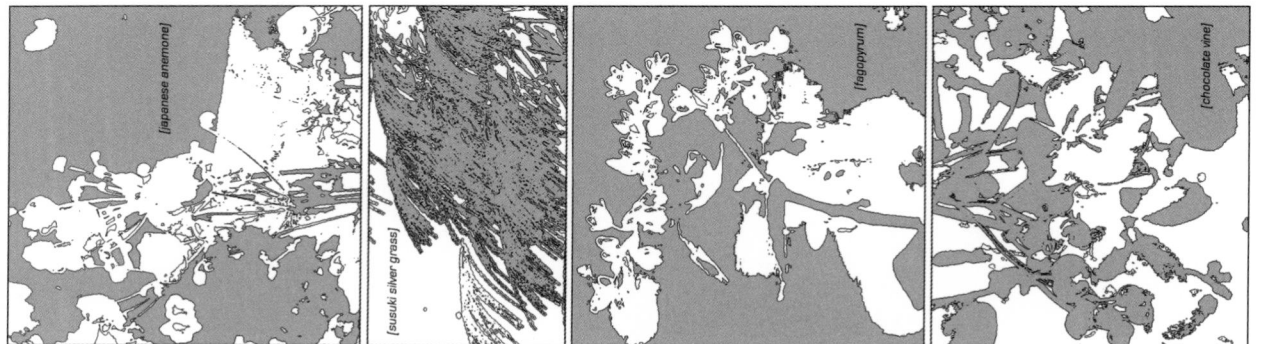

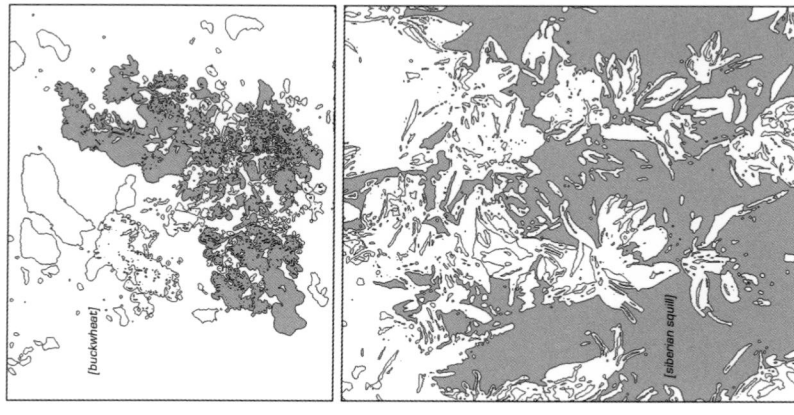

[japanese anemone]

autumn

One of the things Alicia enjoyed doing in her new home was to watch strangers walking past the front yard below, a guilty pleasure that had been denied her at the Liddells' old country cottage, partly because the cottage had been a bungalow, and partly because everybody in the neighbourhood knew each other. At this moment, it so happened that a young man and woman were approaching the forecourt, dodging the puddles that had materialised in the uneven paving. They were quite oblivious of their uninvited observer; Alicia had noticed that people tended not to look up while walking, particularly when it was drizzling. Only a few days ago, the streets had been teeming with T-shirts and sandals but autumn had fallen swiftly, and the pair were swathed like mummies in cardigans, coats and scarves of brown, russet and burgundy - much the same colour as the leaves shed by the trees that lined the pavements. This odd consonance made Alicia wander whether anyone had made frocks and dresses out of leaves.

At the borderland of the Liddells' new home perched the rubbish collection. Peeking out of the over-filled recycling bin was the bottle of pop soda that Alicia had finished earlier that afternoon, sitting atop stacks of father's half-read newspapers. These, Alicia assumed, would go off to a recycling plant to be remade into more paper and bottles. But why make more paper out of paper and more bottles out of bottles? That was no challenge at all. Why couldn't papers and bottles be made into something else? A house, for example, Alicia mused.

CHAPTER 8:
IN WHICH WE COME ACROSS A NOVEL USE FOR NEWSPAPERS AND WINE BOTTLES

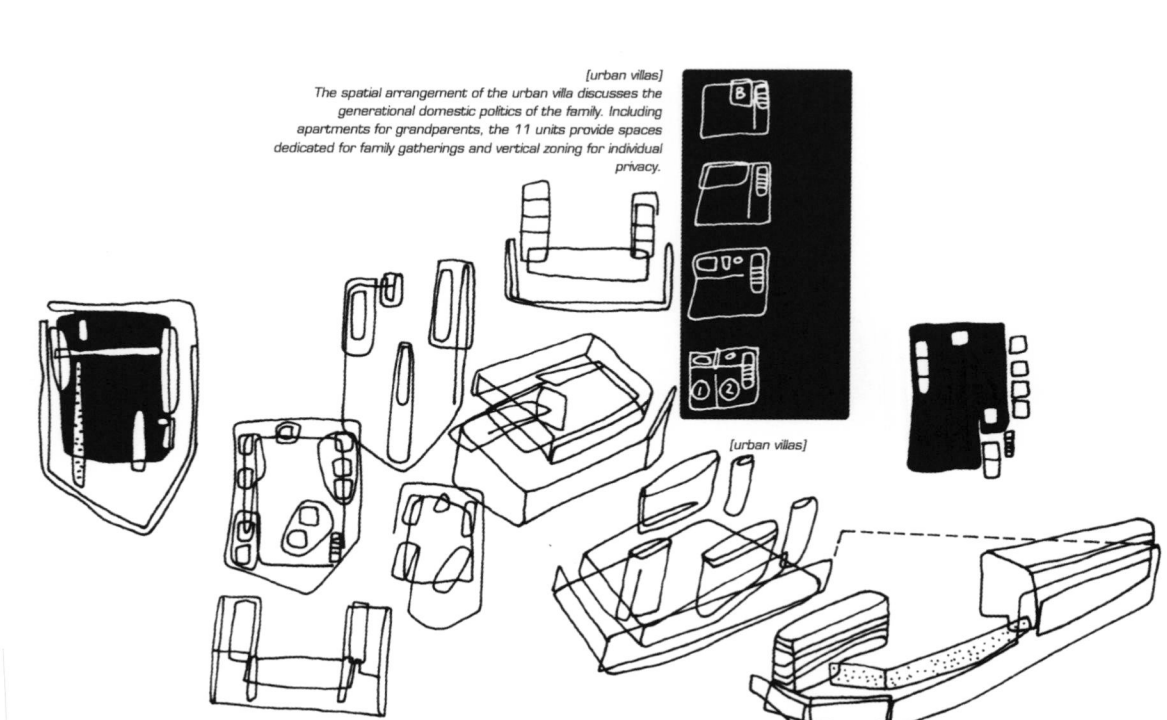

[urban villas]
The spatial arrangement of the urban villa discusses the generational domestic politics of the family. Including apartments for grandparents, the 11 units provide spaces dedicated for family gatherings and vertical zoning for individual privacy.

[urban villas]

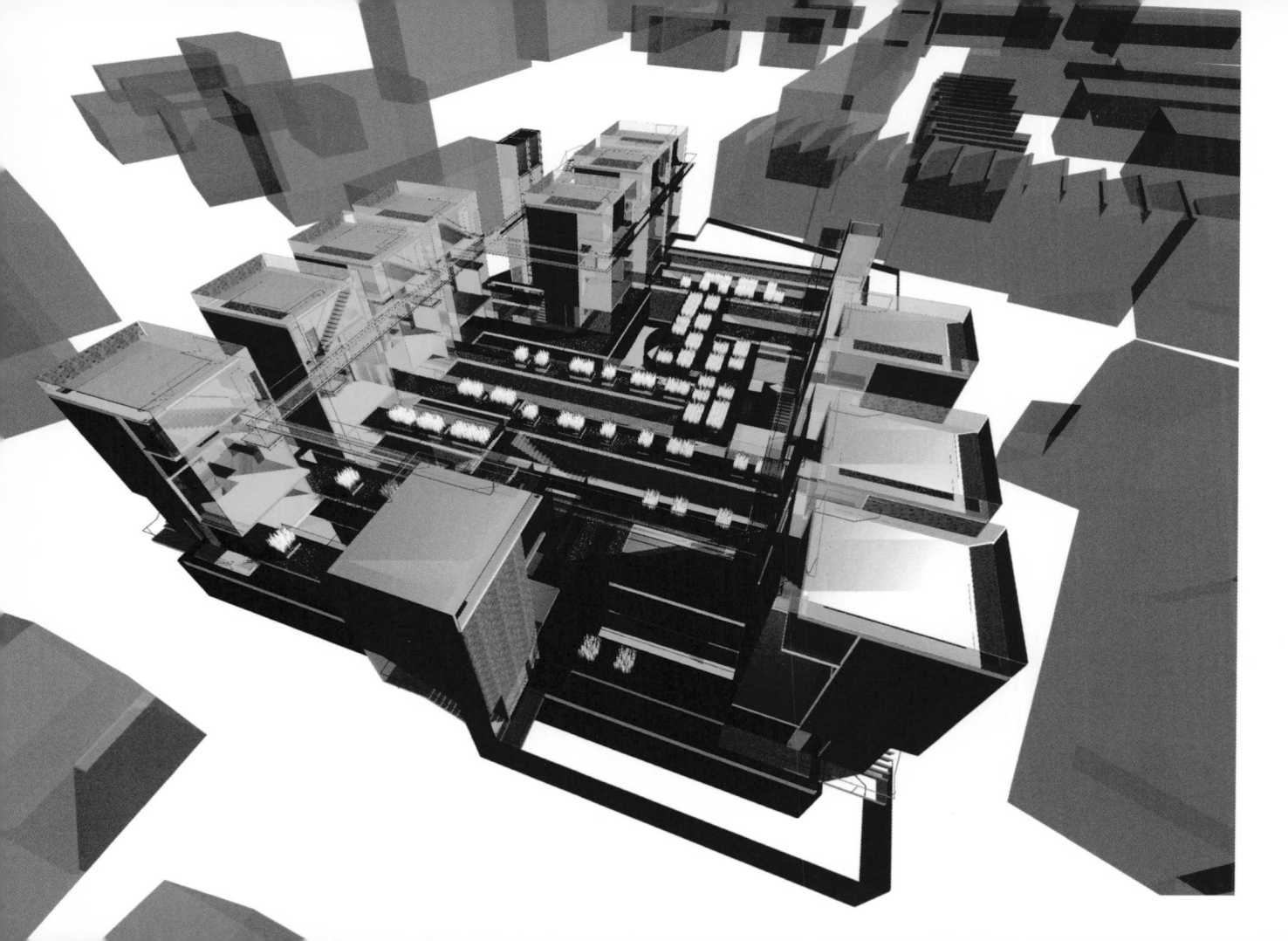

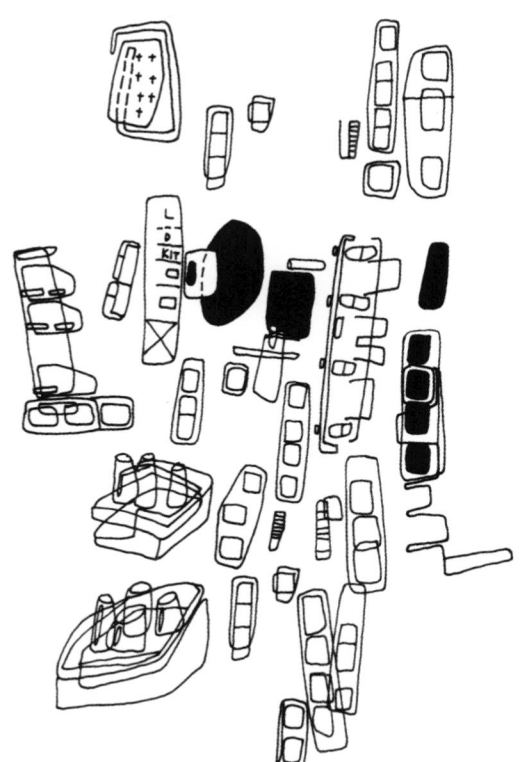

[inhabitable garden]
Floating above the community space is a 3.7m thick slab of planting containing 25 single-bedroom apartments. The concrete shell, clad in sedum is punctured by a series of glass courtyards and bridges. The result is a rich coloured living skin, The hues of the seasons reflecting onto and softening the conventionally harsh surfaces of modern building materials.

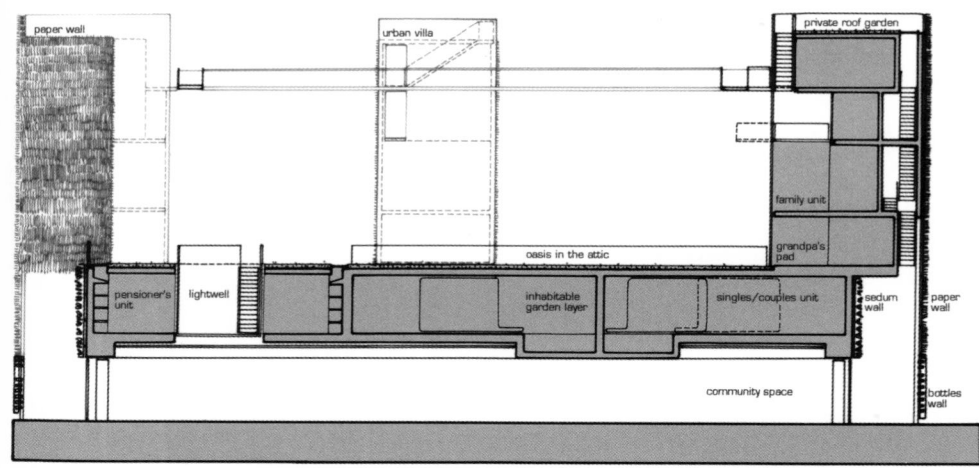

paper wall

urban villa

private roof garden

family unit

grandpa's pad

oasis in the attic

pensioner's unit

lightwell

inhabitable garden layer

singles/couples unit

sedum wall

paper wall

community space

bottles wall

I'm very late!

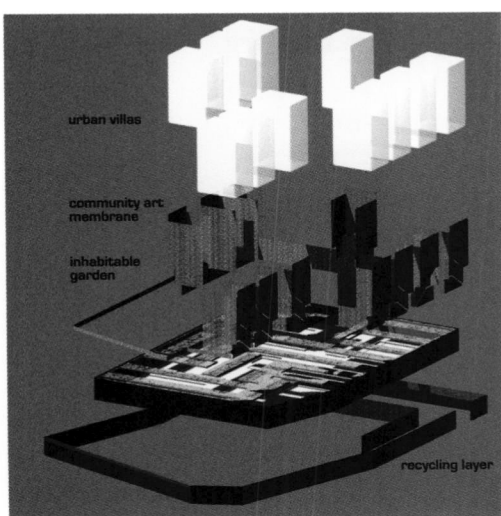

urban villas

community art membrane

inhabitable garden

recycling layer

[Conceived as small individual villas overlooking an green oasis, the design is divided into four constituent layers: (1) communal area (2) inhabitable garden (3) urban villas (4) art membrane.]

The sole area of the flat that remained unexplored was the attic, and Alicia felt duty-bound to investigate. Balancing on a stack of books, Alicia pressed gently on the touch latch of the door in the ceiling and hastily ducked as the panel whooshed over her head. As she let down the telescopic ladder, a piece of cream paper floated down, turning over and over like a sycamore pod. Alicia gingerly stepped down from her impromptu perch and retrieved it. The strip of paper looked suspiciously like the messages found within that abstruse purveyor of the future, the fortune cookie. This one, however, was not much of a prediction:

Climb up to the thirty-third ring.

Was it supposed to be a riddle? It did not seem particularly tricky like finding the 7th face of a cube or the smell of a rainbow, but there certainly were not thirty-three rungs, let alone rings on the ladder. So what did the cryptic message mean? Alicia slipped the note into her pocket and began to climb.

After reaching the 8th rung, at which point she expected to be nearing her destination, Alicia was surprised to find herself only a third of the way up the ladder. When she finally popped her head through the ceiling, she found number seven of the nine gardens distributed amongst a complex of flats, villas, glass courtyards, and bridges. Who would have thought — a green oasis in the attic! And what a wonderful place this would be to live in!

Expertly choreographed by the evening sun, reflected light and colour daubed harsh concrete and glass, softening their edges; the scent of citrus filled the air as Alicia brushed past bundles of stick-like lemon grass. Alicia realised with a start that what she was really smelling and experiencing was not the garden but the abstract notion of change. The mellow hues and fragrances of the turning season lay heavy in the atmosphere.

'Kwauqs!'

Out of the corner of her eye, Alicia saw a black object streaking through the air. Its flight came to an abrupt end as it thudded against the trunk of the oak tree and fell to the earth with a squawk. When it came to a standstill, Alicia recognised it as a bird, albeit a rather dishevelled one. Its flight and crash-landing had been so ungraceful that Alicia could not help but expel a guffaw of unladylike laughter.

'Dna tahw thgim eb os gnisuma?' asked the indignant bird, 'Oh nothing, Mister Bird,' said Alicia, smoothing its ruffled feathers, which were very ruffled indeed. 'Its just that I have never seen a bird land like that before.'

'Llew ouy dluohs yrt gniylf drawkcad.'

'Why do you fly backward? And speaking of which, why do you speak backward?'

'Drawkcab? M'I diarfa uoy era nekatsim. I, eht mulzoo drib, kaeps drawrof. S'ti lla eht rehto sdrib that kaeps drawkcab. S'taht yhw er'yeht os tluciffid

newspaper wall

bottle bank wall

inhabitable garden

urban villas

car park

service zone

glass courtyards

main entrance

service entrance

kitchen

community hall

creche

a

b

c

a

b

a

b

c

structural system

a   a   a
a   b   b   a
a   a
a   a
b   a   a
b   b   a
a   b
a   b

apartment types

kitchen
community dining room
mobile storage wall
rent-a-room
glass wall

glass rooflights

community art membrane

community garden
@ 0.0m

moss garden @ 6.7m

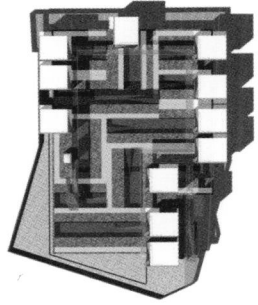

allotments @ 8.70m
in recycled paper
trays

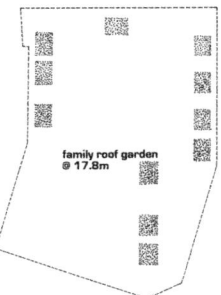

family roof garden
@ 17.8m

ot dnatsrednu. Dna eht nosaer I ylf drawkcab si to
ees erehw I ma gnimoc morf.'

The oozlum bird, Alicia decided, was a shining example of why it was dangerous to keep ones eyes focussed on the past while closing them to the future. It made much more sense to see where you were going than where you were coming from. Her father, or perhaps even Edith might have made some pithy comment about the bird being an alleygory or something or other, but Alicia was a girl whose nose was firmly grounded in reality.

'Where are we?'

'Mmh…Uaetahc RuotaL 1691.'

'1961…Chat..eau Lat..our,' translated Alicia. None the wiser, she gave the bird a quizzical look.

'Yrros,' said the oozlum bird. 'I saw tsuj gnidaer siht lebal. Na yllanoitpecxe enif egatniv. SihT elohw llaw si edam morf eniw selttob.'

'You're right! This wall is entirely made of wine bottles dating back to goodness knows when. Oh, and that wall over there is made from old newspapers! I'll wager that if you could climb high enough, you would be able to find out anything you wanted from the last few decades. What a delightful thing! A building built from time!' (Quickly bored, Alicia had decided that houses made of newspapers and bottles were old hat). 'Years and dates…dates and years…' she mumbled to herself.

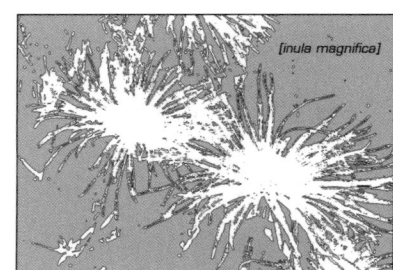

[inula magnifica]

[helenium]

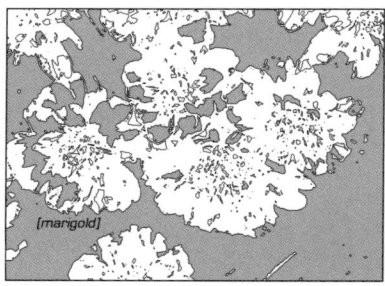

[marigold]

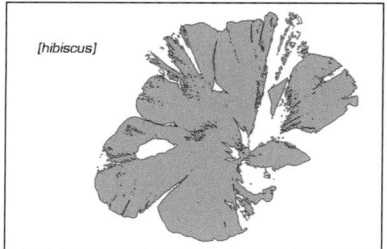

[hibiscus]

[lemon verbena]

[citrus-scented and flavour blossoms]

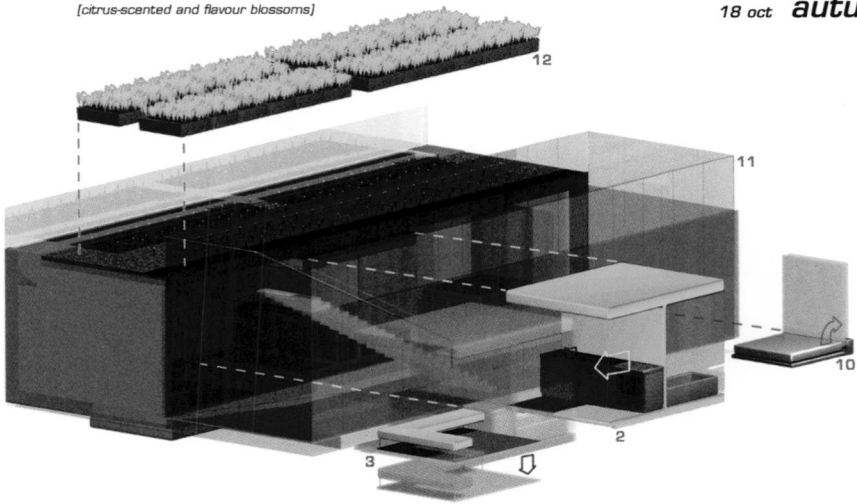

[citrus-scented and flavour blossoms]

18 oct *autumn*   Oasis in the Attic

12

11

10

3   2

[unit for singles/couples within inhabitable garden layer]

A mobile cupboard[1] moves along the entire length of the apartment. This element contains the kitchen, bathroom and utilities; service sockets are provided at various locations. The living room[2] recesses into the floor. The bed[3] folds back into the wall.

The movement of the mobile cupboard is facilitated by an air cushion at its base. The other elements work with pneumatic pistons.

The flexible allotment system[4] comprises recycled paper trays supported on illuminating posts creating a landscape of twinkling lights during winter months.

Glass courtyard[5]

[1]   entrance: anywhere depending on the location of the mobile service cupboard
[2]   mobile service cupboard with bath-toilet, utility and kitchen
[3]   living room area with sunken storage space
[4]   folding bed
[5]   storage with frosted glass panels and roof light above
[6]   glass courtyard threshold
[7]   stairs to garden @+6.7m
[8]   dining area
[9]   optional Stannah lift
[10] bedroom
[11] studio/office

[plan of apartment within inhabitable garden layer]

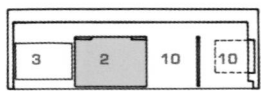

[2 bedrooms apartment]

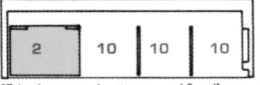

[3 bedrooms + 'rent-a-ground-floor']

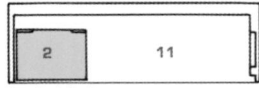

[studio/office]

26.11.95

19.12.75
02.10.81

30.01.72

[paper]

25.09.02

26.07.88
23.08.93

12.08.98
15.05.99

01.01.00

09.06.92

27.05.01
07.03.86

03.09.65

21.11.77
14.12.00
07.03.79

19.05.78

10.09.69

[sedum]

[bottles]

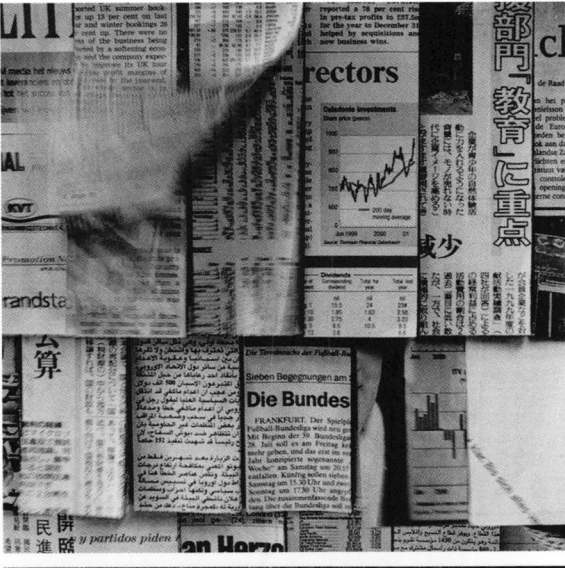

[sedum]

[art membrane]
Fixed to the exterior of the villas is a steel mesh into
which the community inserts coloured elements. As
with the recycling centre, the final appearance of the
building is thus governed by the users of the buildings
themselves.

'Llew, I tsum eb ffo,' said the oozlum bird, flying off in its strange back-to-front fashion. 'Secalp ot evael, elpoep ot pmub otni.'

It was indeed getting late and high time for Alicia's tea (hence, high tea). She reluctantly began her descent down the ladder to Flat Number 8, already remembering the garden in the sky and the scent of time with longing.

[communal area]

The community and recycling centre at ground level crystallise the themes of ecological awareness and communal closeness that give character to the scheme. Defining the boundary of the housing development, bays of acrylic translucent walls form bottle and paper banks; the materials of the architecture is provided by the users themselves, creating a montage of reflection, colour and texture. Enclosed within the walls is a canteen, crèche and community kitchen. A series of flexible screens allow for large and small-scale events.

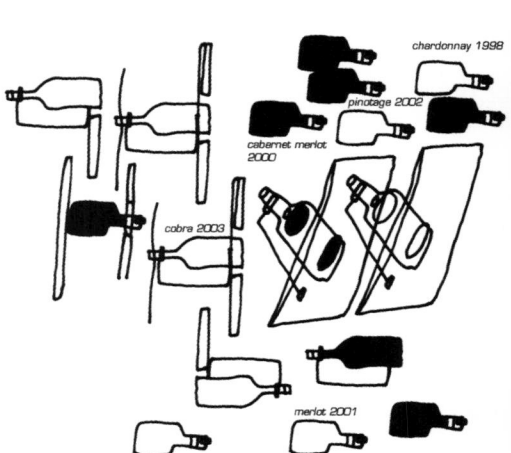

chardonnay 1998

pinotage 2002

cabernet merlot 2000

cobra 2003

merlot 2001

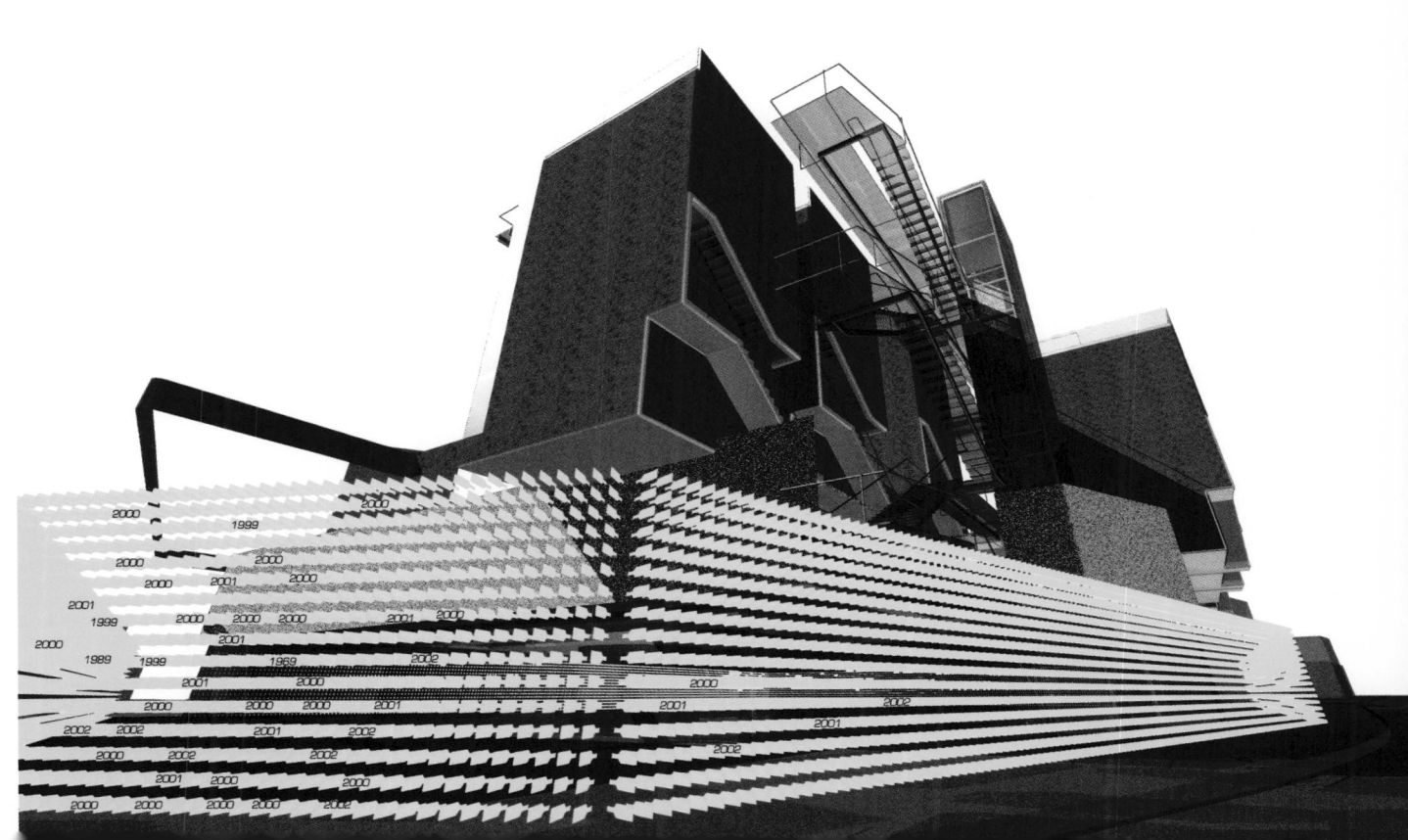

[a green oasis in the attic]

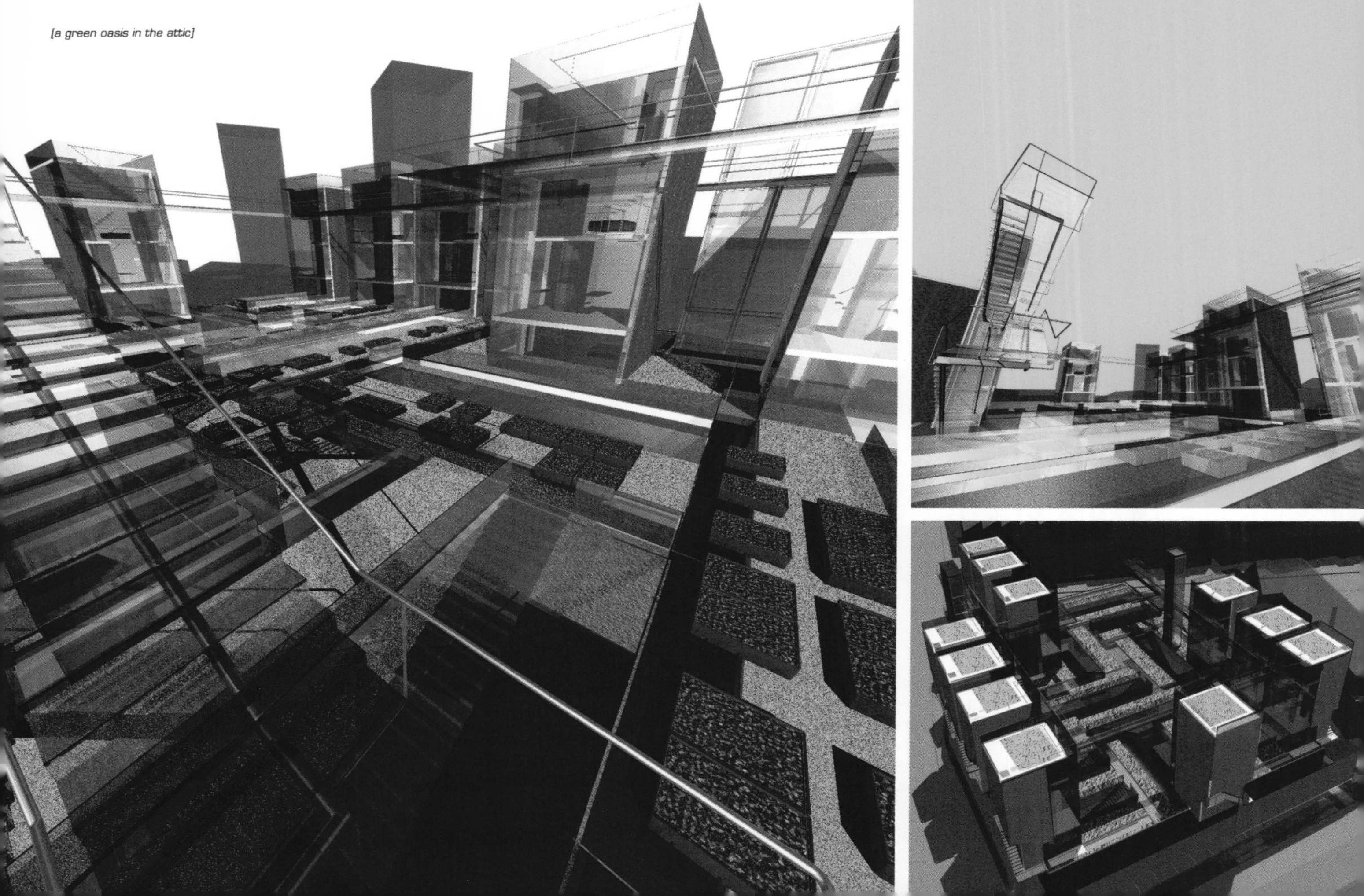

[helianthus 'lemon queen' rendering the courtyard a bright yellow in early summer]

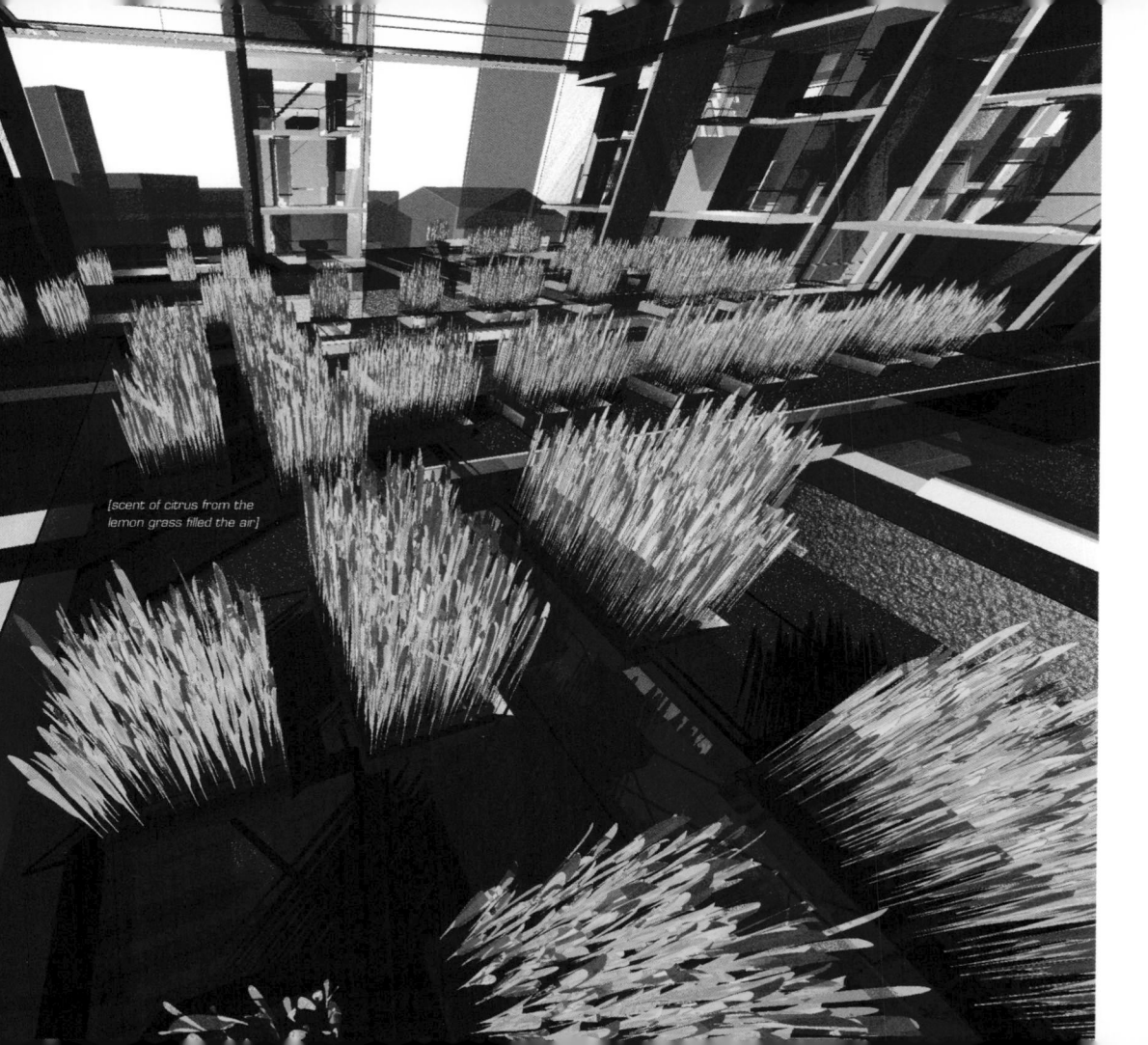

[scent of citrus from the
lemon grass filled the air]

[in winter twinkling lights replace
the lush and colourful blooms]

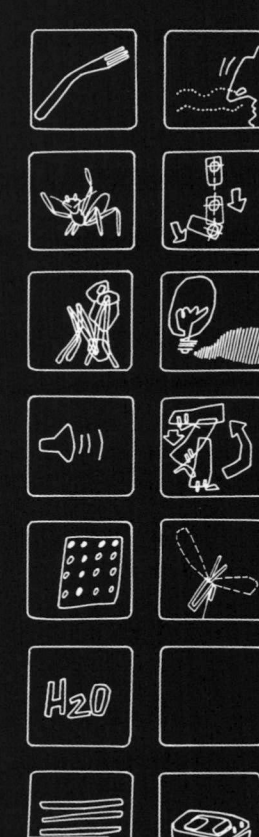

Night had fallen, and Alicia was preparing for bed. Living on the uppermost flat (what used to be the servants' quarters) meant that Alicia's bedroom was extremely hot and sticky, and Mother had left the window open to allow some fresh air to enter. Alicia climbed into her bed and switched on her bedside lamp. Before long, the light was being orbited by a swarm of moths and daddy-long-legs.

'Get away! The moon is over there, outside!' cried Alicia, pointing out of the window. 'And it's a very long way away, so if you wish to get there tonight, you had better get a move on.' The assortment of creepy-crawlies flew out of the open window sheepishly (if that is possible for insects), many of them bumping their heads on the glass before making their way outside.

'Hmph!' frowned Alicia as she opened the little green book to read a few pages before turning in for the night. The chapter began thus:

In the Far East, the grasshopper, along with termites and the large palm weevil grub, is prized as a great delicacy. The grasshopper is fit for consumption only in the imago phase, when it is sexually mature and newly emerged from metamorphosis.

Alicia scrimped up her nose in disgust.

CHAPTER 9:
IN WHICH ALICIA REMEMBERS HOW TO FLY AND DISCOVERS AN UNORTHODOX RECIPE FOR PEST CONTROL

[car parking]

[glass dining
tatami parking]

[kitchen + bar]

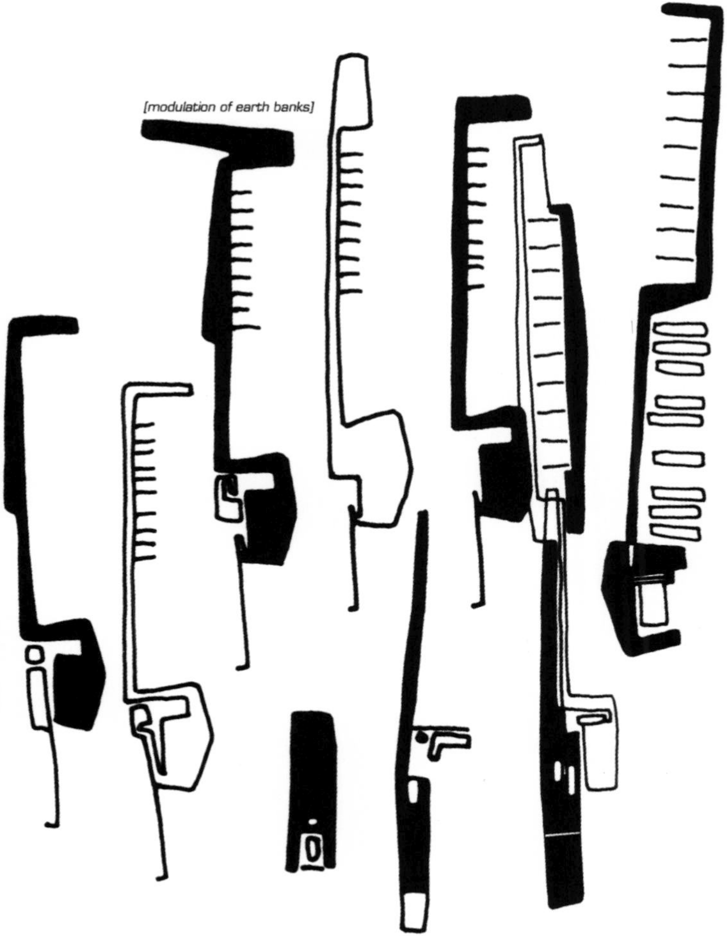

[modulation of earth banks]

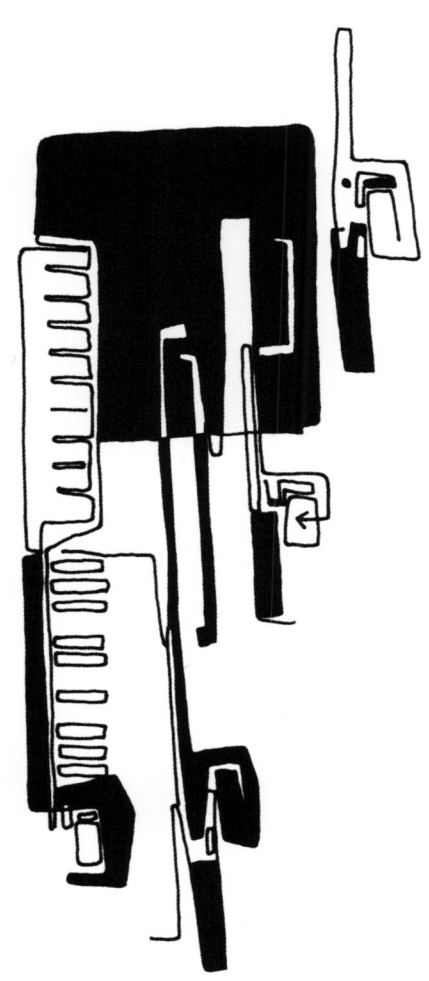

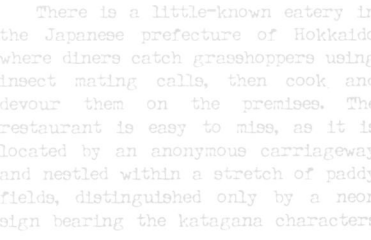

There is a little-known eatery in the Japanese prefecture of Hokkaido where diners catch grasshoppers using insect mating calls, then cook and devour them on the premises. The restaurant is easy to miss, as it is located by an anonymous carriageway and nestled within a stretch of paddy fields, distinguished only by a neon sign bearing the katagana characters

蟲 館

It had been a long day and Alicia was becoming increasingly drowsy, her head nodding its way to the land of nod. The book flopped shut onto the counterpane, jolting her awake just long enough to fumble at the light-switch and bring darkness to the room.

Strange will-o'-the-wisp-like lights bobbed across the black horizon. They flitted and flocked, at times congregating around a single spot, and at others, dispersing to explore in seemingly random vectors, but always within some unseen, intangible boundary. The sight was quite bewitching.

One of the lights was acting quite differently from the others. In the pitch black, Alicia could not be certain whether the light was growing in size or drifting towards her. That was, until, it came to a

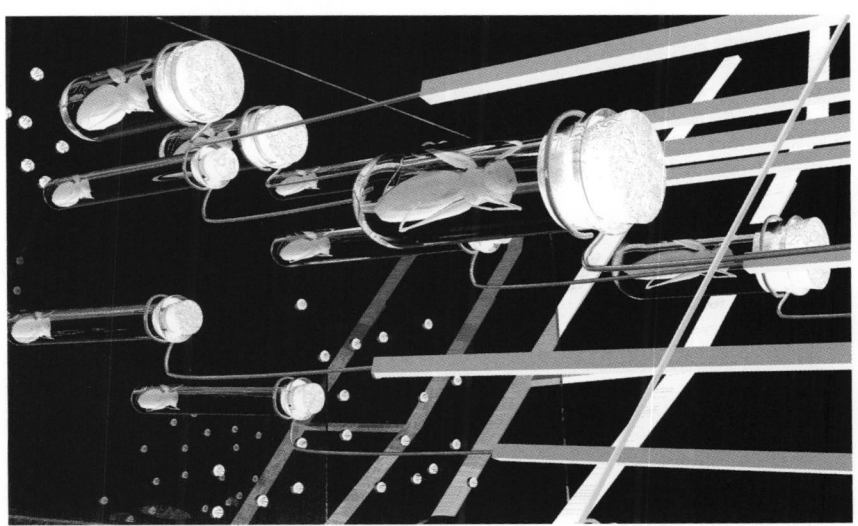

[Restaurant façade: This is made up of bales of straw and rammed earth. The name of the restaurant in glass neon signage adorns the rustic entrance.]

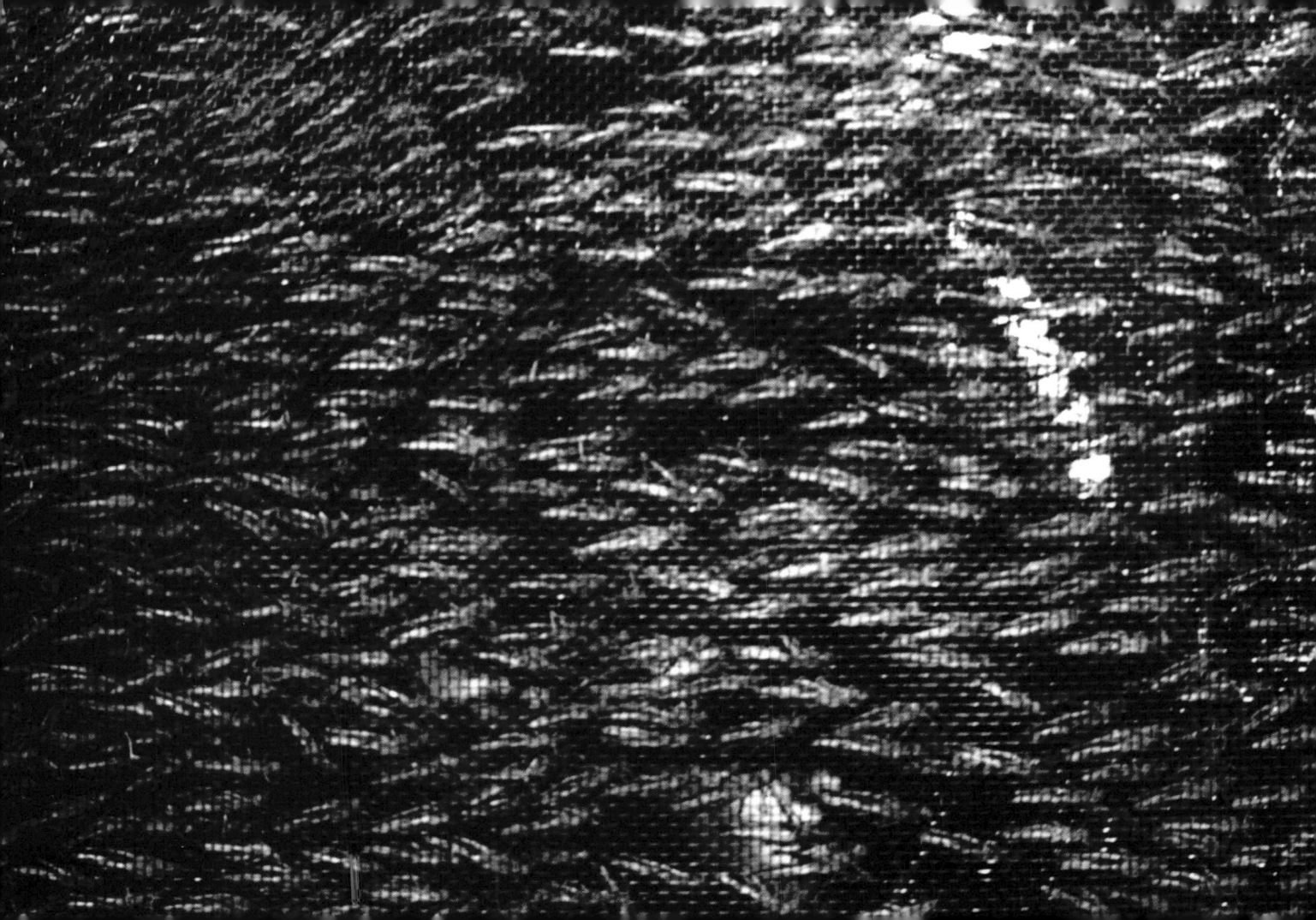

[Menu Board: Glass tubes containing different grasshoppers in season embedded into the hay screen.]

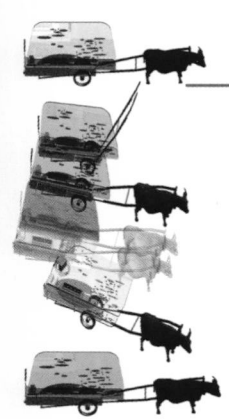

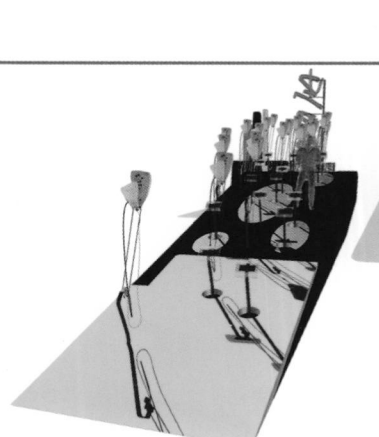

[the brasserie]

[the restaurant]

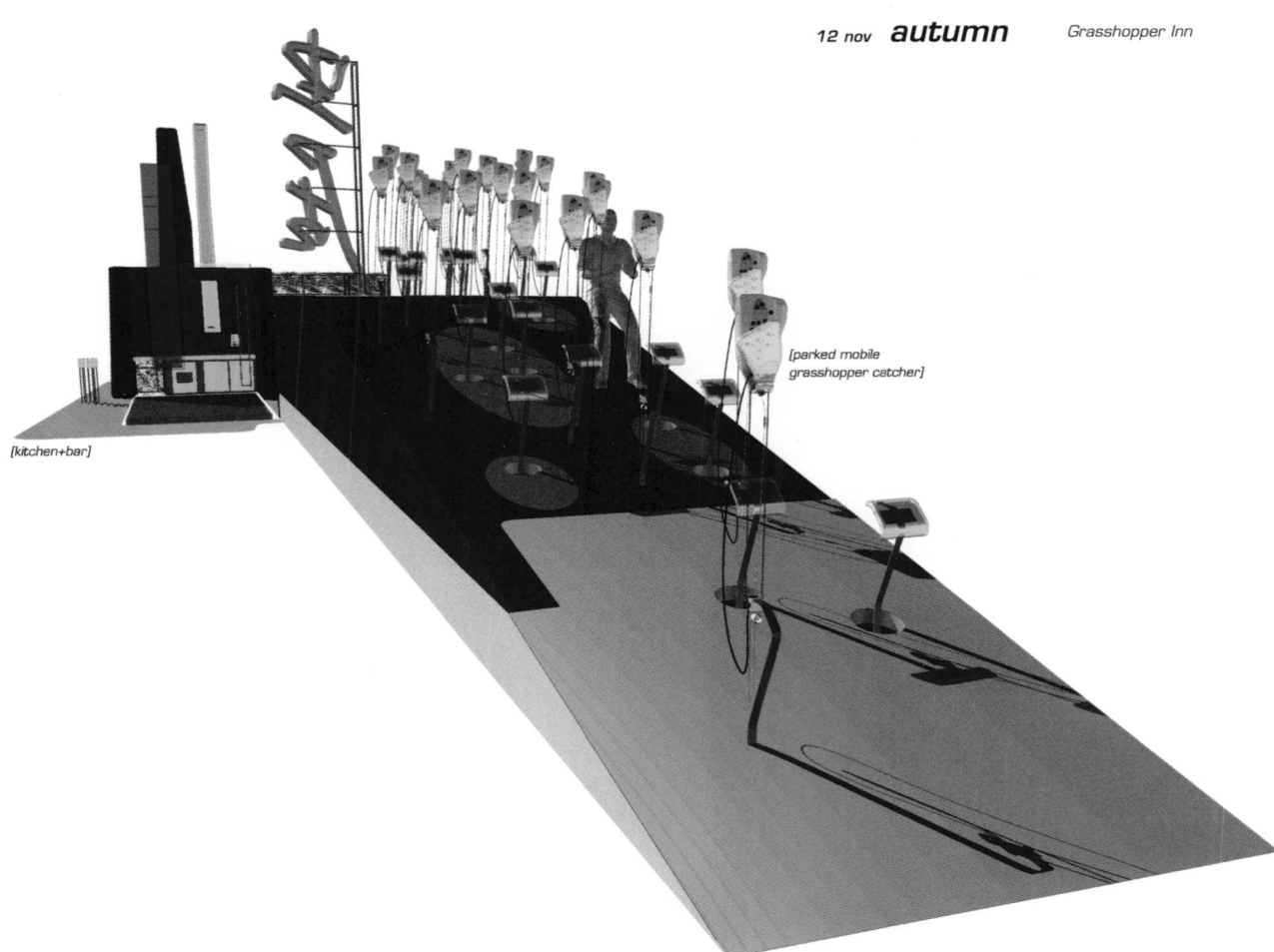

12 nov **autumn** *Grasshopper Inn*

[parked mobile
grasshopper catcher]

[kitchen+bar]

halt beneath her hand. Similar to an octopus in appearance as well as size, it had a gourd-shaped body that pulsated with a technicolour glow. In place of tentacles, however, it possessed a miniature propeller and a long stick-like tail, at the end of which was a rudder. It made both a faint spluttering and a high-pitched clicking sound.

Splut.Splut.Splutsplutsplut Click.Click.Click-click-click.

While the spluts clearly came from a poorly-maintained propeller, the clicks appeared to emanate from within the gourd. Peering inside, Alicia found a small glass tube which held a single grasshopper. Its carapace was a crisp jade green, its eyes a deep ruby red.

'CLICK.CLICK. CLICK-CLICK-CLICK!' said the grasshopper impatiently.

In her state of awakened consciousness, Alicia realised that she could understand what the grasshopper was saying.

'Oh my!' she exclaimed in embarrassed comprehension. 'Oh-my-oh-my-oh-my!' Her hands flew to her cheeks which had flushed a rosy red. 'If Mother hadn't just told me the story of the bird and the bee, I would suspect my ears of grand duplicity!' she exclaimed.

To avoid enflaming your delicate cheeks too, gentle reader, we shall summarise the gist of the insect's utterances as 'follow me!' The grasshopper-gourd, impatient to be off, bobbed out into the ether once more. Compelled by the creature's siren call, Alicia floated after it.

'I must be dreaming,' murmured Alicia, her lips barely moving. 'Because try as I might, I can never remember how to fly in the waking world.'

'Come along!' cried the creature.

And as they roved over the undulating irrigated plains, the grasshopper-lantern hybrid began to gather suitors like a magnet, drawing grasshoppers by the light and call of their lascivious mate.

The light from the gourd grew dimmer and dimmer as it became shrouded with a mass of chittering grasshoppers. When it was completely blanketed, it paused from its roving and tilted to one side, as if cocking an ear. Then, having confirmed some inaudible instruction, the composite creature veered towards a cluster of people gathered on a low glass dais.

Alicia and the grasshopper-gourd alighted onto a red-orange ring embedded into the glass platform, much to the delight of the waiting party. The children capered about, waving their arms in glee; the adults were all smiles. As Alicia wondered idly whether the coloured ring held any special significance, she experienced a warm sensation spreading through her body. In fact, it was uncomfortably warm. At the periphery of her hearing, she heard a snap, a crackle and a pop. In a haze, she thought she saw some wooden chopsticks being snapped and some rice bowls being filled. Alicia sniffed the air and wrinkled her nose. She could smell burning.

This rather unsubtle conflagration of sensory information was further contributed to by the ceramic cooking ring that Alicia was seated upon.

'Ouch!' howled Alicia, as she leapt up, her ethereal bottom singed out of its stupor.

Alicia woke up with a start, hastily withdrawing her posterior from the vicinity of an unaccountably warm radiator. An expression of stark horror adorned her pale young features.

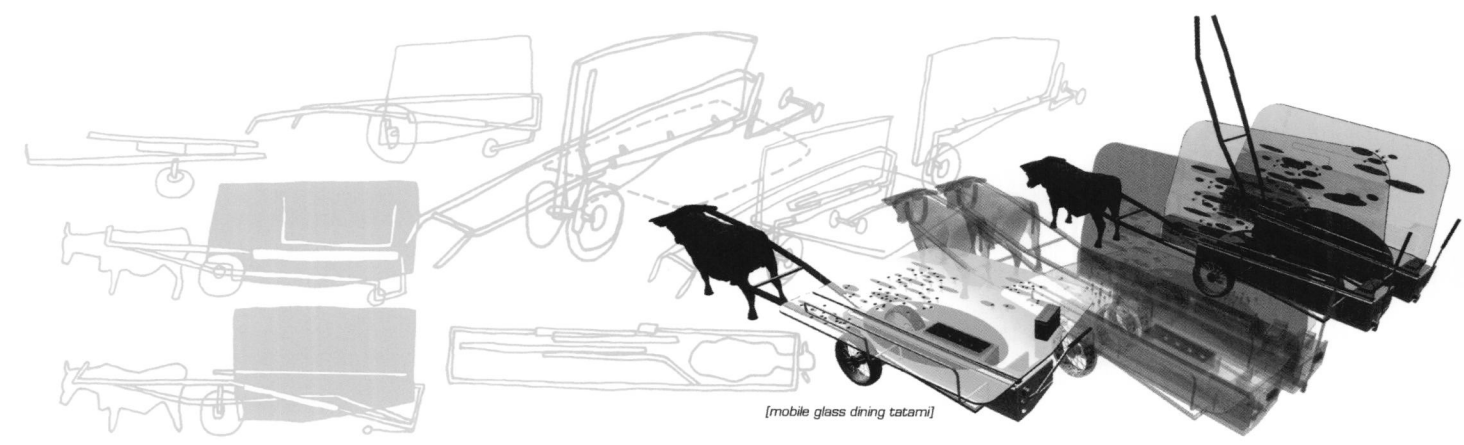

[mobile glass dining tatami]

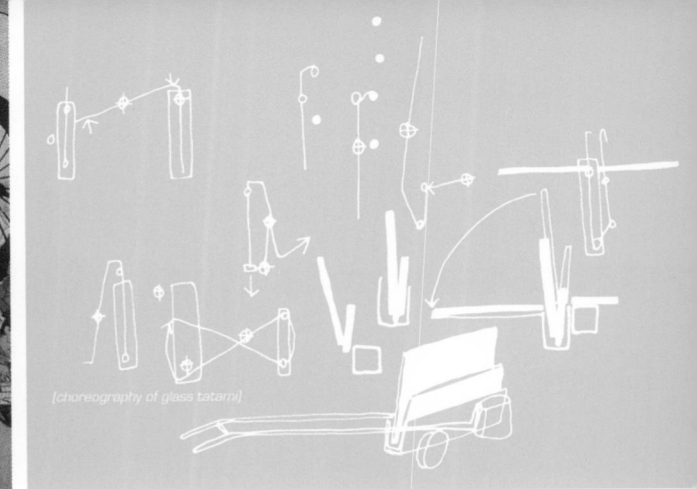

[choreography of glass tatami]

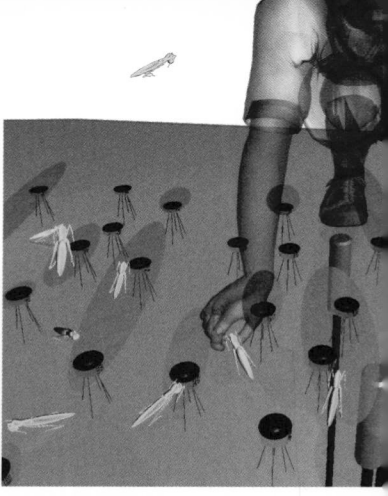

[Speakers emitting female grasshopper mating sounds are used to trap unsuspecting male grasshoppers. A natural method of pest-control for crops without using chemicals.]

I'm very late!

[Glass Dining Tatami: Carried by an ox, each dining table may be located anywhere in the fields. The vertical glass pad rotates to a horizontal position, cantilevering over the crop plains to provide an area for relaxation while diners waiting for their meal to appear. Embedded into the glass surface are cooking elements, loudspeakers and lighting tubes. The grasshoppers are harvested off the glass surface, prepared, grilled and consumed on the glass tatami. In the evening, cooking fires define varying territories of the restaurant on the plain.]

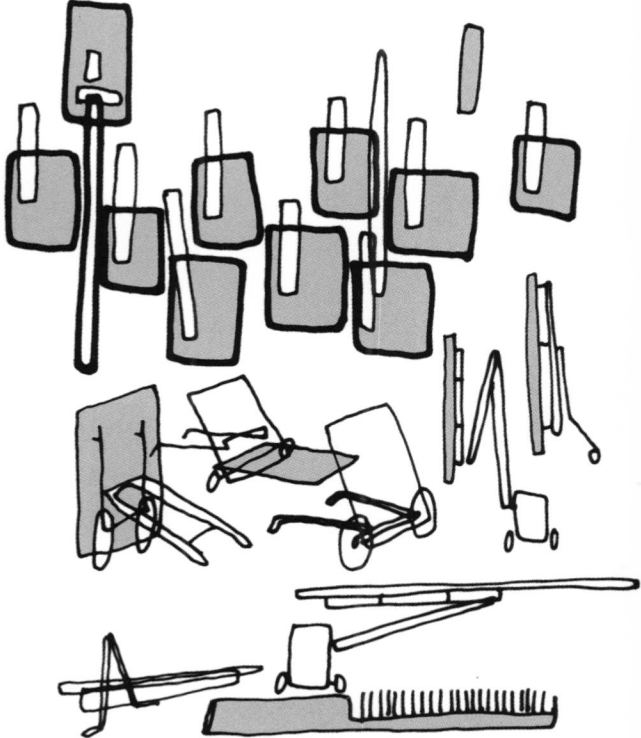

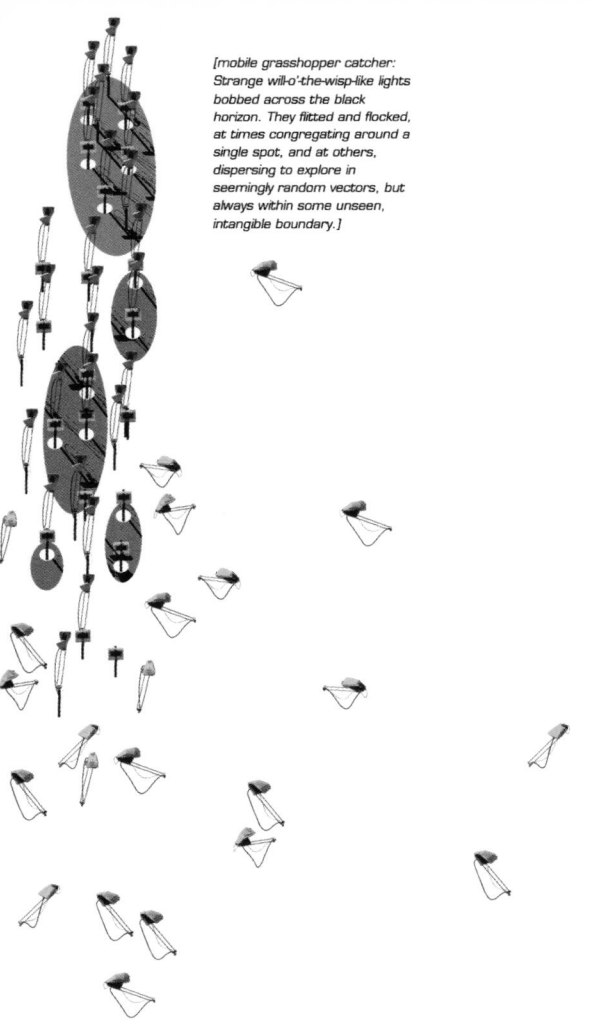

[mobile grasshopper catcher:
Strange will-o'-the-wisp-like lights
bobbed across the black
horizon. They flitted and flocked,
at times congregating around a
single spot, and at others,
dispersing to explore in
seemingly random vectors, but
always within some unseen,
intangible boundary.]

22 nov **autumn** Grasshopper Inn

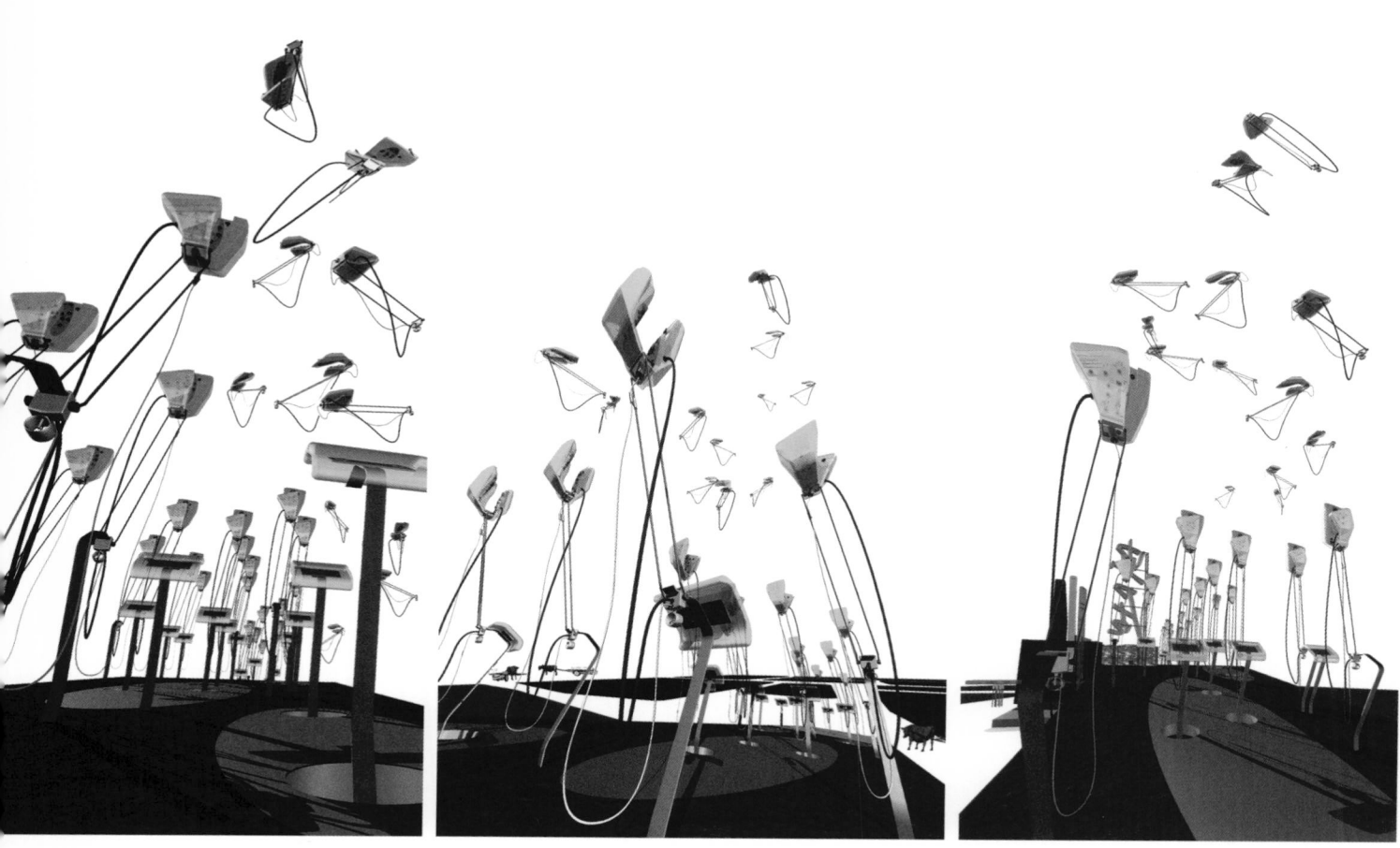

24 nov **autumn** *Grasshopper Inn*

[catch-for-supper]

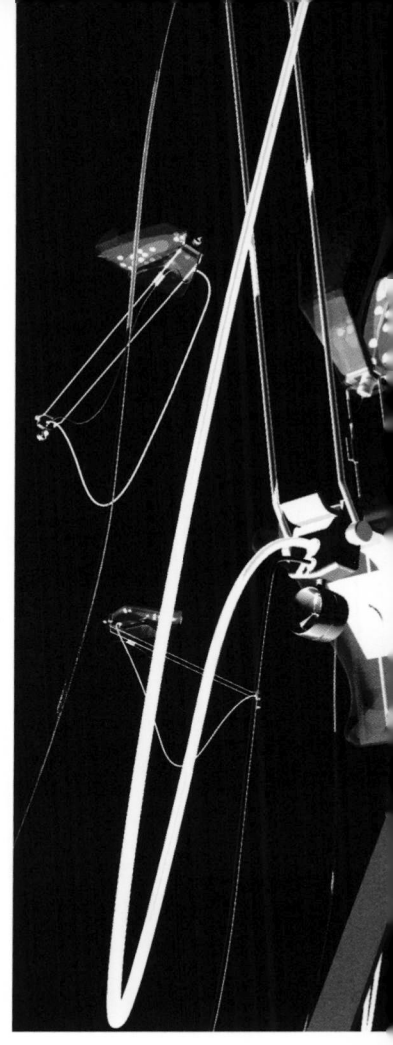

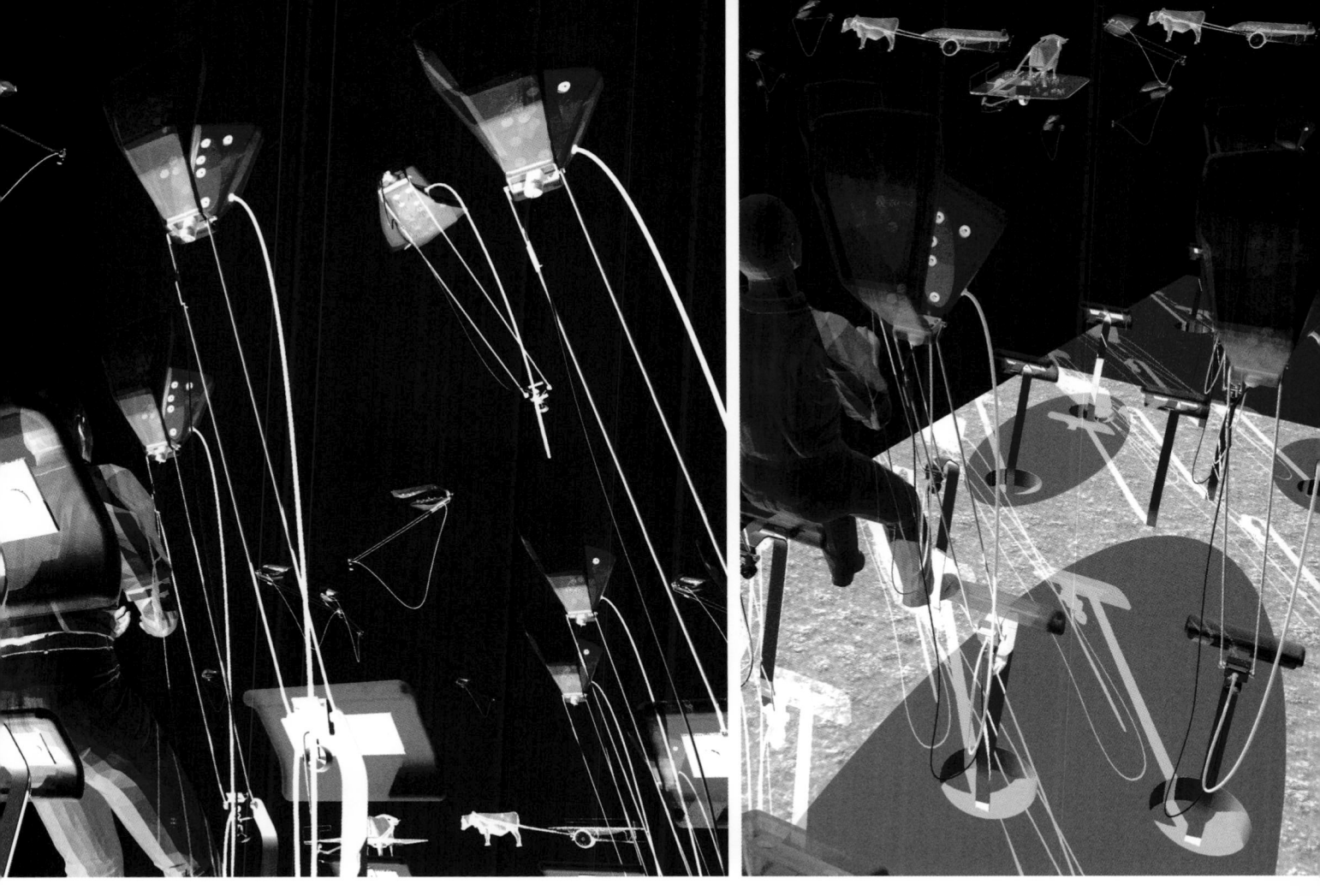

[will-o'-the-wisp]

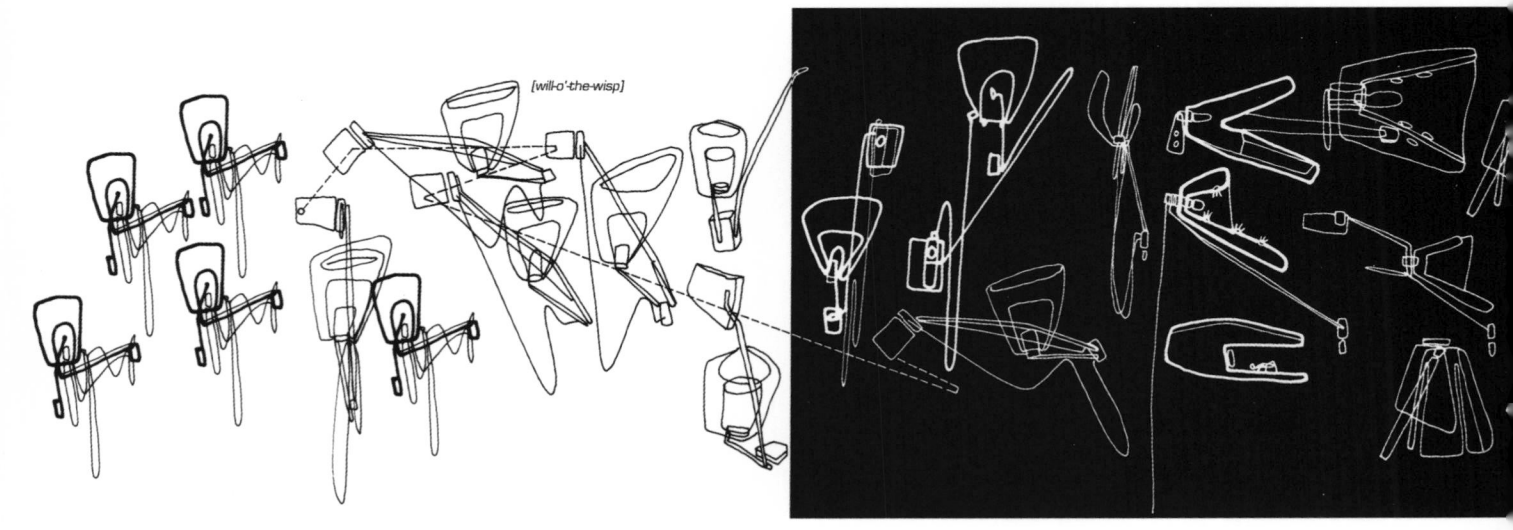

28 nov **autumn**   *Grasshopper Inn*

[plan of mobile grasshopper catcher]

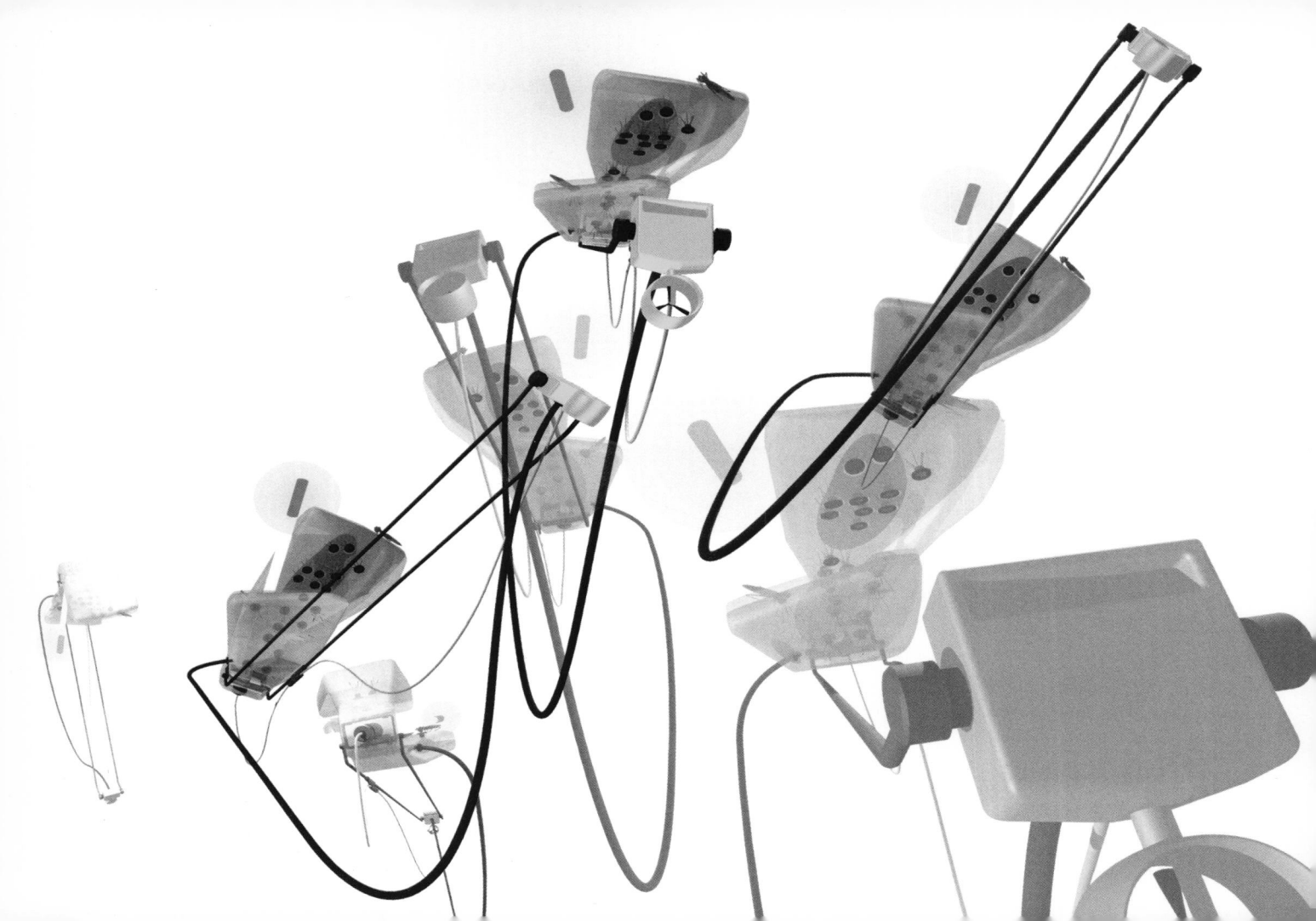

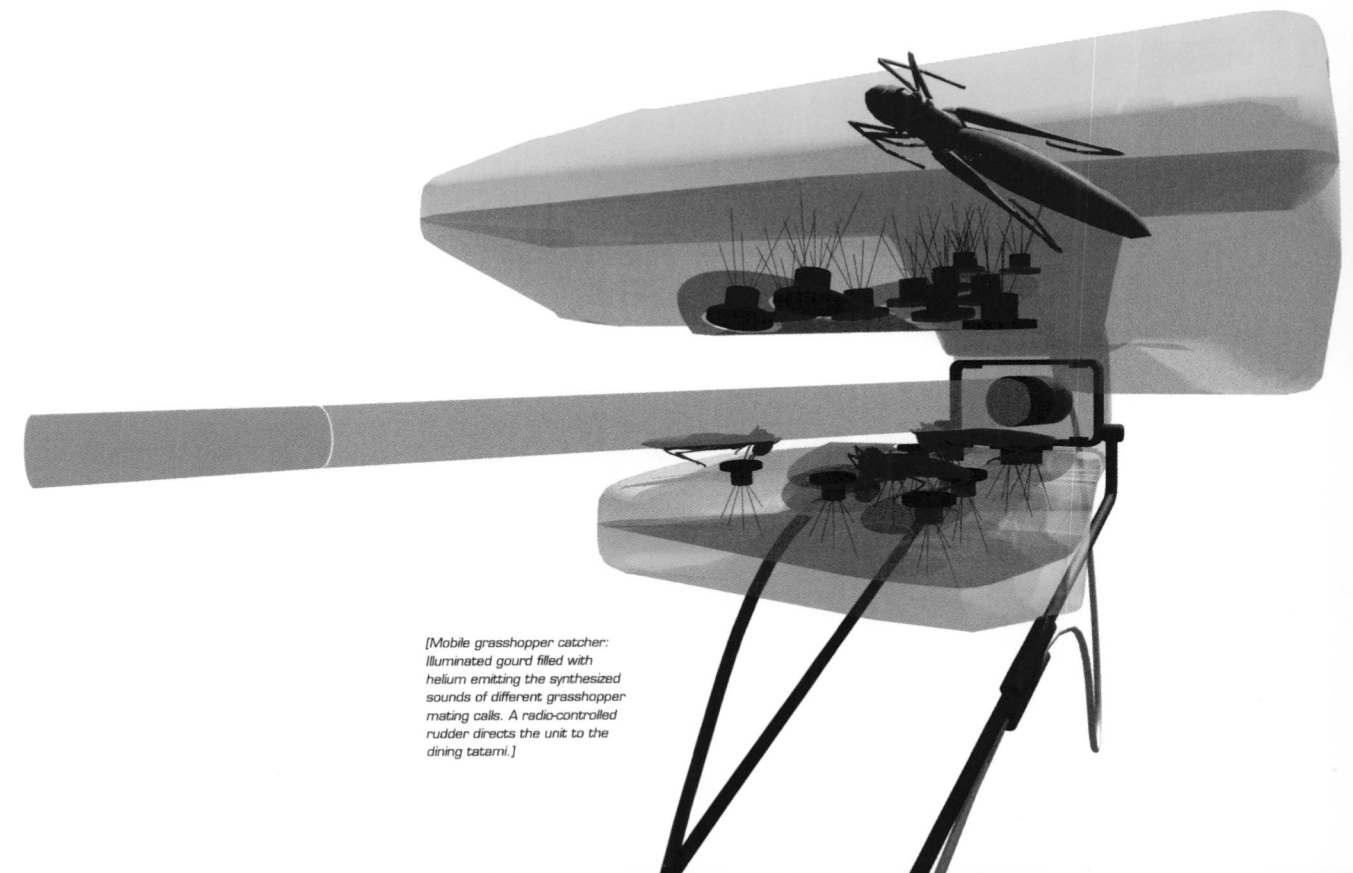

[Mobile grasshopper catcher: Illuminated gourd filled with helium emitting the synthesized sounds of different grasshopper mating calls. A radio-controlled rudder directs the unit to the dining tatami.]

pantone 192
pantone 3935
pantone 185
pantone 299
pantone 317
pantone 304
pantone 3025
pantone 320
pantone 308
pantone 383
pantone 178
pantone 3955

pantone 192
pantone 427
pantone 292
pantone 2975
pantone 185
pantone 291
pantone 297
pantone 317
pantone 178
pantone 2975
pantone 151
pantone 108

pantone 304
pantone 584
pantone 317
pantone 297

pantone 102
pantone 185
pantone 318
pantone 185
pantone 2925
pantone 427

pantone 5767
pantone 427
pantone 3025
pantone 192
pantone 297
pantone 292

pantone 320
pantone 427
pantone 2925
pantone 311
pantone 185
pantone 102
pantone 185
pantone 185
pantone 292

pantone 584
pantone 2975
pantone 584
pantone 192
pantone 291
pantone 2975
pantone 2925

pantone 448
pantone 448
pantone 7547
pantone 7547
pantone 448
pantone 448
pantone 547
pantone 553
pantone 448
pantone 7547
pantone 547

spring

winter

pantone 292

pantone 2975

pantone 108

pantone 304

pantone 584

pantone 192

pantone 304

pantone 584

pantone 297

pantone 317

pantone 2975

pantone 178

pantone 151

pantone 192

pantone 7547

As Alicia walked down the corridor, the fourth step towards the bathroom gave out a groan from beneath her feet. This was followed by a scuttling noise, a second patter of tiny footsteps and then silence. Alicia bent down, pressed her ear to the floor to create a suction cup, and made out two faint but distinct voices:

'It's not his fault, Minerva.' said a squeaky voice. 'It's probably just his way of...of showing affection.'

The second voice was shrill, and if possible, even squeakier. 'Affection? Affection?! I'll give you affection! The very idea of us having a dog in the first place is utterly ridiculous! All he does is defecate on the carpet. I've caught him red-handed this time. This is the last straw, Michael. Either it goes, or I go...'

'Please, Minerva. Keep your voice down! What will the neighbours think?'

Alicia looked up, guiltily, her ears flaming a deep crimson red. She knew she shouldn't be listening to private conversations, but she was a naturally curious creature. What provoked this curiosity even further was that she had met everyone living in the building and couldn't recall any of the residents owning a dog. Pets were, after all, not allowed.

In order to clear up this mystery (and certainly for no other goodly reason), Alicia put her ear to the floor a second time, but as she did so, a mote of dust flew straight into her left eye. Scrunching both eyes up tightly, she rubbed away with her knuckles to dislodge the offending particle. When her eyes opened once more, however, she found herself not in the flat, but floating high above the ground.

What was not immediately apparent was what the ground was made of. From on high, the land resembled the multicolour weave of an African kente cloth, but as Alicia looked closer, she saw that the weave was alive! The little stitches were moving! They could not be ants, for ants were far too small, and they did not amble or trample like sheep or cattle. They could only be one thing — people! A landscape of humans, their clothes coloured the land! Each one, whether single or grouped, had their ear pressed to the ground, listening. Some were sitting; some crouching; others lying down. There were cottons, there were linens, shiny fabrics of every brand or style. There were greens. There were yellows. There were reds. And as Alicia noticed, plenty of bare flesh too!

Alicia blinked once more.

The ground was the same, but at the same time different. No longer spring, winter had come, replete with its hats and its woollies, its gloves and its wellies. Rainbow hues had long disappeared, displaced by sombre browns and silent greys. A different landscape - still human, but spare and thin.

Alicia blinked again. Three times the charm, she was back in the flat. Her morning routine was to check on her coat, and she did just that. The skin of grass was lush and a glorious blue! With a smile on her face, Alicia skipped to the loo.

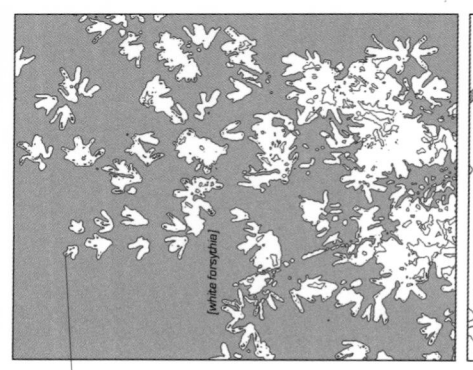

[white forsythia]

[primula mikado]

[white primrose]

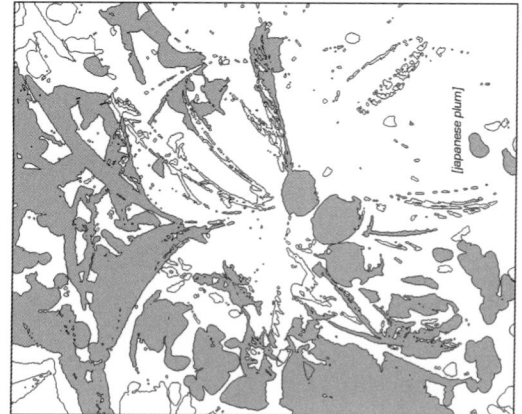

[japanese plum]

winter

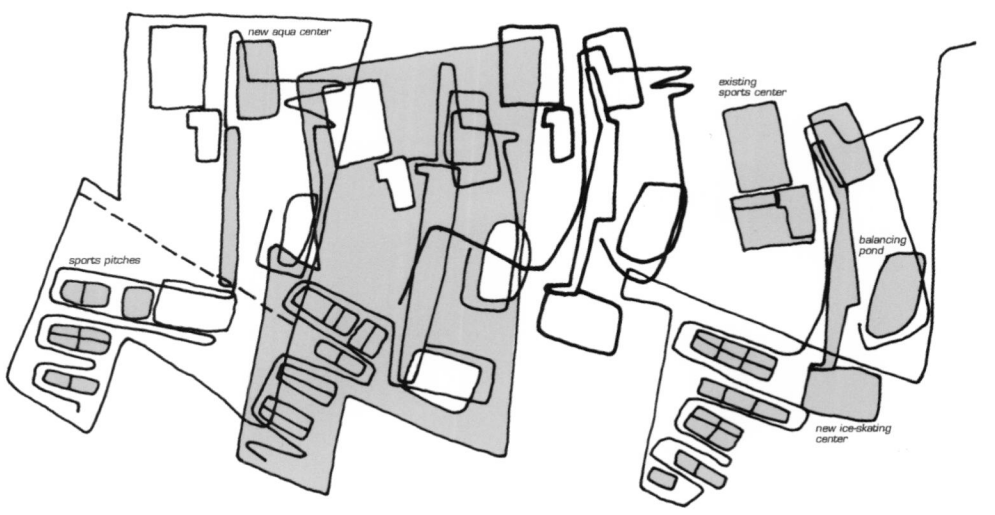

new aqua center

existing
sports center

balancing
pond

sports pitches

new ice-skating
center

[The natural contours are retained as much as possible and a series of routes for cyclists, skaters and pedestrians take
the visitor on routes that lace through land. The Aquacentre has been positioned within the existing contours to allow
access to the planted roof surface, thus offering an additional garden space within the park. Throughout the landscape
are areas shielded by thickets of green willow. Each area offers a different character, from the quiet and contemplative,
to areas that are evidently more colourful.]

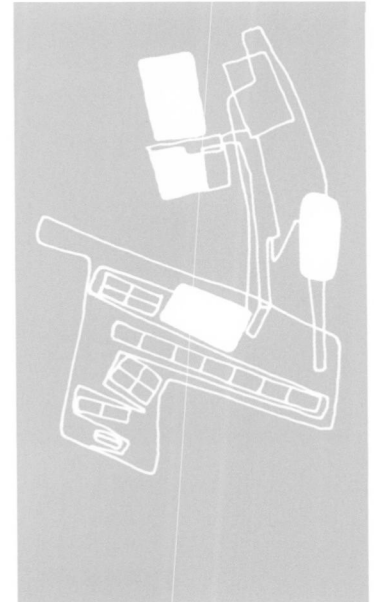

CHAPTER 10:
IN WHICH ALICIA ADDRESSES THE CONFUSING PARADOX OF A LAND MADE OF WATER AND WARMS TO A THERMOMETER MADE OF FLOWERS

Alicia stared at the water in the sink as she braced herself for the first icy splash to her face. Gazing into the water's surface, she saw the unsurprising reflection of her own face and the frame of the sash window beyond, but also captive of the water, was a vivid sky that could not possibly be over London at this time of the year.

The other odd thing about the reflection was that the watery world was inverted not from right to left like in a looking glass, but from up to down. Alicia dimly recalled her science teacher telling her that the universe was handed (although she couldn't quite imagine how a universe might have hands) and that it would be quite impossible to survive in a looking-glass world as the food would be all but indigestible.

Alicia took a deep breath and plunged her face below the water's insubstantial skin. Curiously, she remained bone dry.

'Hmm,' murmured Alicia. 'Water has a fairly good reputation for being wet and by all accounts, its wetness is highly contagious. But I suppose it's hard to tell if you're wet in water, just as it's hard to tell if you're dreaming in a dream,' she reasoned. Although she might be dry, however, Alicia's chattering teeth and goose-pimpled skin told her it was nevertheless very very cold. She was clearly no longer in her bathroom. As far she could see, the earth was a frosty white, interrupted only by a sparse smattering of cobalt and delphinium. Was it possible that winter had fallen already?

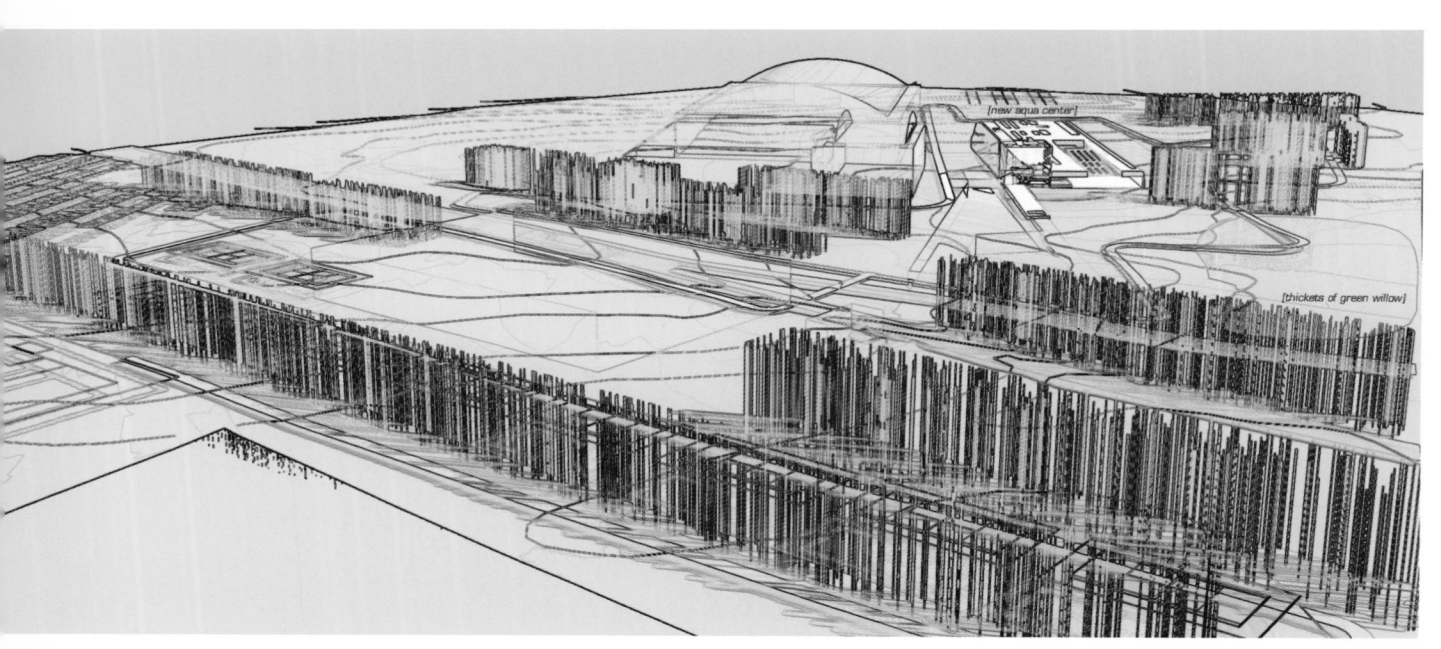

[new aqua center]

[thickets of green willow]

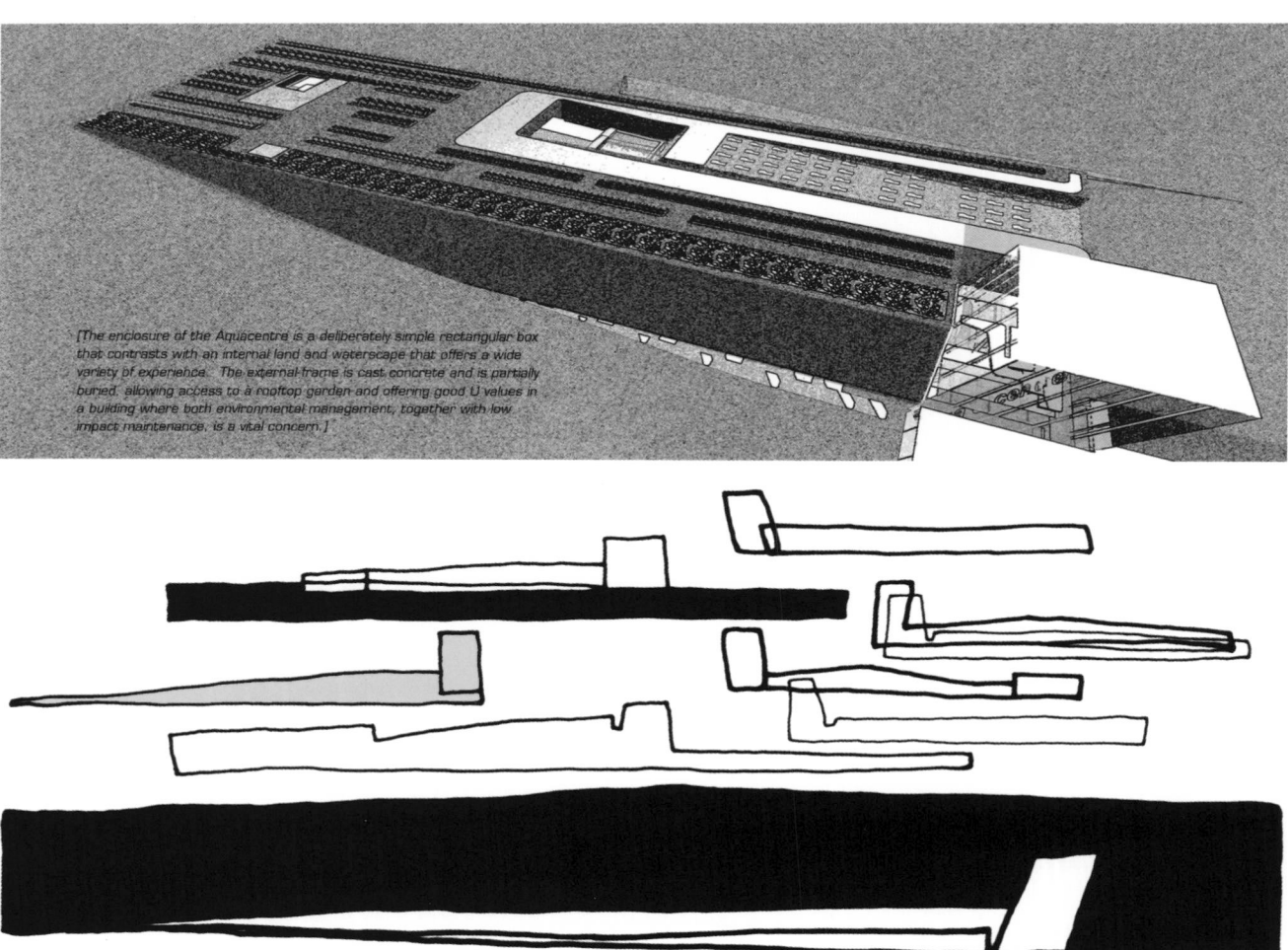

[The enclosure of the Aquacentre is a deliberately simple rectangular box that contrasts with an internal land and waterscape that offers a wide variety of experience. The external frame is cast concrete and is partially buried, allowing access to a rooftop garden and offering good U values in a building where both environmental management, together with low impact maintenance, is a vital concern.]

29 dec **winter**   *Icebergs + Flower Maps*

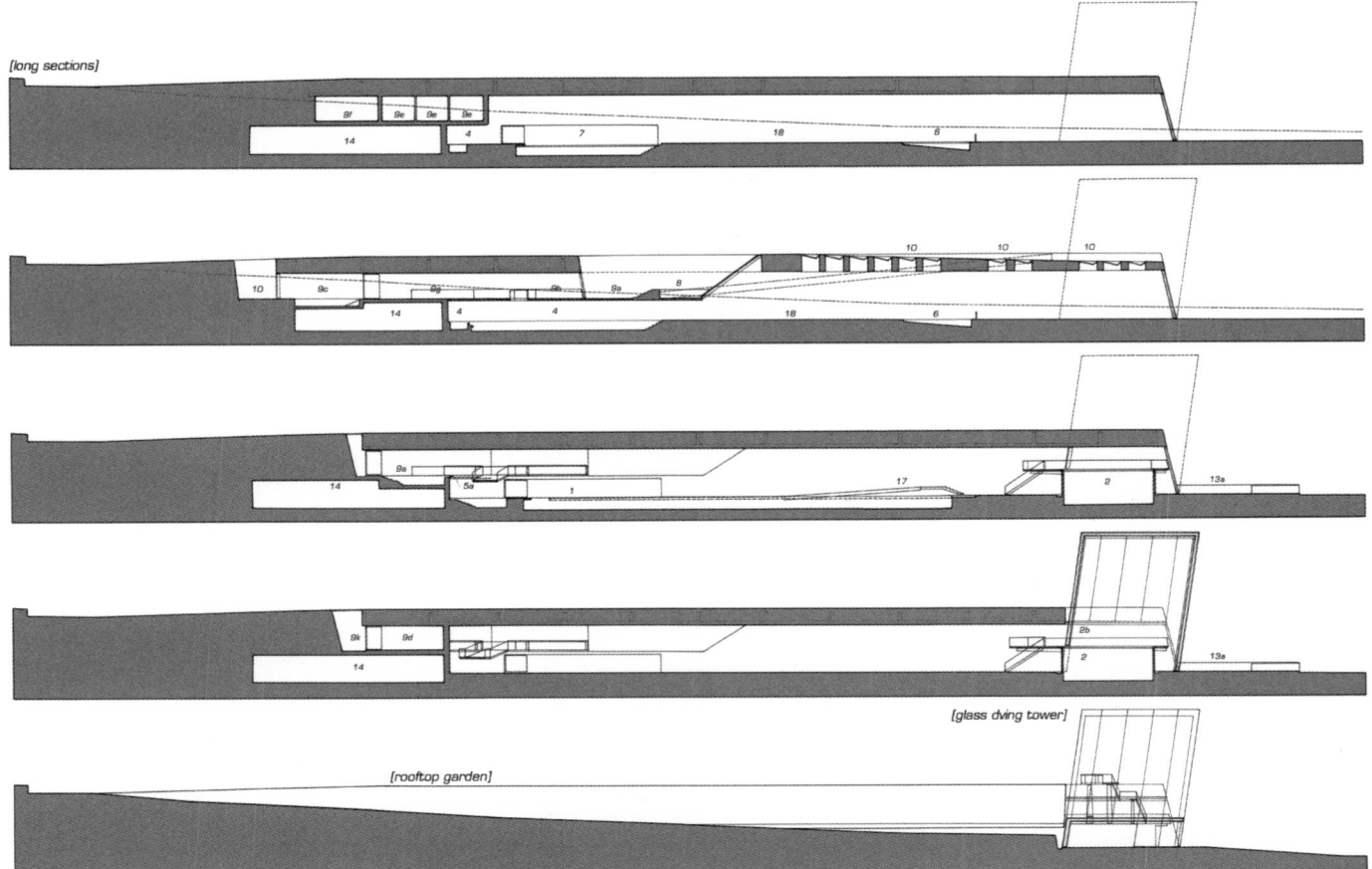

[long sections]

[glass dving tower]

[rooftop garden]

[The circuit pool may either be used in isolation for lane swimming or with inflatable islands to offer a number of configurations for continuous circuit swimming. The inflatable islands have a number of optimum positions so the routes can be varied and they may also be used as landing and diving platforms. All the main pool areas are accessed at ground level and all those of similar temperature are interconnected.]

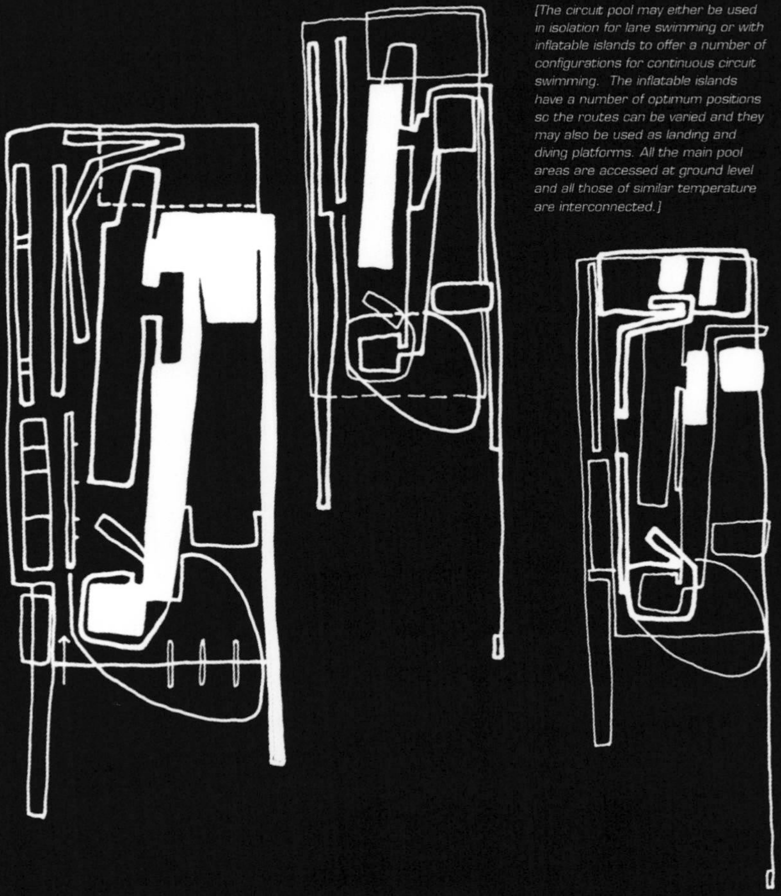

[flower map of the rooftop garden]

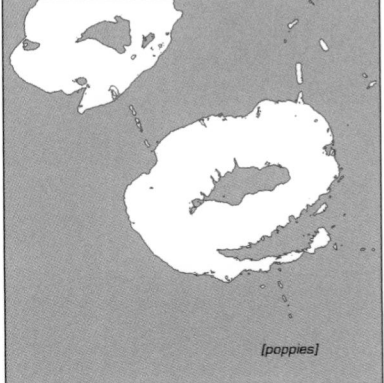

[blood-red tulips]

[poppies]

[the distribution of flowers produces a thermal map drawn in the colour red]

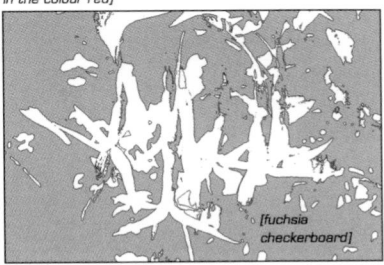

[fuchsia checkerboard]

A concentrated shock of high voltage colour drew Alicia's eye to a crimson oasis amidst a plain of sparkling bluebells, icy snowdrops, barren trees and blue-eyed grasses. On closer examination, she discovered that this island of colour was made up of myriad red inflorescences. But why did they grow only on this particular patch of ground? And although they were clearly untended, how did they grow in such neat patterns? Alicia searched for clues but the only thing she noticed was that her toes felt slightly warmer here than where she first arrived. Alicia consulted her oracle, the little green library book:

The garden located on the roof of the Aquacentre offers a secluded vantage point from which to view the panoramic landscape.

'Ah,' thought Alicia. 'Aquacentre. Aqua is Latin for water and centre is... well centre is English for centre.' As if to confirm its identity, the surrounding land indulged in a fit of spluttering, gurgling, trickling and babbling, speaking all the tongues that water speaks.

'Yes, yes. Very impressive,' said Alicia, as if to a boasting child. 'But what can you tell me about this island of red?'

The 40m-wide roof structure is supported by a series of externally positioned concrete beams. The space

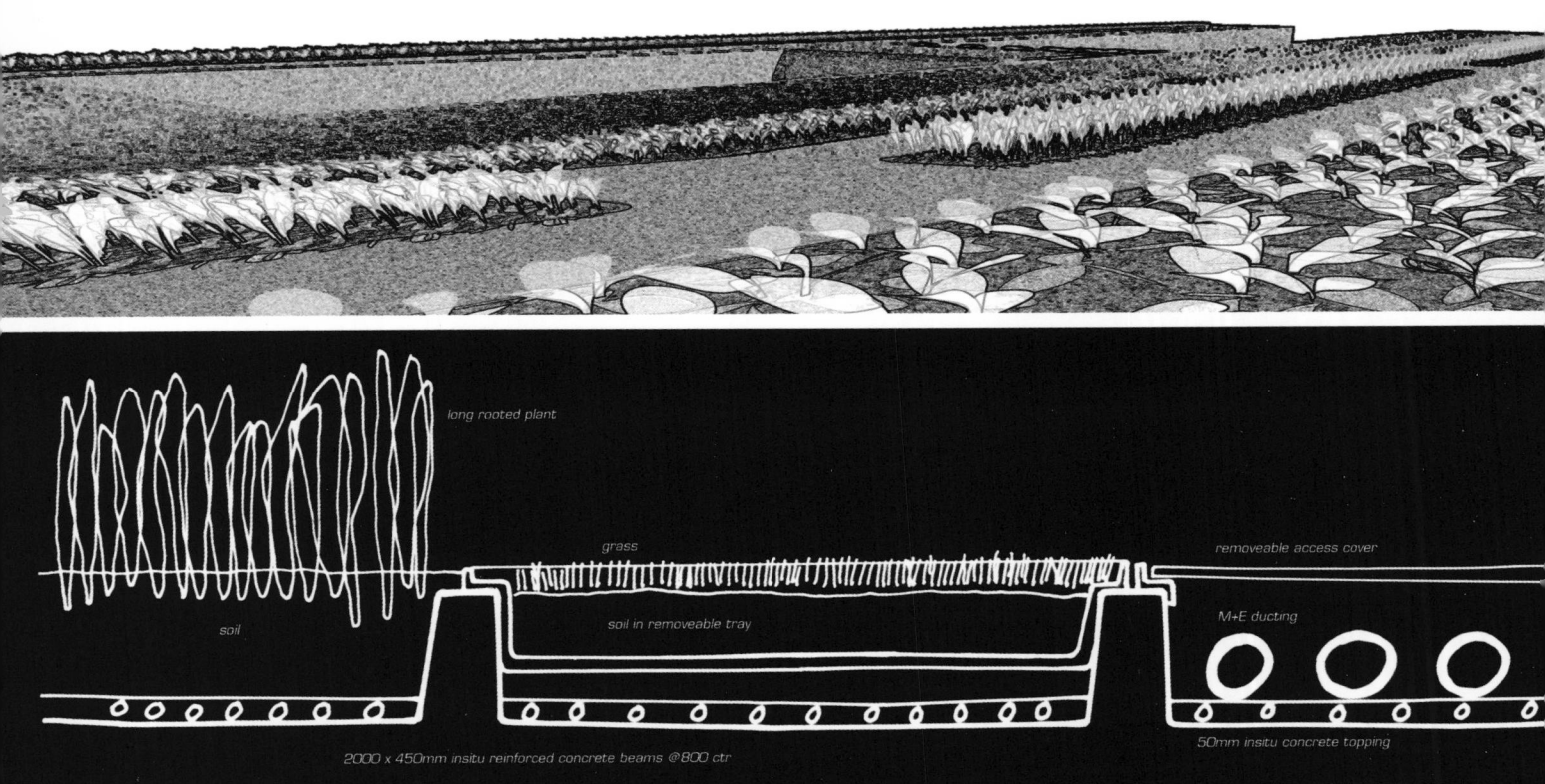

long rooted plant

removeable access cover

grass

soil

M+E ducting

soil in removeable tray

2000 x 450mm insitu reinforced concrete beams @ 800 ctr

50mm insitu concrete topping

between these is partially filled with
hydroponic aggregate, facilitating
the growth of grass and selected
plants. This space also carries heat
exchange capillary tubes that create
a rise in soil temperature and a
microclimate that will allow an
extended growing season. The garden is
envisaged as a three-dimensional
coloured canvas where plants of
different height, texture and colour
provide a place that is vivid and
scented.

Alicia was rather distressed to hear that she was standing on the roof of a building. Roofs were doubly dangerous places to stand as you could both fall off and through them. Having said that, this roof was reassuringly several feet thick and there was no edge in sight to fall off of. Alicia marvelled at the metamorphosis of discharged heat into halos of scarlet life. How could something so poetic grow from something so uninspiring?

What also fascinated her was that the distribution of the flowers produced a thermal map drawn in the colour red. The warmer the soil, the more populous and concentrated the poinsettias, tulips, poppies became, resulting in a deep

burgundy hue. At the periphery of the heat, the colour atoll faded to faint damask as crimson flora grew more and more sparse.

The aquacentre was book-ended by two curiosities. At the south end sat the sole protuberance from the horizon, a beached iceberg. How could it possibly have got there? And how did people get inside? Alicia stifled a shriek as a young girl inside the iceberg stepped off a platform several storeys high (where were the guard rails?!) and plummeted down, tumbling over and over and out of sight. Alicia heaved a sigh of relief when she heard a loud splash and the absence of screaming.

The diving pool is observable from
both within and outside the building.
This pool, with its tall glass tower,
is perhaps the most dramatic feature
of the Aalborg Aquacentre. It is a
clear external marker for the
building as the flight of the divers
can be seen externally. This gymnastic
theatre acts as a self-advertisement
for the building.

explained the book.

The second curiosity, this time at the north end of the complex, was a reflecting pool that was considerably larger than the sink in the Liddell family bathroom. From the centre of this topsy-turvy sky rose a great column of steam that slowly dissipated into the cool morning air. Alicia

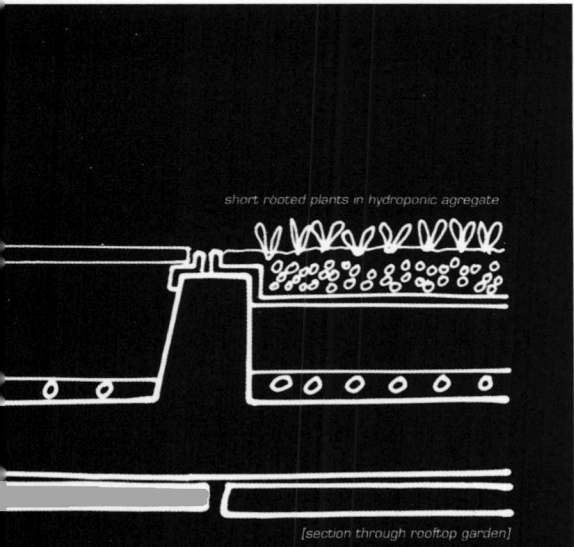

short rooted plants in hydroponic agregate

[section through rooftop garden]

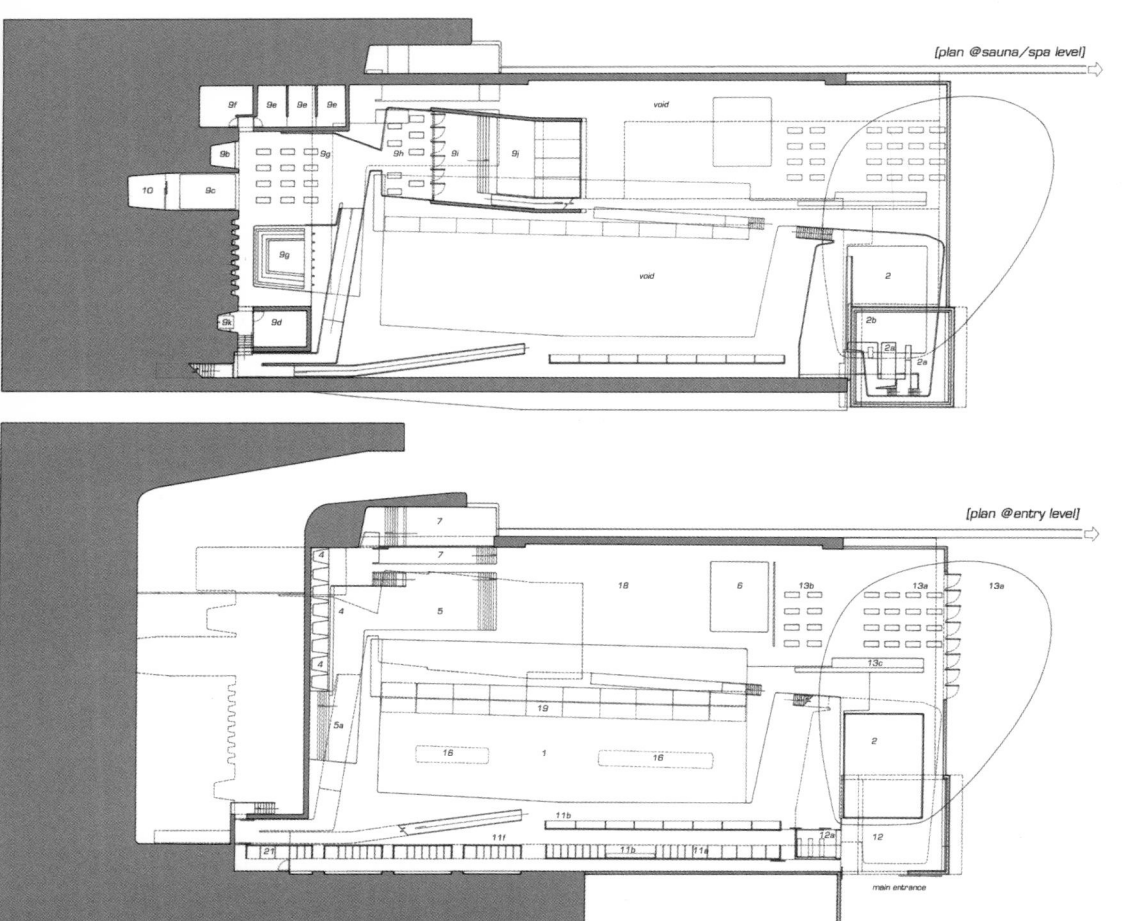

[plan @sauna/spa level]

[plan @entry level]

main entrance

1. Circuit Pool
2. Diving Pool
   a. diving deck
   b. climbing glass wall
3. Play Pool
4. Relaxation Pool + Resting Area
5. Hot Water Pool
   a. water-jets massage area
6. Infant Pool
7. Cold Pool
8. Outdoor Pool
9. Spa + Sauna Area
   a. hot water pool
   b. small cold pool
   c. small warm salt-water pool
   d. sauna
   e. steam bath (3 different temperatures)
   f. hot air bath
   g. sunbeds
   h. rest and massage area (indoor)
   i. rest and massage area (outdoor)
   j. external hot pool
   k. shower-jets
10. External Sun Deck
    a. sunken glass deck chairs/roof lights
11. Changing Area (frosted glass)
    a. disabled changing rooms/lockers/
       toilets/showers
    b. sinks area
    c. cubicle showers
    d. toilets
    e. lockers
    f. changing rooms
    g. family changing rooms
    h. open shower (clear glass wall)
12. Public Foyer
    i. reception / ticket office
    b. toilets
13. Cafe Area
    a. dry area
    b. wet area
    c. bar counter
    d. café tables
    e. kitchen
    f. food store
    g. service yard
14. Plant Room
15. Staff Facilities
    a. mess room
    b. changing/bath/toilets
16. Inflatable Islands
17. Water Shoot
18. Water Mattress
19. Retractable Pontoon
20. Cold Water Stream
21. Equipment Store
22. Plants

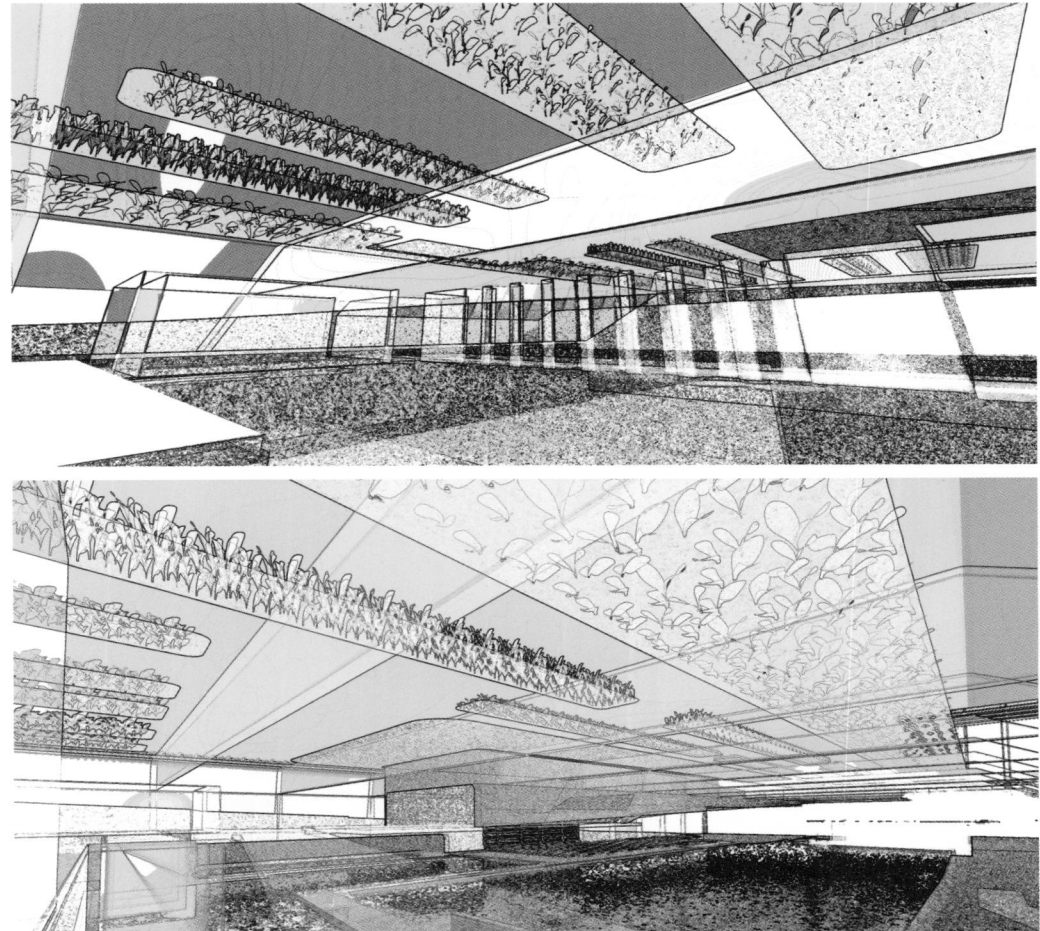

[Within the hot pool, swimmers may sit under the waterfalls that tumble from the higher pool in the sauna or sit in the jacuzzi alcoves. The sun lounger platform receives direct sunlight due to the profile of the roof and also allows views directly into the pool interior. There is stepped access from this area onto the roof "beach", an area for further sunbathing.]

[The water mattress is a wet play zone for children. It is constructed from a series of welded PVC pillows, some of which have water exit nozzles. The impact of pressure on the mattress is sufficient to release the valves and allow thin jets of water to escape. The greater the impact, the higher the jet of water. At certain points the water-feed pipes are bundled together and taken up the east wall to the ceiling so that water jets are activated not only at ground level, but from the wall and ceiling also.]

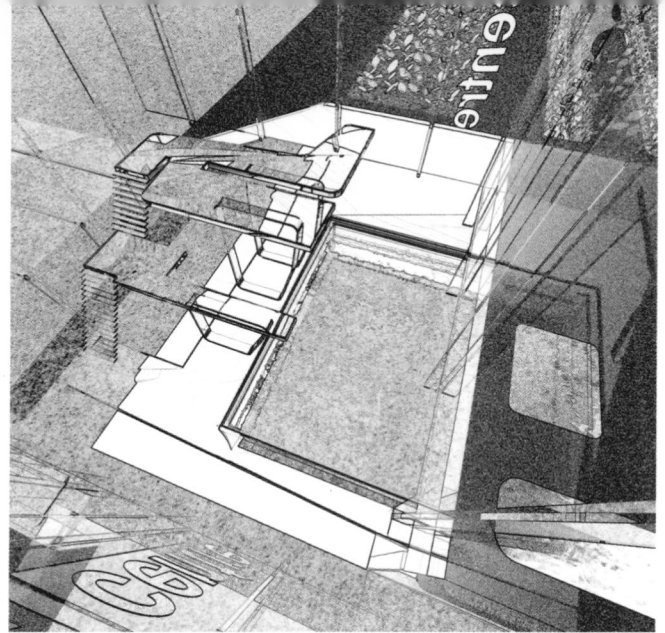

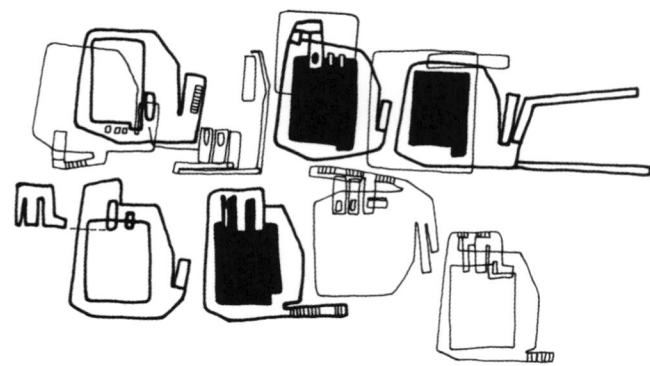

[This diving pool, with its tall glass tower, becomes the only dominant physical presence of the Aquacentre within the landscape. The flight of the divers can be seen externally from a far around the park. It is intended that this gymnastic theatre would be the building's own self-advertisement. The entrance is contained within this inclined glass box]

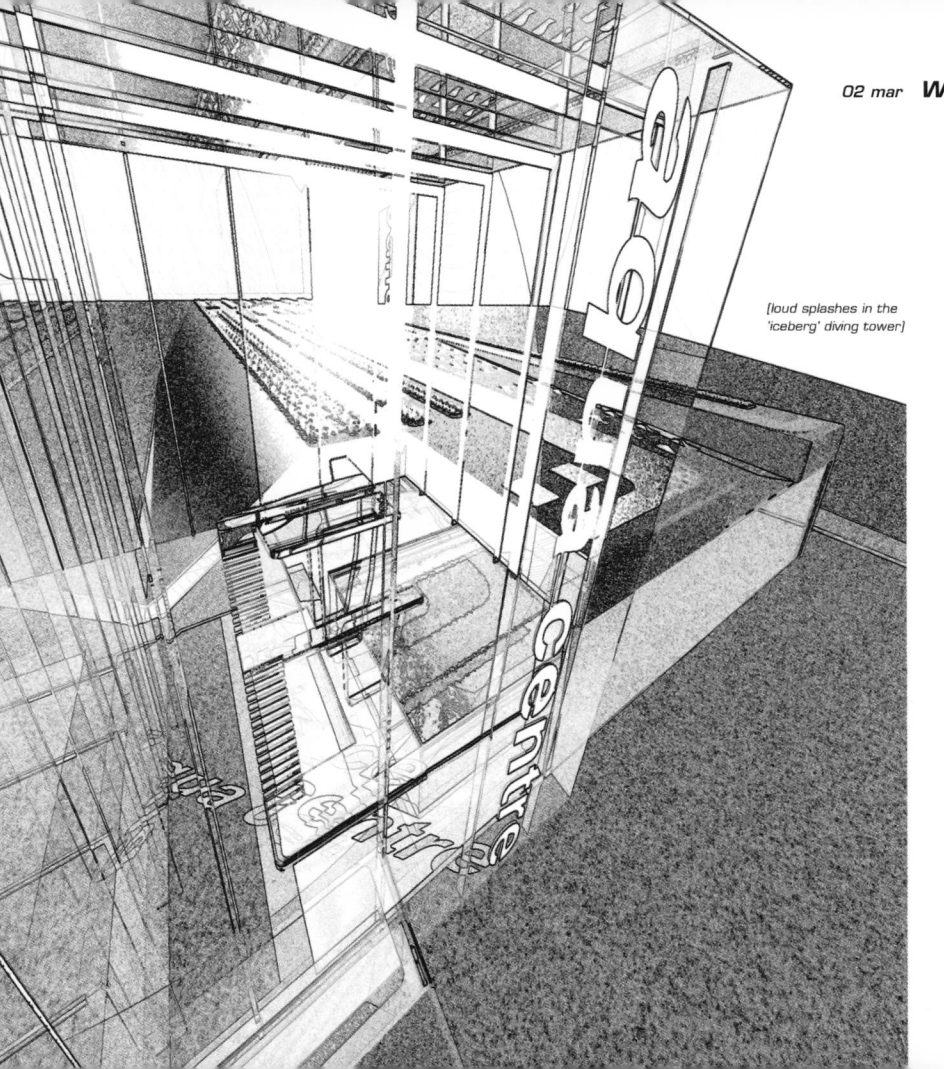

02 mar **winter**

Icebergs + Flower Maps

[loud splashes in the 'iceberg' diving tower]

speculated whether a whale, or worse, some horrid lagoon creature might be clearing its lungs from a blowhole, but the water was clear and disappointingly empty.

She did, however, meet the salesman and the carpenter there. The former was remarkably long in the tooth and bald as a coot (the coot is a Eurasian aquatic bird that strangely enough, isn't bald at all). This combination of features, along with a large drooping moustache, lent him the appearance of an affable walrus. His companion, the carpenter, was a skinny stick of a man who seemed to be, for all intents and purposes, fashioning blocks of wood out of larger blocks of wood.

'Excuse me sir, what are you carving?' asked Alicia.

'Why, isn't it obvious? I'm making floats to teach the little children how to swim,' said the carpenter, pointing to a group of tiny figures cavorting on the water mattresses.

'But… but those floats don't look like they'll float very well.'

'Don't be ridiculous. They're made of wood, aren't they? Boats are made of wood and float. Logs are definitely made of wood and they float too. Wood floats and I only use the finest wood to make my floats. Rosewoods and mahoganies. Only the very best.'

'That's why we do such a roaring trade!' roared the salesman. Alicia remained sceptical. She

shivered again.

'It's so cold. I wish I were home. I've had quite enough of gardens and people who make no sense,' she grumbled. A thought suddenly occurred to her. The little green library book had been extremely reliable describing where she was. If she sneaked a peak at the end, it might possibly have taken her home! She turned to the final page and this is what she read:

The sun came out and the landscape began to thaw, melting the landscape around her, leaving only a sink, an iron bathtub, a lavatory bowl and a yellow rubber duck.

THE END

[The garden located on the roof of the Aquacentre offers a secluded vantage point from which to view the panoramic landscape. The planted areas change according to the season where the fiery hues of summer flowers give way to the more subdued colours of the autumn and winter. The garden is envisaged as a three dimensional coloured canvas where plants of different height, texture and colour provide a place that could be vivid and scented together with areas that are sheltered and contemplative.]

[Roof garden taking advantage of the natural characteristics of the surrounding landscape]

["beach" area for sunbathing]

'Is that all?' asked Alicia, squeezing a lump of toothpaste onto her toothbrush. She counted the number of gardens she had visited on her fingers. 'I started the day in the circular library garden, where I borrowed the book,' she recalled. 'In the second garden I met that mad inventor fellow in the glasshouse and then in the third, I got horribly giddy with the caterpillar on the lorry. After that, I had a rest under a canopy of mechanical flowers. Hmm,' her memory began to fail her.

'Where else have I been?' She turned to the contents page of the book. 'Ah yes, here we are! Chapter 6, the park of sand; chapter 7, the gallery of four seasons; chapter 8, the oasis in the attic; chapter 9, the grasshopper inn and of course, there was the iceberg and the flower map in that last garden.' She turned the page and found a piece of flapping paper. Printed at the top were the words:

Stamped underneath was a date.

'My Goodness! That's today!' exclaimed Alicia. She balanced the book on the rim of the bath and began to brush her teeth. 'I shall go and return it as soon as I've had a wash,' she declared.

'Hmm,' pondered Alicia. 'Perhaps I'll be able to pick up something else by the same author...'

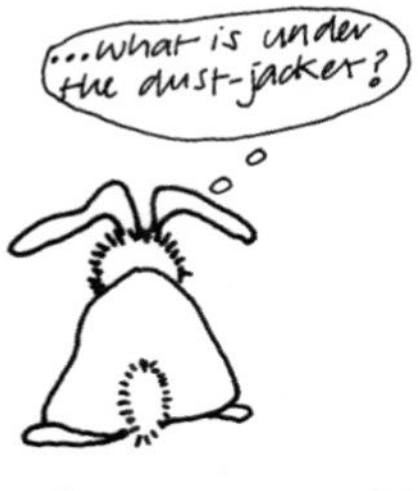
...what is under the dust-jacket?